"It is almost unthinkable that the
brought to the central topic of forgiveness. In this book, Coutts not only fills
this significant gap in Barth research, but does so with the care, sensitivity and
depth of analysis that is a model for any Barth reader. Any student of Barth
and any theologian interested in forgiveness will find much worth in engaging
seriously with this work."

Tom Greggs, Marischal Chair of Divinity, University of Aberdeen

"Jon Coutts has provided us with a brilliant study of the character of forgiveness.
Leaning into the wisdom of Karl Barth, he demonstrates that the church cannot
be the church until it learns to give and receive forgiveness, and that this can
only be learned and offered insofar as the church leans into the forgiveness
offered by God in Christ. This book is a wonderful explication of the pivotal
line in the creed, 'I believe in . . . the forgiveness of sins.'"

Gordon T. Smith, president, Ambrose University, Calgary, Alberta

"What a pleasure to read a work that combines scholarly excellence with pastoral
sensitivity. Jon Coutts serves both the academy and the church by offering a
careful, well-reasoned and innovative theology of forgiveness in conversation
with Karl Barth and a host of contemporary thinkers. The interpretation and
appropriation of Barth will be of special interest to scholars of his theology, but
the constructive account of forgiveness that stands at the heart of this book will
be helpful to anyone seeking to learn how the church can learn to forgive as it
first has been forgiven."

Keith L. Johnson, Wheaton College

"The significance of Jon Coutts's masterful description of Barth's teaching on
forgiveness and the church extends beyond the narrow confines of Barth
scholarship. It deserves to be read by anyone who wants to think seriously
about the logic and practice of forgiveness."

Adam Neder, Whitworth University

"This is the most thorough account we have of Karl Barth's theology of forgiveness
as outlined in *CD* IV. Coutts rightly locates his study within Barth's ecclesiology,
highlighting the fundamentally communal character of Christian forgiveness.
Coutts's careful exposition, critical theological judgment, and charitable practi-
cality come together to advance our vision of what it means to 'forgive as we
have been forgiven.' I'm doubly delighted to acknowledge that Coutts, a former
student of mine, has now become my teacher!"

David Guretzki, Briercrest Seminary

"In this accomplished volume, Jon Coutts presents a bold vision of the theology and practice of Christian forgiveness that navigates this acutely difficult terrain with sensitivity and insight. Operating at the boundary of systematic, ethical, and pastoral reflection, Coutts draws on Karl Barth's doctrine of reconciliation to present a scripturally based and ecclesially attentive account of forgiveness as a reality of grace in a truly reconciled yet still sinful world. The result is a work that offers both consolation and challenge to Christians in their calling to be servants of reconciliation and deserves the careful attention of both theologians and pastors. Highly recommended."

Paul T. Nimmo, King's Chair of Systematic Theology, University of Aberdeen

"Coutts's aim in this tightly argued yet accessible volume is to elucidate the 'practical ecclesial ramifications' of Karl Barth's theology. He does so by reading Barth's doctrine of the church in *Church Dogmatics* IV through the lens of forgiveness, which highlights the church's ministry of reconciliation while anchoring that mission firmly in Jesus Christ's own history. Coutts demonstrates that Barth locates 'interpersonal forgiveness at the beating heart of the church's life.' In so doing, Coutts helps us think through what it means when in the Lord's Prayer Christians ask their Father to forgive them as they forgive others."

W. Travis McMaken, Lindenwood University

"Jon Coutts has provided us with the first substantial and reliable treatment of Karl Barth's theology of forgiveness as it appears in the final volume of the magisterial *Church Dogmatics*. This nuanced exposition and extension of Barth's thought on the theme of forgiveness is astute and generous in its theological judgements, clear in its expression, and practical in its orientation. This is not a blueprint theology but one that engages with Barth's understanding of the gospel of reconciliation in relation to the community ordered and animated by the gift of forgiveness for the sake of the world. Forgiveness, received in justification and sanctification, entails a vocation to share it, since God's mercy in Christ is a shared mercy and a mercy to share."

Richard R. Topping, principal and professor of studies in the Reformed tradition, Vancouver School of Theology

NEW EXPLORATIONS IN THEOLOGY

A SHARED MERCY

KARL BARTH ON FORGIVENESS
AND THE CHURCH

JON COUTTS

FOREWORD BY JOHN WEBSTER

IVP Academic

An imprint of InterVarsity Press
Downers Grove, Illinois

InterVarsity Press
P.O. Box 1400, Downers Grove, IL 60515-1426
ivpress.com
email@ivpress.com

InterVarsity Press® is the book-publishing division of InterVarsity Christian Fellowship/USA®, a movement of students and faculty active on campus at hundreds of universities, colleges and schools of nursing in the United States of America, and a member movement of the International Fellowship of Evangelical Students. For information about local and regional activities, visit intervarsity.org.

Scripture quotations, unless otherwise noted, are from the New Revised Standard Version of the Bible, copyright 1989 by the Division of Christian Education of the National Council of the Churches of Christ in the USA. Used by permission. All rights reserved.

Cover design: Cindy Kiple
Interior design: Beth McGill

ISBN 978-0-8308-4915-4 (print)
ISBN 978-0-8308-9344-7 (digital)

Printed in the United States of America ∞

green press INITIATIVE *As a member of the Green Press Initiative, InterVarsity Press is committed to protecting the environment and to the responsible use of natural resources. To learn more, visit greenpressinitiative.org.*

Library of Congress Cataloging-in-Publication Data
A catalog record for this book is available from the Library of Congress.

P	23	22	21	20	19	18	17	16	15	14	13	12	11	10	9	8	7	6	5	4	3	2	1
Y	36	35	34	33	32	31	30	29	28	27	26	25	24	23	22	21	20	19	18	17	16		

To Angie,

Elijah, Brady, Jesse and Mattias.

Thank you.

Contents

Foreword

John Webster
(1955-2016)

A *Shared Mercy* is a study of Barth's theology of forgiveness as it is to be found in the work of his greatest maturity, the doctrine of reconciliation in the fourth volume of the *Church Dogmatics*. Writing about Barth well is no easy matter. Most of all, it requires command of Barth's lengthy and complex texts—in the case of the *Church Dogmatics*, of a text on which Barth was at work for over thirty years, and that contains all manner of shifts of style, attitude, conversation partners and content. Because the texts are so discursive and often rhetorically as well as spiritually demanding, readers need uncommon presence of mind to absorb, appropriate and reach judgments about what Barth has to say. Alongside this, there is the need to make sense of the setting and development of Barth's theology, without being swamped by genetic and evolutionary questions, and the need to master an enormous secondary literature and a conflicted history of the reception of Barth's work. The best studies of Barth combine awareness of the large structural principles of his theology with sensitivity to the details of his writing; they avoid both deference and suspicion, and demonstrate a free gratitude toward this most generous of theologians; they meet Barth's long-windedness with determined clarity of thought and economy of expression; and, more than anything, they respond to Barth's invitation to take up the theological task in his wake and to think with and on occasions beyond him.

This book has all these virtues. Though other students of Barth have ges-
tured toward the importance of forgiveness in Barth's conception of Christian
faith and teaching, the topic has until now received no full or adequate
treatment. Beyond this substantial enrichment of the literature, the significance of *A Shared Mercy* is threefold. First, it makes a distinguished contribution to the understanding and reception of Barth's ethical thought. Long
considered indifferent or even hostile to moral theology, Barth is now widely
recognized to have demonstrated a deep and abiding concern for human life
and activity in relation to God. The book's study of the human work of forgiveness and its ground and exemplary cause in the divine work of reconciliation provides further confirmation that Barth's theology (especially, but
by no means exclusively, in its later reaches) presents inter alia a lengthy reflection on God and creatures as agents in an ordered moral history. Second,
the book takes Barth's ecclesiology seriously. If Barth's theology is sometimes
considered to lack a sufficient sense of the church as human reality, this
reading of the ecclesiology of *Church Dogmatics* IV demonstrates just how
ample, complex and humanly dense Barth's teaching about the Christian
community in fact is. For Barth, the goods of the Christian gospel are not to
be detached from the common life and activities of the reconciled people of
God in whom forgiveness is embedded. Third, as *A Shared Mercy* unfolds
what Barth has to say, it also invites its readers to reflect on the theology and
practice of forgiveness. Barth hoped that his writings would provoke further
work on the doctrinal and practical-theological work by which he was
himself so deeply engaged. Those seeking to consider the ecclesial work of
forgiveness in relation to the church's troubled cultural locations will find
much profit in what follows.

In short: this book is both a sure-footed and perceptive study of a largely
undiscovered element of Barth, and an astute and at times moving essay in
doctrinal, moral and pastoral theology.

Abbreviations

CD   Karl Barth. *Church Dogmatics*. Translated by Geoffrey W. Bromiley and Thomas F. Torrance. 4 vols. in 13 parts. Edinburgh: T&T Clark, 1956–1975.

ChrL   Karl Barth. *The Christian Life: Church Dogmatics,* IV/4: *Lecture Fragments.* Translated by Geoffrey Bromiley and Thomas F. Torrance. Edinburgh: T&T Clark, 1981.

KD   Karl Barth. *Die kirchliche Dogmatik.* 4 vols. in 13 parts. Zurich: Theologischer Verlag, 1932–1970.

Introduction

THIS IS A BOOK ABOUT FORGIVENESS, and as such it is about the church. To some this statement may seem exclusive, to others even contrary to experience, but by the time this book has been read hopefully the statement will not only make sense but also be found compelling. It is certainly not a new idea. Not only did Jesus tie divine forgiveness closely together with interpersonal forgiveness, but he also made it central to the life and identity of his followers. Thinking about this for a dozen years at varying degrees of intensity as both a student and a pastor has been personally transformative. It is difficult to tell whether it has had a greater effect on my personal life or on my approach to the church. Perhaps it is a good sign that, as a result of this study, I have found it more and more difficult to separate the two. Again, this is a book about forgiveness, and as such it is also a book about the church.

There have been a number of turning points for me in the study of this topic, not the least of which being my years as a seminary student under the teaching of David Guretzki, which in turn led to my encounter with the theology of Karl Barth. So invigorating and insightful was this encounter that it became imperative for me to try to articulate and to share what I was learning from him. This led me to PhD studies under the supervision of John Webster and, finally, to the book in front of you. In this book I believe I have some constructive things to add that should be most evident in the final chapters, but to get there it is best first to analyze the account of forgiveness, ethics and the church that is offered in Karl Barth's *Doctrine of Reconciliation* (*Church Dogmatics* IV). This is, in my view, an aspect of his work that has not yet been fully appreciated by Barth scholars or, more importantly, by the church at large. Some readers may wish to skip to chapter four—and I think they will get the thrust of what is being put forward—but beginning with Barth in chapter one will provide the best backdrop for the argument that follows. We go back to Barth, not for novelty or popularity, but because we listen with the saints and the Scriptures to what the Spirit has to say to the churches today. Because this could be some readers' first substantive inter- action with Barth, allow me to begin with a brief introduction.

Karl Barth is best understood on his own terms: as a witness to Christ and a servant of the church. Born in 1886 in Switzerland to Fritz and Anna, Karl grew up in the home of a professor and former minister and began a pastorate in Safenwil at the age of twenty-five. There he married Nelly Hoffman, and with her served the church into his mid-thirties. During that time, spurred on by friendship with nearby pastor Eduard Thurneyson, he began exploring afresh what he had in one lecture called "The Strange New World of the Bible." In the latter years of that ministry he wrote a com- mentary on Romans that would spark much discussion and propel him into full-time scholarship. With the acceptance of a professorial position in Göt- tingen in 1921, Karl Barth began an influential teaching and writing career that spanned five decades and brought him to three more universities. After Göttingen, Barth served half a decade each in Münster and Bonn before his resistance to Hitler forced him back to Switzerland, where he landed in Basel for the teaching post that would take up the remainder of his career. He became a prolific writer, considering his books less as finalized manifestos and more as ongoing projects—contributions to churchly deliberation at the lead of the living and active Word of God.

From early on Barth exemplified this commitment to an ever-reforming, communal process of faith seeking understanding by revising his Romans commentary for a second edition in 1922, just three years after the first edition had been completed. While revising it even further, Barth moved on to other projects.[1] One of these was a short book on the Apostles' Creed that, in re- flection on the third article of faith contained therein, evocatively declared,

---

[1] See Karl Barth, *The Epistle to the Romans*, trans. Edwyn C. Hoskyns (London: Oxford University Press, 1933), 15, 20. For an excellent introduction to this part of Barth's life, see Kenneth Oakes, *Reading Karl Barth: A Guide to Karl Barth's* Epistle to the Romans (Eugene, OR: Cascade Books, 2011), 1-39.

"The forgiveness of sins or justification of the sinner by faith is *the* gift of the Holy Spirit . . . [and] the common denominator, so to speak, upon which everything that can seriously be called Christian life must be set."[2] Time would tell whether this was rhetorical flourish or whether it was something that Barth could explicate further. But it is notable that by 1940, with early works such as *Credo* and the Romans commentary in hand, Paul Lehmann had already called Barth's theology "a reaffirmation of the great original theological treatise on the gospel of forgiveness . . . and an analysis of its effects upon contemporary culture and religion."[3] We might be tempted to call this hyperbole, except that Barth's subsequent work actually bears the statement out. In the decades that followed, while Barth did not go on to produce a practical theology of forgiveness per se, the culmination of his life's work had much to offer in this regard.

After some stops and starts (beginning in Göttingen with what he called *Christian Dogmatics*), in 1932 Barth published the first part-volume of the theological epic he would work on the rest of his life—*Kirchliche Dogmatik*, or *Church Dogmatics* (as it was gradually translated into English). With the help of assistant Charlotte von Kirschbaum, by the time of his death in 1968 Barth had seen almost four of the planned five volumes (thirteen part-volumes) through to publication. Although he had already broached these topics under other headings, it was in the fourth part—*The Doctrine of Reconciliation*—that Barth followed his christocentric theology through and focused squarely on salvation, sin, the church and mission. Unfortunately the volume went unfinished, but not before three massive part-volumes (and the baptismal portion of another part-volume) had been produced. Together with fragments of what was to be his "ethics of reconciliation"— published posthumously as *The Christian Life*—the approximately three thousand pages of Barth's *Doctrine of Reconciliation* will be the focus of our study on the practical theology of forgiveness.

One could certainly perform this study on other parts of Barth's corpus (or perhaps upon the entirety of it), but our goal is to follow Barth's work through to its most practical, ecclesial ramifications. Thus we will perform a

---

[2]Karl Barth, *Credo* (London: Hodder & Stoughton, 1936), 153.
[3]Paul Louis Lehmann, *Forgiveness: Decisive Issue in Protestant Thought* (New York: Harper & Brothers, 1940), 104. Reinhold Niebuhr concurs with this appraisal in the foreword (x).

close reading of the most acutely pastoral sections of the *Church Dogmatics*, where we see Barth working up a compelling picture of what Christ's reconciling work looks like as it comes to bear on Christian life and community. It is with a certain sense of loss that we read the posthumously published fragments and see Barth's work trail off only a third of the way into the Lord's Prayer, but in the final pages of Barth's magnum opus it can justifiably be said that we see him fine-tuning what he had been describing (or at least gesturing at) all along. When it comes to the task of tracking down the conclusions he seemed to be reaching, it is not as if Barth left us with a shortage of material! While this book will be constructive in nature, its conclusions are not to be considered a speculative reconstruction of what Barth was *about to say*, but an accountably close reading of Barth's work *that builds on what he left us*. What it endeavors to show is that contained within the sprawling ecclesiological vision of Barth's *Doctrine of Reconciliation* there is a coherent theology of forgiveness that, though scattered and often implicit, offers itself up to be extrapolated and appropriated. Indeed, as I will argue, Barth prompts us to form an understanding of Christ's ministry of reconciliation within which the practice of forgiveness most properly finds its home.

In its simplest terms, our goal is to better apprehend what on earth it means to ask *our Father in heaven* to *forgive as we forgive*, and our task is to do so from within a systematic theology particularly attuned to the task (see Mt 6:12 and Lk 11:4). What follows, then, is a critical commentary on the fourth volume of Barth's *Church Dogmatics* that will assess and articulate his account of the place and meaning of forgiveness in Christian life and community. Given that there has been little direct study on this particular question, chapter one will begin with a brief review of some key literature pertaining to Barth's ethics and ecclesiology, wherein gains will be noted and cautions heeded. With this in place, chapters two and three will provide a section-by-section analysis of *The Doctrine of Reconciliation* with a view to the topic at hand, weaving through the first three part-volumes in order to assess what it has to offer. This will lead to chapters four and five, which work out a Christian definition of forgiveness by embedding it along with other aspects of the church's ministry of reconciliation in Christ. There we will see the imperative of sharing forgiveness as a free gift of God in Christ, will explore its connection to other acts of grace and will espouse a definition wherein forgiveness finds its telos in full reconciliation. The sixth and final chapter will then return to Barth's *Doctrine of Reconciliation*, viewing it from the perspective of its unfinished ethics sections in order to read between the lines of the Lord's baptism, Supper and Prayer, spelling out ramifications for the church's common life.

Before we proceed any further, a note about gendered language is needed. Given that much of the source material for this project comes from a culture wherein masculine language was understood to represent both genders, many of the quotations will not be up to today's standards of inclusivity. Where possible, I have abbreviated or paraphrased quotes to match contemporary convictions on the matter, but in many cases the alterations required would have proved awkward and distracting and have thus been left undone. To balance this out to some degree, other third-person pronouns have been employed in the feminine. In any event, let the reader understand that the retained masculine language is in no way meant to communicate or condone patriarchal thinking. In fact, the material content we are discussing should prompt us to an ever-greater vitality of mutual submission between Christian brothers and sisters, springing from a common reverence for Christ (Eph 5:21).

Finally, as this book represents work that spanned nearly a decade, allow me to express some thanks to those who were either intentionally or inadvertently drawn in by its gravitational pull. Their support took many forms, including encouragement, financial backing, prayerful solidarity and substantive counsel. It was in a small town with an early morning reading group in the middle of the Canadian prairies that I was first introduced to Karl Barth. As mentioned, it is David Guretzki whom I have to thank for guiding me to those invigorating discussions and opening up vistas for me to track down and further explore. If it was in the prairies that this project took off, it was in the highlands that it landed and found its legs. I consider myself incredibly fortunate to have had the opportunity to track down my questions in the company of a collegial rather than competitive group of scholars at King's College in Aberdeen, Scotland. For helpful conversations too many to count, I thank Adam Nigh, Darren Sumner, Justin Stratis, Joe McGarry, Graham MacFarlane, Martin Westerholm, Scott Prather, Ben Rhodes, Josh Malone, Geordie Ziegler and Leon Harris, as well as a handful of others. Behind this vibrant research community stood Francesca Murphy, Philip Ziegler, Don

Wood, Brian Brock and Chris Brittain, whom I have to thank not only for their excellent questions, but for showing me how to ask them. Most of all I am grateful for John Webster's encouraging, patient and perceptive supervision. For him to say such kind things about this book is almost as much as I could have hoped for. I am glad to have thanked him in a meaningful way at his Festschrift last year. It was the last time I would see him. He is deeply missed.

As this project gathered momentum and at times threatened to snowball out of control, I found myself frequently benefiting from the support of churches and family and friends. It is impossible to name everyone, but in this regard I express appreciation to Terry Jackson, Jamie Davies, Aaron Gerrard, Chris Smith, Clayton and Tamara Puddicombe, Dale and Dani Harris, the extended Coutts family, everyone at The Mission in Aberdeen, and the good people of Selkirk, Beverly and Richmond Alliance Churches. Special thanks also to Anne Wilma, Andrew, Keziah and Naomi Louden, Melody and Brian Kilbank, Darlene and Fred Zelensky, Dorothea and Stewart Coutts, and all of my brothers and sisters. For reviewing some early drafts I thank David Robinson, Phil Stewart, Dot Coutts, Angie Coutts and Micah Smith. For supporting this work I also give my thanks to colleagues at Trinity College Bristol, and to everyone at InterVarsity Press.

All told, it has been the collaboration and commitment of my wife, Angie, that has made the most indelible impression on me. I am deeply grateful to her and to our sons, Elijah, Brady, Jesse and Mattias, for their sacrifices and solidarity on this journey, and am so glad for the wonderful surprises that awaited us. This book is dedicated to them.

1

What Is It About Forgiveness?

Tensions in the Study of Forgiveness

In recent decades the topic of forgiveness has seen increased attention in the fields of philosophy, psychology, sociology and political science, owing largely to the prevalence of complex interpersonal and geopolitical conflict in the twentieth century. In these studies one often sees Christian theology mined for illustrative and effective content but underutilized in forming premises and reaching conclusions. This shortcoming applies often enough within practical theology as well. Given the centrality of forgiveness to Christianity, it should be of utmost concern to understand and appropriate this rightly.

One of the landmarks in contemporary forgiveness studies came in Hannah Arendt's *The Human Condition*, where she rather famously labeled Jesus the "discoverer" of the human "faculty" of forgiveness, and thereby offered a qualified recommendation of its usefulness in social progress.[1] Building on this in his book *Before Forgiveness: The Origins of a Moral Idea*, David Konstan explores examples of pre-Christian forgiveness and argues that, actually, not even Jesus had the same moral action in view that modern Westerners have today. Tracing back to "differences in the ancient and modern conceptions of the self," Konstan claims that before Immanuel Kant the "ideology of forgiveness" was more general—concerned more with "assuaging anger" than initiating or sealing a reconciliatory exchange.[2]

---

[1]Hannah Arendt, *The Human Condition* (Chicago: University of Chicago Press, 1998), 238, 246; see also 236-47.

[2]David Konstan, *Before Forgiveness: The Origins of a Moral Idea* (Cambridge: Cambridge University

It would seem that Konstan underappreciates both the New Testament's influence on and its resonance with contemporary concerns, but his distinction of modern from premodern and ancient emphases is apropos. According to Charles Griswold's analysis, "forgiveness is not seen as a virtue by the ancient Greek philosophers," mainly because their "perfectionist views" of the moral field obscured the possibility of naming something virtuous that depended upon the presence of imperfection in order to be enacted.[3] In the classic period, John Milbank observes "no real recommendation of forgiveness in a post-Christian sense," noting instead the predominance of "a gesture of pure negative cancellation"—a gesture that could easily succumb merely to "a pragmatic ignoring of [faults] for self-interested reasons, or else to the taking into account of mitigating circumstances and involuntary motions."[4] Such generalizations and gestures are certainly not foreign to the hyperindividualized interpersonal encounters of today. Perhaps the more things change the more they stay the same.

When it comes to the appropriation of forgiveness in church history, Rodney Petersen succinctly relays the mixed legacy we inherit in that regard:

> In the history of the church the practice of forgiveness has been clearly tied to penitence, most often privatized as a part of individual religious practice since the early medieval period. Throughout what became recognized as "Christendom," the public significance of forgiveness often languished as more retributive conceptions of justice dominated social theory, power politics, and practice. Forgiveness was often "spiritualized" and removed from the practice of everyday life. While forgiveness might happen between God and an individual penitent, among persons and groups in society only some lesser form of condoning, dismissal, or forgetting appeared possible. The recovery of particular patterns of religious behavior and theology in the Protestant reforms caused Christians to rethink the topic.[5]

Press, 2010), ix-xi, 81. Konstan suggests that the Old and New Testaments recommend more of a general sense of solidarity within divine forgiveness than a rich interpersonal encounter (see 21-30, 80-81, 105, 118-23).

[3]Charles Griswold, *Forgiveness: A Philosophical Exploration* (Cambridge: Cambridge University Press, 2007), 2, 17. See especially 1-19.

[4]John Milbank, *Being Reconciled: Ontology and Pardon* (London: Routledge, 2003), 48.

[5]Rodney L. Petersen, "Theology of Forgiveness: Terminology, Rhetoric, and the Dialectic of Interfaith Relationships," in *Forgiveness and Reconciliation: Religion, Public Policy, and Conflict Transformation*, ed. Raymond G. Helmick and Rodney L. Petersen (Philadelphia: Templeton Foundation Press, 2001), 4-5.

The difficulty has always been to find the right relation of forgiveness to repentance and reparation. In the face of lethargy toward the imperatives of grace, the tendency has been to motivate repentance by fear of punishment; in the face of oppressive legalism the tendency has been to emphasize the freedom of God's love. As Carl Bråkenhielm reports, Peter Lombard called for *contrition* as the perfect repentance that arose from the love of God, while seventeenth century Pope Alexander VII declared fear-induced *attrition* acceptable as well, reckoning "imperfect repentance" nonetheless apt for God's gracious appropriation.[6] On either side of this tension lies the possibility for abuse.

As will be seen in this book, Karl Barth sought both to retain emphasis on divine mercy and to resist the descent of grace-invoking penitence into self-serving penance. This is no mere Protestant polemic: Barth vociferously warns against the assumption that the Reformation made anyone immune to the temptation to self-manage grace. Indeed, the similarities between pre- and post-Reformation impulses are not difficult to trace. Anachronistic caricatures of the sacrament of penance should not obscure the nuances of grace and accountability that, at the best of times, it aimed to observe. Despite the rise of indulgences and the threats of purgatory, pastoral handbooks show that good intentions and ideas coexisted with and preceded those more infamous church practices. For instance, medieval pastoral advisor Guido of Monte Rochen called penance a God-given way to mend the scars of sins already forgiven, promoting both the meritorious nature of contrition and the belief that it must take place within the activity of God.[7] No doubt looking to retrieve some premodern impulses, John Milbank argues that for thinkers like Aquinas divine forgiveness was freely given but "realized through repentance," thus when "mediated by the Church through the sacrament of penance, it was to some extent the case that . . . to forgive someone was actively to bring about reconciliation through the provision

---

[6]Carl Reinhold Bråkenhielm, *Forgiveness*, trans. Thor Hall (Minneapolis: Fortress, 1989), 27. For concurring accounts see E. Basil Redlich, *The Forgiveness of Sins* (Edinburgh: T&T Clark, 1937), 220, 227, 235-36, 259-61, and W. Telfer, *The Forgiveness of Sins: An Essay in the History of Christian Doctrine and Practice* (London: SCM Press, 1959), 36.

[7]See Guido of Monte Rochen, *Handbook for Curates: A Late Medieval Manual on Pastoral Ministry*, trans. Anne T. Thayer (Washington, DC: The Catholic University of America Press, 2011), 208, 238, 159.

to the other of a positive means of recompense."[8] One must be careful not to overstate retrieval at the expense of the gains of reform, but it is worth noting that, for all the abuses, the proper impulse was to embed forgiveness within Christ's ongoing work of reconciliation via the church.

Indeed, Christians overreacting to institutionalized forms of penance may take it up again in individualistic forms instead. This reality was felt early on in Martin Bucer's attempt to replace priestly mediation with the establishment of *Christlichen Gemeinschaften*. By all accounts the post-Reformation attempts at thriving mutual accountability ran into obstacles and faltered as people found themselves still caught up not only in the power struggles of church and state but also the tensions of personal and corporate interest.[9] As time wore on, these tensions would only be exacerbated by the fragmentations implicit in Enlightenment notions of freedom and the resultant heightening of individuality. Whether institutionalized or privatized, the temptation remains to try to manage grace by manipulating penitence.

Of course, the modern focus on individuality has not been entirely negative. It has also had the advantage of spurring new reflection on the personal and interpersonal implications of divine forgiveness and reconciliation. The most prominently recognized example of this turn has become a pair of sermons preached by Bishop Joseph Butler in 1718 at Rolls Chapel, London, titled "Upon Resentment" and "Upon Forgiveness of Injuries."[10] As explained by Griswold, Butler previewed the way "resentment and forgiveness are routinely linked in modern discussions," signaling an emphasis on inner and interpersonal dynamics that would resound in the social sciences for centuries to come.[11] This focus would only intensify in the twentieth century as the rise of global transport and

---

[8]Milbank, *Being Reconciled*, 45-46.

[9]See Gottfried Hammann, "The Creation of the 'Christlichen Gemeinschaften,'" in *Martin Bucer: Reforming Church and Community*, ed. D. F. Wright (Cambridge: Cambridge University Press, 1994), 129-43, and David Lawrence, *Martin Bucer: Unsung Hero of the Reformation* (Nashville: Westview Publishing, 2007), 138.

[10]See Joseph Butler, "Sermon VIII. Upon Resentment" and "Sermon IX. Upon Forgiveness of Injuries," in *Fifteen Sermons Preached at the Rolls Chapel* (Cambridge: Hilliard and Brown, 1827), 68-83. See also Anthony Bash, *Forgiveness and Christian Ethics* (Cambridge: Cambridge University Press, 2007), 27.

[11]Griswold, *Forgiveness*, 19.

communication coincided with the fallout of colonial injustices and surges in violence the scope of which the world had never seen.[12] Concurrent with this was also an increased sensitivity to psychology and personal healing, which brought questions of forgiveness and reconciliation close to home. In this regard Everett Worthington considers Lewis Smedes's 1984 *Forgive and Forget* to have been a formative influence: it triggered the interest of psychotherapists with its compelling depiction of forgiveness as a benefit to *forgivers*.[13]

In the developments of the last century, what Anthony Bash finds most notable is the fact that forgiveness garnered a wide range of attention *apart from religious conviction*. Desperate for alternate modes of conflict resolution in light of the visibly downward spiral of violence and retribution, more and more people have found the idea of forgiveness profoundly pertinent to interpersonal and sociopolitical affairs.[14]

What should be clear from this brief sketch is that forgiveness is at the same time both elemental and complicated. The notions and practices of forgiveness found in any time or place may present parables (or forgeries) of Christian forgiveness. In any case, one must understand forgiveness *Christianly* in order to see where the similarities begin and end. When George Soares-Prabhu observes analogies to Christian forgiveness in the Buddhist tradition, he rightly maintains that even if mercy and compassion "are not *exclusively* Christian attitudes, the importance given to them in the teaching of Jesus, and the concrete forms they assume in the New Testament, give them a *specifically Christian significance*."[15] With Barth, our goal is to better understand forgiveness within Christ's mission of reconciliation.

---

[12]Key points are narrated in Petersen, "Theology of Forgiveness," 6-8. A prime example of the serious reflection brought about by violent atrocity is Simon Wiesenthal's eloquently narrated conundrum of a Holocaust survivor confronted by a request for forgiveness from a former prison guard. See Simon Wiesenthal, *The Sunflower: On the Possibilities and Limits of Forgiveness* (New York: Schocken Books, 1969).

[13]Everett L. Worthington Jr., *Forgiveness and Reconciliation: Theory and Application* (New York: Taylor & Francis Group, 2006), 1, and Lewis B. Smedes, *Forgive and Forget: Healing the Hurts We Don't Deserve* (New York: Harper & Row, 1984). See Robert D. Enright, "Comprehensive Bibliography on Interpersonal Forgiveness," in *Exploring Forgiveness*, ed. Robert D. Enright and Joanna North (Madison: University of Wisconsin Press, 1998), 165-86.

[14]Bash, *Forgiveness and Christian Ethics*, 29.

[15]George Soares-Prabhu, "'As We Forgive': Interhuman Forgiveness in the Teaching of Jesus," *Concilium* 184 (1986): 57, emphases added.

The Foregrounding of Forgiveness in Barth's Theology

More than a decade before Barth began the fourth volume of his *Church Dogmatics*, Paul Lehmann wrote a book called *Forgiveness: Decisive Issue in Protestant Thought*, which spent a considerable portion of its latter half tracing the trajectory of Barth's thought. Without really delving into practical matters, it certainly promoted serious study of forgiveness in Barth's theology. In Lehmann's view, if Roman Catholics thought forgiveness to be available to humanity naturally, then Reformers had taken the opposite view—only to let the far-reaching implications of this fundamental conviction get temporarily pressed out by other matters.[16] Attending to its retrieval, Lehmann pointed to the assertion of Albrecht Ritschl, who said, "The immediate object of theological cognition . . . is the community's faith that it stands to God in a relation essentially conditioned by the forgiveness of sins."[17] With Barth, Lehmann detected both a renewal and a sharpening of focus. What Barth highlights for us, he observed, is that Ritschl's object of theological reflection is not the God revealed in Christ, but *the faith* of the community and the "*consciousness* of those who believe in Him."[18] This distorts the picture considerably, turning us from apprehension of Christ's mercy to the practice of "self-forgiveness."[19]

As Lehmann saw it, Barth posed a powerful question to Roman Catholics and liberal Protestants alike—namely, "Is forgiveness fundamentally an unheard-of miracle, or is it something other, something less than that?" Well before Barth wrote his *Doctrine of Reconciliation*, Lehmann detected his trajectory and began to track it down: "New horizons of forgiveness open to the eye that inquiringly follows Barth's answer to this question": "What is the significance of the grace of God in Christ for the man to whom it comes?"[20]

Breaking this query into three parts, first Lehmann asked *how* this grace is "to be thought of as coming to man" and suggested that Barth's "answer is that the grace of forgiveness comes to man as the *crisis* of his existence."[21]

---

[16]Paul Louis Lehmann, *Forgiveness: Decisive Issue in Protestant Thought* (New York: Harper & Brothers, 1940), 9-10.

[17]Albrecht Ritschl, *The Christian Doctrine of Justification and Reconciliation*, trans. H. R. Mackintosh and A. B. Macaulay (Edinburgh: T&T Clark, 1902), 3; see also Lehmann, *Forgiveness*, 58.

[18]Ritschl, *Justification and Reconciliation*, 1, emphasis added.

[19]Lehmann, *Forgiveness*, 102.

[20]Ibid., 9, 130.

[21]Ibid., 130, 137.

Second, Lehmann asked what this grace tells us about *those to whom it comes*, and postulated Barth's answer as follows:

> Man exists altogether by the grace of God. When man is forgiven, he is forgiven *in toto* and *from moment to moment*. The consequence of the discontinuity between God and man is that God *forgives* man as the sheer miracle of his love and that when he forgives, man's whole existence is changed. Changed?—yes, but not as the simple moving from one house to another. Forgiveness . . . is the paradox of a futuristic indicative, of a forgiveness that is present as a hope, as a promise, and which in spite of its being a promise is at the same time an event for the man to whom it comes. We have grace. Yes, but in no sense as a possession of our own.[22]

Third, Lehmann moved from the language of crisis to the language of Christian faith and asked *how this grace comes in Christ*. For him, Barth's answer was simple: "Just as the Cross is significant because it is that event which is followed by the resurrection . . . forgiveness is an event in which . . . I actually am that which I actually am not. In Christ, I am a new creature because I am forgiven."[23]

So it was that in 1940 Paul Lehmann thought it possible to indicate the "structure" of Barth's doctrine of forgiveness, even though he himself had not made it explicit.[24] For Barth, forgiveness is provided once and for all by Christ, and as it comes to us in Christ it perpetually intersects with everyday life as an event wherein we are freed from the old self and freed for the new. In comparison with the more robust expression of his later work, it appears that early on Barth's view of the role of *the community* in this life of faith was still underdeveloped—but the foundations were in place for what was yet to come.

In the decades since Barth's *Doctrine of Reconciliation*, the ecclesial ethic of forgiveness entailed in his final volumes has been broached generally but has not garnered direct analysis of its own. Reflecting mainly on *The Doctrine of Creation*, Gerald McKenny observes that, for Barth, forgiveness is a Christ-given "refusal to treat sin as the final word, and thus, in the form of

---

[22]Ibid., 140-41. Aware that Barth was being critiqued as an existentialist, Lehmann asserted that the "resurrection of Jesus really is the starting point for Barth's theological thinking (and not Kierkegaard, as Lowrie would have us believe)" (138). See Walter Lowrie, *Our Concern with the Theology of Crisis* (Boston: Meador, 1932), 43-44.

[23]Lehmann, *Forgiveness*, 165-66.

[24]Ibid., 128-29.

the ethical imperative, it demands an ethos in conformity to it."[25] Analyzing Barth's politics, Todd Cioffi hearkens to his view of church as a "sympathetic communion" in which there is a "straight line" from God's mercy to our "very definite political problem and task."[26] Writing about Barth's account of agape, Caroline Simon suggests that he comes to lean heavily on Augustine's portrayal of the church *as a place of mutual forgiveness*.[27] Insights such as these gesture at something about which so much more could be said.

For Barth, the church as such shares an imperative of mercy, and in every encounter and endeavor looks to resound with John's refrain: "Look, the Lamb of God, who takes away the sin of the world!" (Jn 1:29 NIV). Above Barth's desk famously hung Mathias Grünewald's painting of the crucifixion, which shows John the Baptist pointing to Christ. Barth considered this image an encapsulation of his *Church Dogmatics*.[28] The consistency with which Barth follows this through is worthy of our attention. Our analysis will show that for Barth the imperatives of forgiveness and reconciliation find genuine place and meaning in the context of a christological ecclesiology set within the mission of God. Before we begin, it may be helpful to say a word or two more about the ecclesiology and ethics of his final volumes.

Karl Barth on Christian Life and Community

Any approach to the question of Karl Barth's theology of forgiveness must first recall that for Barth it is Jesus Christ who focuses every doctrine. Some reckon the results rather "constrictive," suggesting a christomonistic distortion of other doctrinal loci, but Daniel Migliore is right that Barth's christocentrism is meant to be more about "precedence" than "exclusion."[29] The

---

[25]Gerald McKenny, *Analogy of Grace: Karl Barth's Moral Theology* (Oxford: Oxford University Press, 2010), 44.

[26]Todd V. Cioffi, "Karl Barth and the Varieties of Democracy," in *Commanding Grace: Studies in Karl Barth's Ethics*, ed. Daniel L. Migliore (Grand Rapids: Eerdmans, 2010), 124-25, quoting *CD* II/1, 386. See also George A. Lindbeck, *The Nature of Doctrine: Religion and Theology in a Postliberal Age*, 2nd ed. (Louisville: Westminster John Knox, 2009), 134-35.

[27]Caroline J. Simon, "What Wondrous Love Is This? Meditations on Barth, Christian Love, and the Future of Christian Ethics," in *For the Sake of the World: Karl Barth and the Future of Ecclesial Theology*, ed. George Hunsinger (Grand Rapids: Eerdmans, 2004), 157; see also Augustine, *The City of God*, trans. Marcus Dodds (New York: Random House, 1950), 708.

[28]See Jürgen Fangmeier and Hinrich Stoevesandt, *Karl Barth Letters 1961–1968* (Grand Rapids: Eerdmans, 1981), 315, and *CD* I/1, 112.

[29]Daniel L. Migliore, "Commanding Grace: Karl Barth's Theological Ethics," in Migliore, *Commanding Grace*, 16. For critiques on this score—less relevant here than in Barth's doctrine of

result is a theological approach that is not immune to error but is certainly more properly illuminating than that which is consciously or unconsciously rooted in anthropology. It is the resurrection of Jesus and not an abstract principle with which Barth is trying to grapple when he focuses doctrines through a christocentric lens. This is well illustrated in his unfinished ethics of reconciliation, in which he insists that the ethical task cannot be generalized or reduced to legalism or casuistry, but must expound the "ever-new event" of "encounter with the living God."[30]

Differentiated in this way, Barth's "special ethics" has a definite appeal to it, but it is worth noting that his approach put him at odds with Catholic and Protestant theologians alike. Some question not only his ethics but also his ecclesiology for offering what appeared to be a diminished account of the continuity (and thus the reliability and accountability) of Christian life and community. While it is not the goal of this book to resolve these questions, it may be helpful to give a positive account of Barth's approach before we proceed.[31] Barth's answer, in short, is that continuity is provided by Christ himself, so that the Christian life is a matter of perpetual renewal in God's grace rather than a possession of achieved virtues or timeless truths. Not only does this construal bring forgiveness into the foreground of Barth's ethics, but it also impacts our understanding of what a forgiving community *does*. Thus it will do us well to briefly situate ourselves in the ongoing conversation of Barth's ethics and ecclesiology.

In 1981 William Werpehowski addressed two complaints that had come to (and still) typify the concerns over Barth's ethics.[32] Even if they are aptly

---

election—see David Gibson, *Reading the Decree: Exegesis, Election and Christology in Calvin and Barth* (London: T&T Clark, 2009), 6, and R. A. Muller, *After Calvin: Studies in the Development of a Theological Tradition* (Oxford: Oxford University Press, 2003), 97-98.

[30]*ChrL*, 5. This is a consistent theme in the *Dogmatics*, beginning in volume one. See *CD* I/2, 561-63.

[31]That is not to say I am indifferent to Barth's approach. My primary aim is to offer a constructive account of forgiveness, but a secondary hope is surely to follow through on ideas that were unfortunately cut short in the penultimate volume of Barth's *Dogmatics*. Thus I will be pleased if this book contributes to Barth scholarship by tracing his christocentric approach through to his ecclesiology and ethics in a theologically coherent and practically compelling manner. Indeed, the topic at hand is a particularly advantageous platform for such exploration precisely because it gets to the practical heart of Barth's focus on the "ever-new" mercy of God.

[32]See William Werpehowski, "Command and History in the Ethics of Karl Barth," *Journal of Religious Ethics*, 9, no. 2 (1981): 298-320, since republished as chapter two of William Werpehowski, *Karl Barth and Christian Ethics: Living in Truth* (Surrey, UK: Ashgate, 2014). Subsequent references will point to the 2014 book.

rebutted, these complaints continue to offer correctives to misapplication. The first, attributed originally to James Gustafson, was that Barth so construed ethics in terms of God's commanding that when it came to moral discernment the human agent was rendered either wholly passive or privately self-assured. The charge (sometimes labelled "occasionalism" or "intuitionism") was that Barth became something of an existential fideist, isolating ethics to the realm of private preparation for an unaccountable message from God.[33] The second (not unrelated) complaint, associated with Stanley Hauerwas, was that Barth's "command-obedience-model" excluded the community to such an extent that Christian life lost its sense of continuity and character.[34] In what remains of this first chapter we will address these complaints in three parts, beginning with Barth's account of human and divine agency, then of the centrality of invocation in ethics, and then of the place of continuity and character in Christian community.

Divine and human agency: Self-control as Spirit's fruit. A careful reader of Barth's *Dogmatics* is led to believe that the paradigmatic tension in Christian ethics might be found in Galatians 5:22-23, where one of the *fruits of the Spirit* is said to be *self-control*. As verse 25 indicates, "we live by the Spirit"—even in self-control. If it is our sinful trajectory to work this out on our own, it is Barth's concern to describe how it remains a work of God.

Barth's attentiveness to this point might be attributed to his particular historical moment: aghast that his mentors in Protestant liberalism did not seem to have the theological equipment to resist the German call to war, Barth turned to Scripture for reorientation.[35] As a result, Joseph Mangina observes, if "Kant and Schleiermacher inaugurated a theological turn to the subject," Barth proposed to steer "away from the human and toward the divine Subject" in the conviction that only there could humanity get its

[33]Werpehowski, *Living in Truth*, 15-17, referring to James Gustafson, *Can Ethics Be Christian?* (Chicago: University of Chicago Press, 1975), 156-57, and *Protestant and Roman Catholic Ethics* (Chicago: University of Chicago Press, 1978), 71, 73-74. See also Joseph L. Mangina, *Karl Barth on the Christian Life: The Practical Knowledge of God* (New York: Peter Lang Publishing, 2001), 93, 96.

[34]Werpehowski, *Living in Truth*, 16, referring to Stanley Hauerwas, *Character and the Christian Life: A Study in Theological Ethics* (San Antonio, TX: Trinity University Press, 1975), 11, 176, 220.

[35]See Nigel Biggar, "Hearing God's Command and Thinking About What's Right: With and Beyond Barth," in *Reckoning with Barth. Essays in Commemoration of the Centenary of Karl Barth's Birth*, ed. Nigel Biggar (Oxford: Oxford University Press, 1988), 102-3.

bearings.[36] This determination to ground ethics in divine agency of course led to the question of whether human agency was swallowed up in God's. But Eberhard Jüngel summed up the logic of Barth's claim rather to the contrary: by commanding invocation as "the basic act of the Christian ethos," God "purges himself from the base suspicion that he is [a] deity whose divine nature condemns him to be the only one at work."[37] Similarly addressing the charge of "divine monergism," Sheila Greeve Davaney points out that for Barth "God's determining knowledge and will do not *cancel* worldly self-determination but rather *establish* it."[38]

On this account, it seems that for Barth there are two expressions of human freedom: there is the designated freedom of living in obedience to the Creator, and there is the permitted shadow freedom in which humanity can opt not to so live. Humanity is ontologically determined by and for the creaturely freedom of obedience, but entailed in this is the freedom to reject the relationship as given. Daniel Migliore reckons that living outside of God's designs is a given prerogative, but that it sells the notion short to call this freedom.[39] Indeed, for Barth it amounts to an "impossible possibility"— apart from divine givenness humanity's freedom becomes tragically ironic; it assumes autonomy and ends up in slavery to what Barth calls "lordless powers."[40] As John Webster puts it, humanity "loses its proper agency in grasping after omnicompetence"—and "*suffers*."[41] In Barth's words, "God is indeed everything but only in order that man may not be nothing."[42]

What about the objection, then, that in this construal the human agent disappears altogether? This is, of course, not a problem unique to Christian theology. As Charles Taylor noted, *all* accounts of human freedom come against

---

[36]Mangina, *Christian Life*, 1, 19. See also Karl Barth, *Protestant Theology in the Nineteenth Century: Its Background & History* (London: SCM Press, 1972), 537, 397, and *The Theology of Schleiermacher: Lectures at Gottingen, Winter Semester of 1923/24*, ed. Dietrich Ritschl, trans. Geoffrey W. Bromiley (Edinburgh: T&T Clark, 1982), 276.

[37]Eberhard Jüngel, "Invocation of God as the Ethical Ground of Christian Action: Introductory Remarks on the Posthumous Fragments of Karl Barth's Ethics of the Doctrine of Reconciliation," in *Theological Essays*, trans. John Webster (Edinburgh: T&T Clark, 1989), 162. See also *ChrL*, 64.

[38]Sheila Greeve Davaney, *Divine Power: A Study of Karl Barth and Charles Hartshorne* (Philadelphia: Fortress, 1986), 44, emphasis added. See this point in John Webster, *Barth's Ethics of Reconciliation* (Cambridge: Cambridge University Press, 1995), 7.

[39]Migliore, "Commanding Grace," 1-29.

[40]See *CD* IV/1, 69, 547, and *ChrL*, 213.

[41]Webster, *Barth's Ethics*, 203.

[42]*CD* IV/1, 89. See also Webster, *Barth's Ethics*, 88-89, and *CD* II/1, 409.

the problem of "relating freedom to a *situation*," so that the most thorough-going arguments for "complete freedom" tend to render the human subject cut off and "situationless."[43] With this in view Joseph Mangina avers, "By grounding human identity solely and exclusively in Jesus Christ, Barth exposes the lie at the heart of both modernity's self-absorbed hubris (I can/must be everything) and postmodernity's self-absorbed despair (I am after all nothing)."[44] In Barth's statement that "God does not will to be God without us," Webster says, we should not hear "the *limitation* of divine freedom, but rather its *specification*": it is a freedom that "*specifies* rather than *hems in* the creature"[45]

This account of human freedom is certainly not original to Barth, but it does stand to be more fully appreciated for what Webster calls its "ethical import" for the "reciprocal active life of humanity."[46] With a view toward critical appropriation of Barth's ethic of forgiveness and reconciliation, we must thus attend briefly to his chosen rubric of invocation, and then to what Mangina refers to as the "social character" of the in-breaking kingdom of God.[47]

Invocation and moral discernment: A tale of two trees. One of the most provocative lines in Barth's *Dogmatics* has to be in the first part of volume four, when he gestures toward the Garden of Eden and suggests that what the tempting serpent had in mind was "the establishment of ethics."[48] We will misread this rhetoric, however, if we hear in it a degrading of ethical discernment rather than a denouncing of ethical presumption, or its mastery apart from invocation of God. As David Clough observes, Barth is often misunderstood on this score in three ways: he is thought either to be recommending "a voice in our head telling us what to do," to be denying the activity of discernment, or to be perpetuating postures of moral superiority.[49] In Clough's view, Barth's account does not shut up but *enlivens* the ethical endeavor by insisting "that we never stop seeking out God's word to us":

---

[43]Charles Taylor, *Hegel and Modern Society* (Cambridge: Cambridge University Press, 1979), 155, 157, emphasis added. See also John Webster, *Barth's Moral Theology: Human Action in Barth's Thought* (New York: Continuum International, 2004), 122, 115.

[44]Mangina, *Christian Life*, 201; see also 32, 101, 121.

[45]Webster, *Barth's Ethics*, 188; see also 185. See also *CD* II/1, 314; *CD* IV/1, 7; and *ChrL*, 103.

[46]Webster, *Barth's Ethics*, 46.

[47]See Mangina, *Christian Life*, 24, 27.

[48]*CD* IV/1, 448.

[49]David Clough, *Ethics in Crisis: Interpreting Barth's Ethics* (Aldershot, UK: Ashgate, 2005), 127-28.

It is straightforward to concede the point that ethicists do not speak with the voice of God, and so may make errors in their method or conclusions. It is harder to let go of an ambition for Christian ethics to develop solid and reliable principles and values that will in turn generate conclusions that can be depended upon. Barth maintains in this second claim that Christian ethics must not aim so high. We must free ourselves of the temptation "to win clear of the occurrence, the freedom and the peril of this event, to reach dry land, as it were, and to stand there like God, knowing good and evil."[50]

For Barth, God's command is always freshly discerned. This construal may sound disconcertingly open to arbitrariness and abuse, but is this not the case with any ethical system? As Nigel Biggar observes, it is just as easy to pour "the dictates and pronouncements of [one's] own self-will into the empty container of a formal moral concept."[51] Attuned to the voice of the living Lord who is trusted to be self-consistent, Barth contends, the church is most prepared to resist both fixed traditionalism and fickle trendiness.

For all his resistance to making an "anticipatory judgment," Barth does not think that the "ethical event" of the day-to-day Christian life is left to be tackled apart from "instructional preparation."[52] Christians trust that God's commands will not be ultimately discontinuous with what has been relayed in Scripture and heard by the church. Barth certainly emphasized the "final mystery of the encounter" with God, but in the face of this he also sought to counter the notion that there could be "no definitive statements" made or "certain lines" taken.[53] In fact, Barth said, "To draw these lines, to give these directives, is, in a general way, the task and theme of special ethics."[54] Thus there is license given by Barth himself for the final chapters of this book, wherein the implicit shape of his ethic of reconciliation will be drawn out more explicitly and built upon.

Before venturing into this, however, it is worth returning to the conditions Barth places on such an ethic. For him, Christian obedience means attending to biblically traditioned imperatives without freezing them in prescriptions or digging beneath them to secure timeless principles. As Simon puts it, this calls for "prayerful, open inquiry concerning how to be

---

[50]Clough, *Ethics in Crisis*, 130, citing *CD* III/4, 11.
[51]Nigel Biggar, *The Hastening That Waits: Karl Barth's Ethics* (Oxford: Clarendon Press, 1993), 8, 9.
[52]*CD* III/4, 18. For an excellent account of this, see Werpehowski, *Living in Truth*, 25-30, 43.
[53]See *ChrL*, 6-7, and *CD* IV/2, 372-73.
[54]*ChrL*, 7.

God's lovers in . . . concrete places and shifting times."[55] None of this need completely preclude the use of reason, the place of social norms, or the tutored reflection upon lives well lived, but it does embed these things within the primary activity of asking and listening for God's command together.[56] Barth did not think we could reason our way *to* God's command, but he did think we could reason *with* it.[57] As Werpehowski explains, our understanding of the "givens" of daily life and history will surely be challenged by God's self-revelation, but those "givens" will still be relevant. While it may offend presuppositions, Christ's command will be *knowable* to those seeking understanding in faith, and even *intelligible* to those seeking understanding without.[58] Nonetheless, in the "ethos" of the Lord's Prayer, believers are freed for action in a manner that in a vital sense "can never at any stage or in any form be anything but the work of beginners."[59]

Furthermore, because it takes place in a sphere that is not only *contingent* but *fallen*, Biggar is right that such an ethic is "epistemologically erroneous" when it abstracts moral discernment from *both* the condition of creaturely freedom *and* the situation of human sin.[60] For this reason it is especially interesting to note that before deciding to use the Lord's Prayer as a framework for his ethics of reconciliation, Barth considered utilizing the rubric of the "pardoned sinner."[61] Surely the move was a step up rather than sideways, since the content of the latter is well contained in the former. For our purposes, Joseph Mangina captures the import that remains: "To act morally is not to step into a vacuum, but into an ontological space defined by the events of the cross and resurrection. . . . To ground ethics in prayer is therefore to set it under the mark of the forgiveness of sins."[62]

---

[55]Simon, "What Wondrous Love," 145.

[56]Migliore, "Commanding Grace," 6-8, 14-16.

[57]See Biggar, *Hastening That Waits*, 41, 30; see also *CD* III/4, 29-30. God is free but this does not mean God is arbitrary; God operates intelligibly within the orders of the created sphere. For more on this see Matthew Rose, *Ethics with Barth: God, Metaphysics and Morals* (Surrey, UK: Ashgate, 2010), 59; see also *CD* III/1, 228.

[58]See Werpehowski, *Living in Truth*, 28-31. See also Biggar, *Hastening That Waits*, 2. Of course, to say Christian ethics will be *intelligible* does not mean it will be immune to charges of fideist insularity.

[59]*ChrL*, 79.

[60]Biggar, *Hastening That Waits*, 11; see also *ChrL*, 24.

[61]*ChrL*, 6-7. Attention is drawn to this in Biggar, *Hastening That Waits*, 86, 87n137.

[62]Joseph L. Mangina, "The Stranger as Sacrament: Karl Barth and the Ethics of Ecclesial Practice," *International Journal of Systematic Theology* 1, no. 3 (1999): 326-27.

For this reason Stanley Hauerwas rightly insists that "there can be no ethical use of scripture unless we are a community" that is "morally capable of forgiveness"—but in Barth's view it is precisely at this point that we must be careful not to be thrown back on our own capacities and conventions.[63] Such would be the ethic of the forbidden tree in Eden rather than the emptied cross of Calvary. One of the fruits of the Spirit is certainly self-control, but Barth's point is that if it does not remain a fruit of the Spirit the self-control in question may stem more from the First than the Second Adam's tree.[64]

For Barth this is no reason for ethical paralysis. In everything it does the church "will always need the forgiveness of the sins which it commits," but it is better to do "something doubtful or over bold, and therefore in need of correction and forgiveness, than nothing at all!"[65] On this account, Christ's mercy is to be invoked in the church's common life not only in the event of its potential failures but as a constitutive propellant in the ethical pursuit itself. Before we set our teeth into Barth's *Doctrine of Reconciliation* it will be helpful to consider how he approaches questions of continuity and character as it regards that common life.

On church growth: Continuity, character and mission. At the outset of the *Dogmatics'* fourth volume Barth indicates that "God with us" is "not a state, but an event." As such the church must not "degenerate into . . . an ecclesiastical form" that is "self-resting and self-motivated," or an "ethical system" that is "self-justified and self-sufficient," because "when this happens, the Christian message as such will no longer have anything individual or new or substantial to say."[66] This "event" characteristic is highly relevant to the way we construe the church's inner life, not to mention its witness.

The most prominent early attempt to grapple seriously with Barth's ecclesiology came from Hans Urs von Balthasar. The *Church Dogmatics* were only

---

[63]Stanley Hauerwas, *A Community of Character: Toward A Constructive Christian Social Ethic* (Notre Dame: University of Notre Dame Press, 1981), 4, 71, 69; see Eph 4:32. See also Hauerwas, *The Peaceable Kingdom: A Primer in Christian Ethics* (Notre Dame: University of Notre Dame Press, 1983), 89-90, and *Dispatches from the Front: Theological Engagements with the Secular* (Durham, NC: Duke University Press, 1991), 88, 57. For further distinction between Hauerwas and Barth on this point see Werpehowski, *Living in Truth*, 32-35; George Hunsinger, "A Response to William Werpehowski," *Theology Today* 43 (1986): 354, 359, and Biggar, *Hastening That Waits*, 138.
[64]See CD IV/1, 448; see also Gen 2:15-17; Rom 5:12-21; 1 Cor 15:45-58; Rev 22:1-5.
[65]In fact, "only as it makes this venture can it be sure of the forgiveness of its sins." CD IV/3.2, 779-80.
[66]CD IV/1, 5-6, 21.

half-finished when he called fellow Catholics to take note of this theology that presented the "deepest drive" of the Reformers' protest with "immense constructive power."[67] For his part, von Balthasar's reservations revolved around the question of how the church's life might be viewed analogously to Christ's. Where *analogia entis* located the analogy at the level of *form*, Barth's *analogia fidei* located it at the level of *orientation*, such that revelation remains reliant on God's revealing, and action on God's activity. With this von Balthasar did not entirely disagree. He wrote that "the essence of the Church is the *promise* of salvation and not its 'guarantee.'"[68] However, where von Balthasar pointed to the incarnation as the establishment of sin-cleansed forms of human life, Barth pointed to the resurrection as the validation of the incarnate Son's perpetual submission to the Father.[69]

So it is that Barth read the body of Christ metaphor in terms of ongoing reliance on a living Head, and von Balthasar in terms of solidity of representation on earth. As the latter theologian puts it, a "body simply cannot consist of isolated moments of actuality"; God is "free enough" to endow social structures with a form analogous to himself rather than make moments and individuals the locus of his reconciling work.[70] In reference to another metaphor, von Balthasar explains, "the Church is not only the *Body* of Christ but also his *Bride*"; for all her dependence on Christ she has still been given the integrity of "relational otherness."[71] To some it may seem like splitting hairs, and to others an overreaction to the problems of the sixteenth or the twentieth century, but in contrast with von Balthasar, Barth rigorously maintains God's

---

[67]Hans Urs von Balthasar, *The Theology of Karl Barth: Exposition and Interpretation*, trans. Edward T. Oakes (San Francisco: Ignatius, 1992), 39-40.
[68]"Christianity is no abstract affair. . . . Karl Barth is absolutely right that the problem of analogy in theology must finally be a problem of Christology." Ibid., 53-55. See also *CD* IV/2, 408-13.
[69]Kimlyn Bender specifies this further as the "analogy to obedient human activity" that is found in the way "Christ's human life mirrors and indeed represents the divine life of God in its own proper sphere of being and activity." Kimlyn J. Bender, *Karl Barth's Christological Ecclesiology* (Aldershot, UK: Ashgate, 2005), 5-7.
[70]Von Balthasar, *Theology of Karl Barth*, 387-88. Von Balthasar thought Barth had merely deflected everything to the register of individual autonomy (see 30-36), but later volumes to which he had not been privy made clear that Barth felt church and believer *both* found their Christian character in the rhythms of invocation rather than the means of mediation. See also *CD* IV/1, 650-52, and *ChrL*, 44-46, 71.
[71]Von Balthasar, *Theology of Karl Barth*, 107. What "the Protestant considers to be human overreaching in the Catholic church is actually for her the sign of the most extreme condescension of divine grace" and "the very high point of grace's power" (387).

freedom in the church's enablement, insisting that the church retain the character of an event, not an institution. God freely binds God's self to humanity in the person of Jesus Christ, without instituting or establishing a secondary mediator. This self-binding retains the fundamental character of an ongoing relation in history. God is no more inclined to hand over the reins at any point than to have Adam and Eve take for themselves from the tree of the knowledge of good and evil. In other words, the Bride is Bride precisely as she submits to her Groom, and the Body is Body inasmuch as it relies on its Head.[72]

After von Balthasar, theologians have tended to defend Barth's ecclesiology by highlighting how it applies christological correctives to good effect.[73] In this, the working premise is not that the hypostatic union has natural parallels in creation, but that divine self-consistency leads us to see in the relation of Christ's divinity and humanity a pattern for perceiving the relation of Christ and his church. It is not unusual to make the point that just as Jesus is born to a virgin, so the church is divinely initiated. What Barth presses further is the point that just as Jesus is the Christ in submission to the Father by the Spirit's power, so the church is the church precisely in its submission to Christ. The *origin* and *nature* of the church are not treated as two separate aspects but one. Barth speaks of the church in historical terms "as an event that must be constituted again and again through the work of the Holy Spirit."[74] This is the mystery he refuses to explain away: the church by definition has duration not *in itself* but *from outside itself*.

Kimlyn Bender traces this theme from Barth's *Epistle to the Romans* right through to his Calvin lectures and *Church Dogmatics*: in the former the true church on a sin-soaked earth is pictured as a tangent touching a circle, and

---

[72]Inasmuch as the first metaphor is relational and the second organic, exegetical analysis of the passages involved leads to a preference for Barth's dynamic account. See Mt 25:1-13; Rom 12:1-8; 1 Cor 12:1-31; Eph 4:1-16; 5:21-33; Rev 21:2, 9; 22:17. What is said here should in no way be taken as an affirmation of what is today known as a "complementarian" view of marriage, which institutes one-way submission of wife to husband. That the patriarchal norm is taken up to illumine the church's relation to Christ does not necessitate the blessing of that norm for all times and places. Note how submission is specifically "to one another" in Eph 5:21.

[73]See Bender, *Christological Ecclesiology*, 2-13, and George Hunsinger, *How to Read Karl Barth: The Shape of His Theology* (New York: Oxford University Press, 1991), 85, 173-80 and 286-87. See also von Balthasar, *Theology of Karl Barth*, 106-7, and Kimlyn J. Bender, "The Church in Karl Barth and Evangelicalism: Conversations Across the Aisle," in *Karl Barth and American Evangelicalism*, ed. Bruce L. McCormack and Clifford B. Anderson (Grand Rapids: Eerdmans, 2011), 177-200.

[74]Bender, *Christological Ecclesiology*, 153. See also pages 9, 104, 158-61, and *CD* IV/1, 151.

in the latter it is depicted as a vertical line perpetually intersecting a hori-zontal.[75] In retrospect, each of these images is probably best when they are held together. Since one could theoretically zoom in on such a mathematical point indefinitely without ever seeing a point of contact, the tangent illus-tration can lend itself to Docetism. Thus the image may be best combined with that of vertical intersection, especially if it is imagined as a motion picture rather than a snapshot. To explain, Bender helpfully appropriates von Balthasar's counterpoints in order to argue that the church's "recog-nition that it lives only in constant dependence upon a divine power" is precisely what gives vitality to its "confidence even in the precariousness of its historical existence." Thus it must "commit itself to ordering its external life in correspondence to its inner reality."[76]

One can see why the question is repeatedly raised as to whether Barth leaves himself any room to speak of the church in terms of an enduring form. For his part, Bender acknowledges a potential deficiency in Barth's work on this point, while maintaining that it was occasioned by a contex-tualized need to be adamant against the reduction of theology to soci-ology.[77] When the church forgets this, its efforts tend to be "emptied of their divine power and thus profane: preaching becomes instruction; sac-raments become religious rites; theology becomes philosophy; and mission becomes propaganda." Extending the still-relevant caution forward, then, we may find space to further specify Christian practices of forgiveness and reconciliation while nonetheless heeding Bender's (Barthian)

---

[75]See Bender, *Christological Ecclesiology*, 59, 71, 163; Karl Barth, *The Epistle to the Romans*, trans. Edwyn C. Hoskyns (London: Oxford University Press, 1933), 30; Barth,*The Theology of John Calvin*, trans. Geoffrey W. Bromiley (Grand Rapids: Eerdmans, 1995), 45-49, and *CD* IV/1, 643-47. Bender finds this idea in the *Gottingen Dogmatics* as well, where a merely *invisible* church is pejoratively referred to as a "cloud-cuckoo-land," but a merely *visible* church is rejected for a rendering wherein the church is always "becoming-visible" by the faithfulness of Christ. Bender, *Christological Ecclesiology*, 61, 72, and Karl Barth, *The Göttingen Dogmatics: Instruction in the Christian Religion*, vol. 3 (Grand Rapids: Eerdmans, 1991), 363-64.

[76]Bender, *Christological Ecclesiology*, 177.

[77]This is the last of Bender's four rejoinders to the objection, the only one to make a concession. The first points out Barth's willingness to in fact describe the church's ministry in terms of twelve basic forms, and the second and third rejoinders commend him for showing appropriate reserve. Systematic theology must hold back from prescribing "a timeless system of . . . practices" in order to describe the framework of timely Christian ethics. Ibid., 274-77. See also *CD* IV/3.2, 859-60, 864-901.

reminder that there is no "intrinsically sacred sociology."[78] Such is the explicit endeavor of this book's final chapters.

In Nicholas Healy's view, Barth's theology pushes us *not* to settle for "abstract ecclesiology" at the point when it calls for specificity.[79] Retaining Barth's adage that it is *the world* that "exists in self-orientation" and *the church* that "in visible contrast cannot do so," Healy nonetheless suggests we "retrain ourselves to . . . still talk about the configurations of practices that make us who we are."[80] Without this our account of the visible church might look less like the "rock" Jesus pictured in Matthew 16:18 and more like a piece of driftwood furtively popping up in the rapids. Joseph Mangina sees the latter "occasionalistic" reading as a failure to account for Barth's "unsparing . . . rejection of ecclesial docetism," not to mention his construal of the sacraments as God-ordained shapers of the church's common life.[81] With particular relevance for the argument of this book, Mangina explains,

> To paraphrase Stanley Hauerwas only slightly, the eucharist does not just imply a social ethic, it *is* a social ethic. . . . Implicitly, we would have to go on from an account of the eucharist to what may be called the church's "politics of forgiveness," the enactment of reconciliation in its common life, and to talk about possible parables of such reconciliation in the wider world.[82]

With comments like these in mind one can see why, in the chapters that follow, I explain Barth's theology of forgiveness within the context of his ecclesiology, and the practices of forgiveness within the ministry of reconciliation. Neither is properly understood without the other.

Before we proceed, it is worth highlighting how integral all of this is to Barth's missiology. For Barth, the church is nothing if not a witness to Christ. Furthermore, if we divide the external witness of the church from its internal identity and action, the church quickly becomes a mediator in too strong a sense. As missiologist J. C. Hoekendijk explained, we run into

---

[78]Bender, *Christological Ecclesiology*, 187.

[79]Nicholas M. Healy, "Karl Barth's Ecclesiology Reconsidered," *Scottish Journal of Theology* 25, no. 3 (2004): 296. See also *CD* IV/3.2, 772 and 854. Healy had previously been critical of Barth's ecclesiology on this score. See Nicholas M. Healy, "The Logic of Karl Barth's Ecclesiology: Analysis, Assessment and Proposed Modifications," *Modern Theology* 10 (1994): 253-70.

[80]*CD* IV/3.2, 780, and Healy, "Ecclesiology Reconsidered," 297-98.

[81]Mangina, "Stranger as Sacrament," 329, 331, 337.

[82]Ibid., 338-39.

problems of the sort where "God is recognized in an almost deistic fashion
as the great Inventor and Inaugurator of the Mission, who has since with-
drawn and left the accomplishment of the mission to His ground personnel."[83]
The church looks to its own inner life as the thing to be *duplicated*, rather
than conceiving of that life within the eccentric movement of God. As Nate
Kerr has argued, this kind of thinking leads the church to conceive of its
set-apartness in terms of distance or superiority rather than particularity of
its "ongoing solidarity *with* the world" in the event of Christ's reconciliation.[84] In Barth's view, as this book will argue and further explain, the grace
and love of Christ are *shared* and *received* in the same motion.

Hopefully it is clear that the topic of interpersonal forgiveness makes for
an ideal point at which to test the reach of Barth's special ethics and ecclesiology, and that the latter gives context for a better understanding of the
former. In the chapters that follow my contention is that practices of forgiveness and reconciliation are right at the heart of Barth's "ever-new" and
eccentric view of Christian life and community. Decades ago Paul Lehmann
rightly identified forgiveness as a vital theme in Barth's theology. What this
book aims to do is further explicate its place and meaning in the church's
common life and witness.[85] We begin in the next chapter with a thematically
attentive guide to *The Doctrine of Reconciliation*.

---

[83]J. C. Hoekendijk, *Kirche und Volk in der deutschen Missionswissenschaft* (Munich: Chr. Kaiser
Verlag, 1967), 335-36, quoted in John G. Flett, *The Witness of God: The Trinity, Missio Dei, Karl
Barth, and the Nature of Christian Community* (Grand Rapids: Eerdmans, 2010), 45.

[84]Nathan R. Kerr, "Das Ereignis der Sendung: The Word of God, Apocalyptic Transfiguration, and
the 'Special Visibility' of the Church" (paper, Princeton Theological Seminary, June 2010). See
also Mangina, "Stranger as Sacrament," 335-36, 338. As John Webster explains, "The church's
true being is located outside itself." Thus, even if we distinguish "acts of the *church in gathering*
and acts of the *church in dispersal*," neither stands free of the other, or from "reference to the
action of God." John Webster, "The Church as Witnessing Community," *Scottish Bulletin of
Evangelical Theology* 21, no. 1 (2003): 29-30.

[85]To my mind the best account of Christian forgiveness in recent decades has been L. Gregory
Jones, *Embodying Forgiveness: A Theological Analysis* (Grand Rapids: Eerdmans, 1995). Interest-
ingly, when Nicholas Healy speaks of the tendency to develop ethical concretions independent
of "well-rounded accounts of more central doctrines," for an example he points to Jones's book.
Healy, "Ecclesiology Reconsidered," 296. I take encouragement from this that a thoroughly
Barthian ethic of forgiveness may yet have something to contribute.

2

Forgiveness in
Church Dogmatics IV

IN ORDER TO ASSESS Karl Barth's understanding of *interpersonal* forgiveness within the life and witness of the Christian community, it is crucial to recognize how he set it in the context of the *divine* forgiveness central to God's reconciliation of the world to himself in Christ. Thus in this chapter we will investigate *The Doctrine of Reconciliation* (*Church Dogmatics* IV) by being attentive to the internal logic of Barth's account, following the outline paralleled within each of the three completed part-volumes (and echoed loosely in the posthumously published ethics section as well). As illustrated in table 1, Barth told the story of reconciliation by cycling three times through Christology, hamartiology, soteriology, ecclesiology and spirituality.[1] In this thrice-repeated fivefold arrangement Barth gave mutually complementary portrayals of each topic under consideration, building a systematic theology more symphonic than linear.

In order to retain Barth's rhythms of thought without being overly confined to them, this chapter and the next will weave freely through Barth's five recurring themes—Christ, sin and salvation in this chapter, church and spirituality in the next—before gathering up, explaining and building on what has been found. This formal adherence to the flow of Barth's argument does not

---

[1]Similar outlines are given in Eberhard Jüngel, *Theological Essays*, trans. John Webster (Edinburgh: T&T Clark, 1989), 159-60; Joseph L. Mangina, *Karl Barth on the Christian Life: The Practical Knowledge of God* (New York: Peter Lang Publishing, 2001), 176; and Paul D. Jones, *The Humanity of God: Christology in Karl Barth's Church Dogmatics* (London: T&T Clark, 2008), 266.

require material restriction to each section. I will take into account the relevant nuances of each part-volume as appropriate so that theological commitments can be traced to church imperatives. Indeed, by tracing forgiveness back to its roots in divine election and through to its telos in final redemption, we will see why Barth thought that only in the context of Christology could forgiveness be properly understood.

Table 1. Arrangement of *Church Dogmatics* IV

Volume	IV/1	IV/2	IV/3	IV/4
Overview	§57–§58			§74
Christology	§59 Lord as Servant: Jesus Christ, true God (priest)	§64 Servant as Lord: Jesus Christ, true human (king)	§69 Jesus is Victor: Promise of life with humanity (prophet)	§75 The Lord's baptism *§76 Invoking "Our Father"*
Hamartiology	§60 Sin as pride and fall, seen in light of obedience of Son of God	§65 Sin as sloth and misery, seen in light of active reign of Son of Man	§70 Sin as false-hood and condemnation, seen in light of True Witness	*§77.1/78.1 Honoring God with us* *§77.2/78.2 Revolt against false peace and lordless powers*
Soteriology	§61 Justification: Jesus frees from sin, as Judge judged in our place	§66 Sanctification: Jesus frees for life of discipleship and self-giving	§71 Vocation: Jesus calls to serve as witnesses to ends of God	*§77.3/78.3 We hallow the Name and pray God's kingdom will come*
Ecclesiology	§62 Holy Spirit gathers for Christian community	§67 Holy Spirit builds, grows and orders the community	§72 Holy Spirit sends, tasks community for the world	*§77.4/78.4 Hear God's command, seek God's justice*
Spirituality	§63 Holy Spirit awakens for life of faith	§68 Holy Spirit quickens for self-giving love	§73 Holy Spirit enlightens life in hope	*(§__ The Lord's Prayer)*
Note: The fourth column does not correlate with the rest, although some patterns can be detected. Sections in italics were posthumously published. Sections in parentheses were never written.				*(§__ The Lord's Supper)*

CHRIST: WHO FORGIVES AND WHY?

Sinfulness is not the same as creatureliness, nor is forgiveness the totality of God's grace. Sin or no sin, God is already being gracious not only when he creates but also when—in free self-commitment before the creation of the world—he decides, "I will be their God, and they shall be my people" (Jer 31:33). When we read of this covenantal decision in Jeremiah 31, however, the prophet immediately indicates that on this side of the fall into sin God can only be known by way of his further self-determination: "I will forgive their iniquity, and remember their sin no more" (Jer 31:34).[2] In this Barth is intent on observing that, in responding to sin, God remains self-consistent. God's being and act are united, as seen in Exodus, where God is self-revealed by saying, "I AM WHO I AM" and "[I] will show mercy on whom I will show mercy" (Ex 3:14; 33:19).[3] God's self-giving love is both the ground and telos of his forgiving mercy, even though the love is now only known through the mercy.

Nothing can be said of the primordial love of God except by way of the incarnate Son's overcoming not only of the "infinite qualitative distinction" between Creator and creature but also of the creaturely rebellion.[4] This is not to say that sin was needed for knowledge of God. Barth is at pains to avoid casting God in a merely reactionary role wherein sin is afforded inordinate credit as a conditioner of reality, or as a necessity for revelation. God is free, and God is free in his love. As prefigured in the old covenant and fulfilled in the new, from first to last God "does not will to be God without us."[5] God's response to sin is not Plan B, but the extent of his gracious resilience with Plan A. To understand what this means for forgiveness, a threefold insight will be pursued in this christological section: "God with us" is (1) the free self-commitment of God's being and activity (2) that commits humanity to a certain mode of being and activity and (3) unfolds in a particular history.

Lord as servant: God's free self-commitment to humanity (§59). The faith that seeks understanding in Barth's work begins and ends with the belief that

---

[2] See also Jer 7:23; 11:4; 24:7; 30:22; 31:1; 32:38. Barth says much on this in *CD* II/1, 257-321. For more on this see *CD* IV/1, 22, 33, 36-37, 42, 46-47, 64, 69-70, as well as Lev 26:12; Ezek 11:20; 37:23; Zech 8:8; 13:9; 2 Cor 6:16; Eph 1:4; Heb 8:10-12; 10:15-17.

[3] See *CD* II/2, 219-20.

[4] *ChrL*, 70-71.

[5] *CD* IV/1, 7 and 61. See Hos 2:23; Rom 9:26, as well as *CD* II/2, 292, and *CD* IV/1, 166, 172.

what we get in Jesus Christ, this crucified Jew of Nazareth, is God. We imagine our gods, but the Lord is revealed a servant. Reflecting on John 1, Barth says,

> In the beginning, before time and space as we know them, before creation, before there was any reality distinct from God which could be the object of the love of God or the setting for His acts of freedom, God anticipated and determined within Himself (in the power of His love and freedom, of His knowing and willing) that the goal and meaning of all His dealings with the as yet non-existent universe should be the fact that in His Son He would be gracious towards man, uniting Himself with him.[6]

In this there has yet to be any mention of sin or forgiveness, but there is the free and loving self-commitment of God in eternity past to not only create humanity but to take it into his very existence. In Christ, God is not only *revealed* but also *united to* humanity. With Barth we read Philippians 2 and understand gratefully that though he was free to do so God did not cling to *divinity alone* but condescended to give of self and to join with humankind. Furthermore, in this free grace God has gone so far as to pursue humankind even when it returned the favor by grasping tragically at *humanity alone*. Divinity alone is not empty or incomplete but triune and holy, whereas humanity alone is not only lonely and destitute, but absurd.[7]

Nonetheless, as both the electing God and the elected human Jesus takes on sinful flesh and submits to death on a cross, thereby holding humanity in union with God *in, through and despite* its deathly stab at autonomy.[8] So it is that in Jesus' life, death and resurrection it is revealed simultaneously that there is a rift in the union of God with humanity and that there has been a merciful crossing of that rift from God's side to ours. Divine forgiveness shows us both the *fact* and the *extremity* of God's self-commitment to the world. This was not a necessity for God, but neither was it discontinuous with God's character: "The word 'forgiveness' . . . does not speak of a new purpose or disposition or attitude on the part of God."[9] Although the difference between God's creative grace and reconciling mercy has everything to do with the entrance of enmity into God's creation, divine forgiveness is

---

[6] *CD* II/2, 101-2. See *CD* IV/2, 342.
[7] See Phil 2:6-8 as well as *CD* II/2, 121-25; *CD* IV/1, 158, 180, 201-4; *CD* IV/2, 92, 100 and *ChrL*, 125.
[8] See *CD* II/2, 3-11, 94-95, 124-25.
[9] *CD* IV/1, 94; see 47, 64.

not grounded in that to which it responds. The gift of creaturely communion with God and one another overflows freely from the perfection of God, and this is understood only through the specific event of grace in which the Lord became Servant to reconcile the world to God.[10]

An account of Christian forgiveness must be rooted to this Christ event. This is forgotten to the detriment of both theology and practice. As Barth says,

> It is a terrible thing if at this point, at the last moment, we ignore [Jesus Christ] as though He were only a means or instrument or channel, and look to something different from Him, some general gift mediated by Him . . . [by] developing an anthropological concept which we have found elsewhere and to which we have simply given a christological superscription.[11]

God is love, but a "general idea of love" is not God.[12] So too Jesus forgives, but a general idea of forgiveness is not necessarily what Jesus brings. As Barth wrote in response to Berkouwer's *Triumph of Grace*, "Grace is undoubtedly an apt and profound and at the right point necessary paraphrase of the name Jesus," but since "the statement needed is so central and powerful . . . it is better not to paraphrase the name of Jesus, but to name it."[13] Otherwise we end up with a principle precisely where the person matters most. To understand forgiveness we speak not of grace generally, but of participation with Christ.

Servant as Lord: God's exalted definition of humanity (§64). In Jesus Christ we see not only God's self-commitment *to* humanity but also his commitment *of* humanity to a particular mode of being and activity.[14] The humble self-giving of Christ is divine, and also *determinatively humane.* When Philippians 2 extols Christ's extreme servanthood as the highest expression of God's glory *it calls us to have the very same attitude.*[15] That the Lord surprises us by coming as a servant says as much about us as it does about him. We have fallen from love. Thankfully, the divine love is not only an "electing love" but also a "purifying love" and a "creative love"—it "causes

---

[10]See *CD* IV/2, 345-46, and *CD* II/2, 166.

[11]*CD* IV/1, 116; see also 124.

[12]*CD* II/1, 276; see also 275, 281-82, and *CD* IV/1, 4, 203.

[13]*CD* IV/3.1, 173, referring to G. C. Berkouwer, *The Triumph of Grace in the Theology of Karl Barth* (London: Paternoster, 1956).

[14]See *CD* IV/1, 304, *CD* IV/2, 32 and *CD* IV/3.1, 356-57.

[15]See Phil 2:1-11, and *CD* IV/1, 635.

those who are loved by Him to love."[16] Because divine forgiveness is not a mere patch-up job—discontinuous with God's nature or plan for humanity—we must be diligent against the construal in which it is rendered a means to some ambiguously related end (such as a so-called second chance or clean slate).[17] It is not simply the case that Jesus is the prime example of a human ideal that we are independently capable of discerning and achieving. In showing us true humanity Jesus also shows us the insurmountable impediment of our fall from grace that could only be overcome by God on our behalf. *All* humanity is judged at the cross of Christ, and there all humanity is atoned for in God's self-giving love.

Barth is not one to confine himself to categories, but it is clear that he holds to a view of the atonement as unlimited, and that this informs his view toward an indiscriminate and free sharing of Christ's grace between persons. As Tom Greggs summarizes, "What is important for Barth is that the Christian cannot view the non-Christian as anything other than the person for whom God elected, who is elected in Christ and whose rejection is all too well known by the reality of the faith community as well."[18] The scope of this project does not allow a full-scale treatment of Barth's doctrine of election, but the question arises as to whether his account of interpersonal forgiveness depends upon his views of election and unlimited atonement (on the basis of which some speculate he is a proponent of universalism). When it comes to questions of how many will be saved, Barth insists that on this side of the eschaton the mystery must remain. However, his treatment does not leave the question in the same condition in which it was found.

Rather than locating the mystery in the pretemporal decision of God, Barth finds it in the temporal persistence of sin itself. Given that God is revealed in Christ, Barth shifts perplexity from God's side to ours. There is no misgiving that somewhere behind the back of the God known in Christ stands a God who decides a fate for individuals other than what he asks believers to hope for and work toward.[19] That there are sinners and rebels against God is the

---

[16]See *CD* IV/2, 766, 771 and 776.

[17]See *CD* II/2, 110-11.

[18]Tom Greggs, "'Jesus Is Victor': Passing the Impasse of Barth on Universalism," *Scottish Journal of Theology* 60, no. 2 (2007): 212; see also 197, 199, 205-6 and 211. See also *CD* IV/3.1, 91, and *ChrL*, 200, 211, 270-71.

[19]This could be countered by such biblical passages as Isaiah's call to "go and tell this people" to "be

quixotic absurdity. It is not to be trusted. Given what we know about God's unlimited grace, when he weighs the biblical evidence and theological factors, Barth calls universal reconciliation a legitimate hope but maintains that such a thing can only be grace and thus never an entitlement or expectation.[20]

Which returns us to this question: Could a person share Barth's account of interpersonal forgiveness who held alternate views such as limited atonement, double predestination or open theism? The short answer is "probably, yes," but it is worth noting that Barth's emphasis on the universality of Christ's reconciliation affords him unique opportunities. Prompted by several biblical texts (e.g., Mt 18:35; Rom 15:7; Eph 4:32; Col 3:13; 1 Jn 4:19), one who holds to limited atonement might generally be inclined to say, "I forgive *you* because God has forgiven *me*." Prompted by others (e.g., Mt 6:14-15; Jn 20:23; 2 Cor 5:15-20; Col 3:11-13; Jas 2:12-13; 1 Jn 4:7-21), however, those who hold to universal atonement might be more inclined to say, "I forgive *you* because God forgives *us*." By locating the conundrum on our side rather than God's, with Barth we reckon interpersonal forgiveness freely extended on the basis of what we *know* rather than on the basis of what we do not. Whatever we think of Barth's view on these matters, we take from it a vibrant call to get caught up in the victory of Christ and to "enter into this history and therefore this conflict of His" with hope.[21]

The God-man Jesus Christ: God comes with a history (§69). For Barth, God's being is known in his act: "He tells us what He does and He tells us as He does it."[22] To know God is to know him as a man with a history. In this we are referred back to the Law and the Prophets that Jesus fulfilled and forward to the day-to-day reality in which the risen and ascended Jesus meets us on his way to our full redemption. God's primordial mercy unfolds into a history that is ongoing and engaging *because* it is accomplished once for all.[23] Now is the time for the "modest praise of God" that is our "little

---

ever hearing, but never understanding" (Is 6:9-13 NIV), but even there the final word is that "this people will not come to an end with this judgment." *CD* IV/3.2, 581.

[20]See *CD* IV/3.1, 477–78.

[21]See *CD* IV/3.1, 173, 175, 179-80, 477-78, and *CD* IV/3.2, 485, 490.

[22]*CD* IV/1, 143; see also 177, and *CD* II/1, 32.

[23]See *CD* II/2, 191, 194. As Barth said in his *Doctrine of Creation*, "The man Jesus has his own time, but He also has more than that: Risen and exalted He is the Contemporary of all." *CD* III/2, 440. This works prominently into volume four. See *CD* IV/1, 312, 249-50; *CD* IV/3.1, 43-45, 105-6 and *CD* IV/3.2, 483.

human Yes" to the "great Yes which God has spoken" in Christ and continues to speak by his Holy Spirit.[24] In this we do not actualize a latent human possibility, as if Christ opened the door to a goal that could have been attained by human beings on their own. Instead we move with Jesus, whose reconciling work is once for all, both in the sense of being completed in our past and in the sense of being present to us in perpetual newness.[25]

Because God and humanity really are united in Christ, and because Jesus lives toward the full sharing of that union by his Spirit, Barth considers knowledge of God to be inseparable from its ethical import.[26] This does not mean that knowledge of God *rests on* human action, but that the grace of Christ *entails* and *enables* it. This is the grace of *God with us*: "He wills to give us a share in His work in our independence as the creatures of God summoned to freedom, as those who are justified and sanctified in Him."[27] Further, because knowledge of God comes to people who have turned away from him and turned against each other, it comes not within the context of God's pristine original grace but within the perfecting work of his forgiving love.[28] To be a Christian is to follow Christ in the midst of a history of conflict that has been given space and time to exist—not because God *needs* this space and time, but because he has graciously *willed* it. This is no accident; it is a testimony to the fact that "He does not will to be alone, but to have fellow-participants and witnesses of this life."[29]

From this it follows that refusing to share or extend God's mercy in our particular circumstances is tantamount to refusing to be part of God's movement toward us in the first place.[30] The church's indiscriminate extension of God's love in the world is not for Barth an *imitatio Christi* owing to the human inability to discern who is or is not elect, but is a *participatio Christi* stemming from a conviction that *all* are *elect in Christ*. We forgive not because we give someone the benefit of the doubt, but because we hold

---

[24]*CD* IV/1, 353; see also *CD* IV/3.1, 3, 10.
[25]See *CD* IV/1, 284-85, 312, and *CD* IV/3.1, 223-24.
[26]See *CD* IV/1, 169, 188.
[27]*CD* IV/3.1, 332. See *CD* IV/2, 280-1.
[28]See *CD* II/1, 44.
[29]*CD* IV/2, 325. See *CD* IV/3.2, 542.
[30]A plethora of Scripture references could be rallied in support of this. See Is 58; Hos 6:6; Amos 5:21-24; Jon 1-4; Mt 5:7, 23-24; 6:9-15; 12:1-12; 18:12-35; Mk 12:28-34; Jn 20:21-23; Rom 15:5-7; 2 Cor 5:15-21; Eph 4:25-5:2; Phil 2:1-11; Col 3:8-17; Jas 2:12-13; 1 Jn 4:7-21.

to it in faith that "in Christ" God truly was (and is) "reconciling the world to himself" (2 Cor 5:19).[31] As explained, this is a doctrine of unlimited atonement, not a dogmatic universalism. The qualification "in Christ" leaves open a construal that would describe the "reprobate" as those who forsake their elected existence for an eternity in the terror or nothingness of that "impossible possibility."[32] For our purposes, the key point is that there should be no doubt about the life for which all persons are elected. Those who reject it live in the pain of rejection, not some other option of their choosing. Those who accept it share it.

SIN: WHAT NEEDS FORGIVING?

Before we move to a further understanding of forgiveness in Barth's *Doctrine of Reconciliation* we must first consider what divine forgiveness reveals and overcomes, thus allowing the light of Christ to expose that which is parasitic on his ethical and ecclesiological imperatives. This is a move to be made with care. Too often it is assumed that humanity has a latent awareness of its sin that simply needs to be amplified so that salvation in Christ may be introduced. Barth exposes and resists this tendency, insisting that humanity does not grasp the nature of its problem unless God reveals it for what it is. Humanity is of course aware of a tension in its existence, but does not have the means to separate the appropriate limits of finitude from the perversions of fallenness. At best it has a nagging awareness of evil waiting to be revealed as such by Christ, a "sleeping knowledge" of its enmity that it exasperates in flailing discontent, knowing not what it does.[33]

When it comes to a doctrine of sin, then, it will not do to simply "stir up a sense of . . . the *infinitely qualitative difference* between God and man" when

---

[31]"Dogmatics has no more exalted or profound word—essentially, indeed, it has no other word—than this." *CD* II/2, 882. See also *CD* IV/3.2, 607.

[32]*CD* IV/3.2, 484. The best treatments of Barth on this topic can be found in Oliver D. Crisp, "'I Do Teach It, but I Also Do Not Teach It': The Universalism of Karl Barth (1886–1968)," in *"All Shall Be Well": Explorations in Universalism and Christian Theology, from Origen to Moltmann*, ed. Gregory MacDonald (Eugene, OR: Cascade, 2011), 305-24, and Tom Greggs, *Barth, Origen, and Universal Salvation: Restoring Particularity* (Oxford: Oxford University Press, 2009). For a connection with ethics and witness along the lines drawn here, see Paul T. Nimmo, "Barth and the Christian as Ethical Agent: An Ontological Study of the Shape of Christian Ethics," in *Commanding Grace: Studies in Karl Barth's Ethics*, ed. Daniel L. Migliore (Grand Rapids: Eerdmans, 2010), 216-38.

[33]*CD* IV/3.1, 192. See also *CD* IV/1, 173, 360-61, 372-73, 387; *CD* IV/2, 379-83 and *CD* IV/3.1, 84, 145.

what is needed is explicit "knowledge that man finds himself *in contradiction against God* (and therefore against his neighbour and himself)." If we hold ourselves to "the abstract law of an abstract god" we can expect that the "resultant knowledge of human sin will correspond to" the "free speculation of the human reason and of arbitrary human imagining."[34] In that case, Barth asks, could humanity not simply be excused for being what it is? Barth departs from a Hegelian scheme, insisting that sin is not a necessary "middle act in a drama" or "point to be passed through," but something alien and opposed to God that is overcome by Christ in favor of an "incomprehensibly new beginning."[35] It is when the Son of God takes flesh that the goodness of creatureliness is revealed and a demarcation is made between the proper interdependency of finitude and the broken relations of fallenness. So to offer a doctrine of sin apart from a christological doctrine of creation and reconciliation would be, Barth says, "to sin again—theologically!"[36]

The true horror of evil is seen in the manner of God's response to it: the Son of God himself is given over to death by crucifixion. In this we see not merely a *reaction*—as if the good were defined by the evil—but the extent of the Son's willful obedience to the will of the Father. The cross is taken up in love—not because sin and death force his hand. "Whatever sin is, God is its Lord. We must not push our attempt to take evil seriously to the point of ever coming to think of it as an original and indeed creative counter-deity."[37] Instead Barth referred to sin as *das Nichtige*, prompting Berkouwer to suggest he was "robbing evil of its sting," to which Barth replied that rather than denying sin's existence he was refusing to grant it the respect that is due to God alone.[38]

Evil is best understood in terms of privation; it has no power or being of its own. It is creation curving in on itself and thus negating itself as such. Evil is the paradox that makes God appear paradoxical: "It is not paradoxical or

---

[34] *CD* IV/1, 363-64, and *CD* IV/3.1, 369.

[35] *CD* IV/1, 373, and Karl Barth, *Protestant Theology in the Nineteenth Century: Its Background & History* (London: SCM Press, 1972), 418, 402. See G. W. F. Hegel, "The Consummate Religion," in *The Lectures of 1827*, ed. P. C. Hodgson (Berkeley: University of California Press, 1988), 450-54.

[36] *CD* IV/1, 141; see also 144 and 360. That there is both contrariety and harmony within nature speaks of "the imperfection of the world which even as such belongs to its perfection as the creaturely world of God." *CD* IV/3.1, 145.

[37] *CD* IV/1, 408; see also 258, 266 and 411-12.

[38] *CD* IV/3.1, 177, and Berkouwer, *Triumph of Grace*, 247-54. See also *CD* III/3, 289, and *CD* IV/2, 411.

absurd that God becomes and is man. . . . But it is certainly paradoxical and absurd that man wants to be as God."[39] As Barth explains it, evil is that to which God implicitly said no when he explicitly said "let there be"; it is the nonwill of God.[40] The God who created *ex nihilo* and brought form from *toho wabohu* can make good come out of evil, but there is nothing good or necessary about evil as such. There is therefore no *felix culpa*, as such. Sin redeemed is still "inexcusable," even an "impossible possibility."[41] The reason it has a *history* is because God leaves room for creaturely participation. There is an ongoing "history of conflict" between the Yes and the No, but the conflict is "decided" and God has not kept his distance from those who are in it.[42]

Caught up in this conflict, humanity is at every moment in need of a total reorientation corresponding to the manner of its intended creatureliness, and this only comes by new creation in Christ. Barth prefers to speak of sin in dynamic rather than static, hereditary language in order to refer to "original sin" not in a fatalist but a perpetually cooperative sense.[43] The doctrines of original sin and total depravity can be inadequate to describe the real problem here, which is not a loss of the goodness of being human but a turn to that which contradicts it. It is not so much that the human nature is "poisoned" but that it "poisons" itself repeatedly.

Even though Barth insisted that sin is known in light of Christ and not vice versa, it will help to clear the ground for a positive description of Christian forgiveness and reconciliation by describing the impostors exposed by Christ along the way. Each part-volume of *The Doctrine of Reconciliation* focuses on sin from an angle corresponding to one of the three offices of Christ. Sin is seen as pride in light of Christ's humble priestly service, as slothful self-care in light of Christ's royal lordship and as falsehood in light of Christ's self-revealing, prophetic presence in the world.[44] By considering the thrust of each of these sections we will not only get a sense of what Barth thinks is forgiven in Christ, but also of the fraudulent forms of the ministry of reconciliation that might be taken. Just as common renderings of the

---

[39]*CD* IV/1, 419; see also 46-48, 74, 140, 249, 409-13, and *CD* IV/2, 408-12.
[40]See Gen 1 and *CD* IV/3.1, 178.
[41]*CD* IV/1, 69, 547.
[42]*CD* IV/3.1, 168, 172, 237. See also *CD* IV/1, 480-82, and *CD* IV/3.1, 271.
[43]*CD* IV/1, 500; see also 492-96, 509-11.
[44]See *CD* IV/3.1, 369.

Lord's Prayer refer to sin in terms of both debts and as trespasses, so believers know that they will sin even in their successes. In fact, even our acts of interpersonal forgiveness themselves will stand in need of divine mercy.

Self-forgiveness: Pride in light of Christ's humility (§60). In John 3:16-18 we see that Jesus comes for the entire world, not to condemn but to save. In this saving act, however, is found the indictment of all. Were there no such judgment there would be no such Savior. Apart from God's self-revelation our concept of sin is as malleable as our concept of deity. Jesus Christ reveals that we play god and do not even get God right. We set ourselves up as false gods and succeed in the attempt, thereby also perpetuating a false humanity. Barth observes, "It is tempting to ask whether man does not usually invent and deck out for himself this idol just because he knows that he cannot be compared with it and therefore that there is no risk of his being put to shame by it."[45] Meanwhile, God humbles himself, takes on flesh and submits even to death at human hands for our sake. No matter what our myths of human progress or regress, Christ's death on the cross exposes them as the "strange human vacillation" of our sin, the predictable "monotony of pride."[46]

As Barth describes it, even an amplified account of evil's monstrosity can be a form of pride. Our predilection to posit sin as something with a radical, ontological existence can lead to a superficial account of its pervasiveness. Distanced from radical evil, we project a gradation of perceived sinfulness wherein we can always find "disproportionately more evil in others than ourselves." Presuming to be more able than others to offer a "counter-movement" to sin (either by willpower, disposition or advantage of socio-structural circumstances), we are then set up to repeat the fall and "accelerate its headlong course to the abyss." This all takes place under the guise of social tolerance, which is a provisional cease-fire always on the brink of breaking out in self-vindicating judgments and their correspondent shamings.[47] The old saying is that pride goes before a fall, but it follows after with self-granted amnesty too.

With this we heed a warning that concerns our topic. Faith in a forgiving God is not a license to perform our own sin management. Taking up

[45]*CD* IV/2, 385; see 403, 407. See also *CD* IV/1, 422-23, and 132, 437, 446, 463.
[46]*CD* IV/1, 507-8; see also 404.
[47]Ibid., 404, 213 and 447. See also *CD* IV/2, 385, 420-21, 443-44.

Feuerbach's charge that religious moralism finds its self-righteous strength in the *projection* of a forgiving god, Barth's account of Christian faith is careful to condemn the self-forgiving Feuerbach thinks is at its essence.[48] When it is turned toward interpersonal relationships, the proclivity to "retreat into the fantasies of stricter or milder self-judgments" unleashes competitive accounts of self-worth and the production of further enmity.[49] The church is certainly not immune to this—even when one member or another appears to be benevolently granting forgiveness. In the most insidious of self-forgiving communities one finds a tendency to isolate in enclaves of nonthreatening like-mindedness and to call them churches. The church misunderstands itself if it chooses simply to "console itself with the idea that everything human is imperfect, or the recollection that its sins are forgiven."[50] We will have more to say about this later when we return to the topic of false peace in chapter six, but some of what it entails may also be seen in Barth's second hamartiological section, concerning the sin of sloth.

Self-help: Sloth in lieu of Christ's movement (§65). In the light of Christ's obedience to the Father we see in humanity that penchant for self-help that Barth calls the sin of sloth. Though it is often perceived merely as a sin of passivity, Barth speaks of sloth in both an active and a passive sense. If creaturely freedom is found in obedience to the Creator, the reasoning goes, then sloth is the anxious self-care that either *opts out* or *acts out* on its own.[51] Had Jesus fallen to this temptation in the wilderness, Barth says that even he would have "betrayed the cause of God by making it His own cause, by using it to fulfil His own self-justification before God"—thus leaving "in the lurch the world unreconciled with God."[52]

On one hand, sloth can take the passive form of a seemingly defensible resignation; on another, it can take the form of an "activism" bent on self-projected visions of success.[53] Perhaps most commonly it takes the form of

---

[48]See Ludwig Feuerbach, *The Essence of Faith According to Luther*, trans. M. Cherno (New York: Harper, 1967), 59, 82, 84, 100, and *CD* IV/2, 422.

[49]*CD* IV/2, 395-96, 458, 461. See also *CD* IV/1, 238, 325, 361, 366-67, 404-5, 489, 507.

[50]*CD* IV/2, 709.

[51]Barth describes sloth as *die Sorge*, which is translated "care" but may be rendered more clearly in English as "anxiety" or, with the right theological overtones, "anxious self-help." *CD* IV/2, 469-72. See also *CD* IV/1, 463-64, as well as Mt 6:34 and 1 Pet 5:7.

[52]*CD* IV/1, 263, and 278. See also Mt 4, Mk 1 and Lk 4.

[53]See *CD* IV/2, 473-75, and *CD* IV/3.1, 243-44.

poise, wherein a self-struck balance is sought between the two. When Barth reflects on the biblical account of the fall and calls it "the establishment of ethics," he has in mind this temptation to *establish and possess* knowledge of good and evil apart from the command of the living God. Rather cleverly he explains, "If man will not be helped by the fact that he is helped by God, the only alternative is to be his own helper and to try to have in God the One who helps him to help himself."[54] Personal crises and societal tragedies may shake such self-reliance, but may also bolster its resolve.

According to Barth, sloth manifests itself in many ways, the worst of them religious.[55] It can even have a cruciform piety to it, wherein one finds inspiration in Christ's atoning work but acts as if Jesus were still dead. To descend into soul-scrubbing introspection in face of this indictment would only prove the point. Barth insists that while "we have to ask soberly and honestly" who we are and what we are doing, the answer is always "decided in the hearing of what God has to say to us concerning ourselves in the Word of His grace." Otherwise we are back in the realm of a presumed natural knowledge of sin that can easily "be only a dramatised form of the self-knowledge of man left to himself."[56] An ethos of mere moralism is easily established wherein heroes and platitudes form a hierarchy of holiness, such that the whole enterprise of Christian ethics comes crashing down around the very community that is meant to subject itself to the righteousness that comes from above. As Barth puts it, "The old game of self-reconciliation and anxiety and indifference still goes on."[57]

When sloth such as this prevails, a convenient philanthropy takes the place of love, and anonymous targets for self-assuring benevolence are set up in place of confrontations with actual neighbors. These slothful attempts at fellowship are deceptive when they succeed, and devastating when they are exposed.

> We can and will make constant appeals to the solidarity of [fretful care], and
> constant attempts to organise anxious men, reducing their fears and desires to
> common denominators and co-ordinating their effects. But two or three or even

---

[54]*CD* IV/1, 448 and 462. See also *CD* IV/2, 476-67, 609.
[55]See *CD* IV/2, 406, and *ChrL*, 128-29, 130-31.
[56]*CD* IV/1, 497-98 and 387.
[57]*CD* IV/3.1, 253. See also *CD* IV/1, 451.

millions of grains of sand, however tightly they may be momentarily compressed, can never make a rock. . . . [Fretful concerns] can never be organised and co-ordinated in such a way as to avoid mutual disappointment and distrust and final dissolution. And behind disappointment and distrust there lurks, ready to spring, the hostility and enmity and conflict of those who are anxious.[58]

Here is another warning to be heeded in the appropriation of forgiveness. Love and mercy are active, but in the movement of Christ they are not to be abstracted and put in the service of human autonomy. This concern will reemerge when we discuss forgeries of forgiveness and reconciliation in chapters four and five, but for now we proceed to the third of Barth's hamartiology sections, which focuses on falsity itself.

Self-soothing: Falsehood in evasion of Christ's ministry (§70). The third type of sin Barth finds fully exposed in the revelation of Jesus Christ is falsehood. As the privation of truth, falsehood provides nothing of its own, but only utilizes truth in order to evade it. Because it is relative to the truth that has been revealed, Barth suggests that of the three types of sin, falsehood is at its most mature mutation in the time following the resurrection and ascension of Christ. The Holy Spirit guides into truth, and falsehood scrambles to avoid or detract from it. Falsehood will "canalise and transform" truth in order to "confirm it emphatically," recommend it as "tolerable and useful," and "champion it" in a form "divested of the distinctive menace" it poses to false humanity. This can be the stuff of self-soothing piety or biblical scholarship; if we usurp "the truth in the name of truisms," we reduce the living Christ to an overseer of principles that we can harness in a self-serving system.[59] Falsehood is related to sloth in the sense that it provides its rhetorical and intellectual support. It is the evasion of the living Word of God.

Contrary to those objectors who see in Barth an almost naive monism of grace, in his doctrine of sin we see him so attuned to the pathology and pervasiveness of our human disorientation that we might be tempted to call it the triumph of despair. It could certainly drive us further into anxious care. Indeed, in each part of the doctrine of sin it has been clear that both our wanderings and (even at the best of times) our worship leave us utterly dependent

---

[58]*CD* IV/2, 476-77, and 438-40, 475. My own renderings of *Die Sorge* are in the brackets. See *KD* IV/2, 539.
[59]*CD* IV/3.1, 436 and 438. See 435, 442, 448 and 475, as well as Jn 16:8. See also *ChrL*, 152.

on the mercy of God.[60] This is another warning to be heeded for our topic. Sin pollutes every human being and act, not just the obviously bad ones. The danger of pointing at ourselves rather than Christ may actually be highest precisely at the point of our well-doing. For divine forgiveness we are in constant need. So Barth issues a call for confession and invocation of Christ's forgiveness in circumstances of *both* abject failure *and* apparent success.[61]

The warning against sacrosanct triumphalism is no push to the ditch of despondency. In the Yes and Nonetheless of God is the grace that overcomes sin, so that all service can be rendered to the living Lord with the positive hope in his faithfulness to the task he has given.[62] As Barth put it, the work of the Christian stands "upon the foundation of Christ, and on this foundation it is forgiven for all its uselessness"[63] In faith we confess that grace is greater than law, mercy triumphs over judgment and love covers a multitude of sins.[64]

So it is that in his frank sensitivity to evil's paradoxical presence in the world, Barth refuses to let sin become the defining axis even of his hamartiology. Instead these sections resound with something like optimism but richer, a hope born not from human experience but the mercy and promises of God. Based upon Barth's depiction of sin and its attendant pathologies, our appropriation of forgiveness will either have to argue against his warnings or heed them. Convinced enough to attempt the latter, it will be our goal in this project to articulate an ethic of forgiveness and reconciliation without making it a self-sufficient system or scheme. In doing so we must not settle for ambiguities where clear contours are required, nor turn Christ's *ministry of reconciliation* into little more than a *method of self-help*. Before we get to that, however, we must focus on Barth's soteriology in the remainder of this chapter (and his ecclesiological ethic in the next), from which will emerge a constructive account of his theology of forgiveness.

SALVATION: WHAT DOES GOD'S FORGIVENESS ENTAIL?

The soteriological sections of the *Church Dogmatics* follow a threefold pattern focusing on the justification, sanctification and vocation of those taken up

---

[60]See *CD* IV/2, 492.
[61]See *CD* IV/1, 262, and *CD* IV/3.2, 904, 906.
[62]See *CD* IV/1, 17; *CD* IV/2, 464; and *CD* IV/3.2, 904.
[63]*CD* IV/2, 637-38.
[64]See Rom 4:16; 5:20; 6:14-15; Jas 2:13; 1 Pet 4:8.

into Christ's work of reconciliation. Where a study of forgiveness might easily relegate itself to the realm of justification, with Barth this is decidedly impossible. By articulating justification, sanctification and vocation as intertwined aspects of the one reconciling event—"more closely united than in a mathematical point"—Barth aims not to conflate them but to understand them in their connectedness.[65] In his view it is when they are pulled too far apart that they tend to eclipse each other, thus leading to "false statements" and "corresponding errors in practice" along the lines of the "cheap grace" warned against so vociferously by Dietrich Bonhoeffer.[66] As an introduction to this section, we evaluate this differentiated integration of the aspects of soteriology by looking at Barth's treatment of the *ordo salutis*.

In two rather telling excurses toward the middle and the end of *The Doctrine of Reconciliation*, Barth decries the notion of an *ordo salutis* and insists on the "simultaneity of the one act of salvation."[67] Where theologians and practitioners have attempted to describe the salvation experience in terms of a temporal, logical or experiential sequence, Barth argues that they have done so to the diminution of "its truly spiritual character," the abstraction of the Christian experience and the transgression of the freedom of God.[68] Observing the "awkward" and "divergent multiplicity of such attempts," Barth calls to mind the fact that "the Bible does not offer any such schema" and seems entirely uninterested in a "mystical ladder" or "psychological genetics of the Christian state."[69] Surely there are "different 'moments' of the one redemptive occurrence," but they come "in the *simul* of the one event."[70]

This does not mean that *justification* and *sanctification* may be treated as interchangeable terms. In fact, Barth relates them to each other in a variegated priority, depending on what the topic under discussion is. Justification is primary in terms of salvation's *basis*, sanctification is primary in terms of its *aim* and in Barth's third part-volume we see that they are both misunderstood if they do not include vocation. So it is that Barth is able to show that,

---

[65]*CD* IV/2, 503.

[66]Ibid., 505. See Dietrich Bonhoeffer, *Discipleship*, ed. Geffrey B. Kelly and John D. Godsey, trans. Barbara Green and Reinhard Krauss, Dietrich Bonhoeffer Works, 4 (Minneapolis: Fortress, 2001), 43.

[67]*CD* IV/2, 502-3. See the excurses in *CD* IV/2, 502-11 and *CD* IV/3.2, 505-7.

[68]*CD* IV/2, 502, 505-6.

[69]*CD* IV/3.2, 505.

[70]*CD* IV/2, 503, 507.

even if justification is not *dependent* on the fulfilment of sanctification or vocation, it is nonsensical to conceive of it apart from participation in God's reconciling work.[71] Christ's end, Barth insists, is not only the holiness of individuals, but the reconciliation of all. This telos gives definition to holy life in this world, and it is for a part in this that one is saved.

As we can see, Barth finds it helpful and important to distinguish these soteriological aspects, but misleading to distill them to a chronological or psycho-social system. In this project his point will be well taken. At the same time it must be asked whether—in a similar vein to Barth's threefold construal of salvation, and with the proper caveats and clarifications—an illustrative "order of reconciliation" might be outlined in order to clarify the interrelation of indicatives and imperatives involved. If Barth can speak of relations of "basis" and "aim" between the different aspects of Christ's reconciling work, then even in his construal there remains some merit to detailing how they pertain to the interpersonal relationships and sociopolitical activities of believers. In chapters four and five, then, we will push the issue of an "order of reconciliation," not for the sake of positing a definite temporal sequence or psycho-sociological account but for the sake of apprehending the variegated and interrelated aspects of Christ's ministry of reconciliation. This will occasion reflection on whether there are some ordered relations to be observed (e.g., between confession and forgiveness), even if not legalistically. What will be seen is that Barth's dynamic construal enables us to fruitfully embed interpersonal forgiveness within the whole of the gospel. First, however, we attend to each aspect of Barth's threefold soteriology.

Justification: Freed from sin for good (§61). When he comes to the doctrine of justification, Barth does not get caught up in a knock-down treatment of atonement theories, but uses the "forensic" as a gathering point for insights from *Christus Victor*, substitution and ransom theories.[72] In the fullest sense of the term, he says, "atonement is the fulfilment by God of the covenant broken by man."[73] In the process of elucidating this, Barth questions Anselm's

---

[71]See ibid., 499-507, and *CD* IV/3.2, 507, 517 and 565.
[72]Barth sees slender reference to the "financial" ransom theory in the New Testament, calls the *Christus Victor* view "military" and suggests that the "cultic" imagery of the Old Testament that was so commonly used by the early church is more remote to us today (and so not as comprehensive as a guiding theory). *CD* IV/1, 274-75.
[73]Ibid., 138; see also 295.

depiction of atonement as the mere satisfaction of divine conditions: "Is the incarnation of God," he asks, "really no more than the fulfilment of a prior condition which enables God to forgive in a manner worthy of himself? Is it not itself the real accomplishment?"[74] As part and parcel of this presentation, in his opening foray into *The Doctrine of Reconciliation* Barth challenges an anemic notion of justification in which it is merely "a verbal action, with a kind of bracketed 'as if,' as though what is pronounced were not the whole truth." Justification *is* "a declaring righteous," to be sure, but it is *also* and *at the same time* "a making righteous."[75]

For Barth, justification entails both the negation of sin and guilt as well as the positive gift of Christ's righteousness; it is the theology of cross *and* resurrection. Since it means *freedom from* "the claim and the power of death and nothingness and chaos," it is precisely not freedom into a vacuum but into the righteousness of Christ. Pressing the issue further with rhetorical questions, Barth asks, "What is the forgiveness of sins (however we understand it) if it is not directly accompanied by an actual liberation from the committal of sin? . . . And conversely: What is a liberation for new action which does not rest from the very outset and continually on the forgiveness of sins?"[76] Borrowing from John Milbank, we might ask the questions this way: Does forgiveness merely "decreate"—in which case we unwittingly admit evil's radicality—or does it have a "positivity" corresponding to the creative supremacy of God's self-giving love in Christ?[77]

It is important to note that in all of this we are not yet talking about sanctification, but are reckoning with the character of justification. For Barth this is no mere slate clearing, it is an *actual reorientation*. Claiming Martin Luther an ally, Barth aims to break not only the conceptual but also the temporal gridlock within which justification is often bound. In his view, justification is accomplished *both* "once and for all in Christ" *and* "day by day in us."[78] These assertions are ripe with ramifications for our project. To that end it is worth elaborating further on Barth's view of Christ's justification in terms of its temporality, its historicity and its eccentricity.

---

[74]Ibid., 487; see Anselm of Canterbury, *Cur Deus Homo?* book 1, questions 11, 13 and 14.

[75]*CD* IV/1, 95. Here Barth argues that justification effects what it announces and creates what it reveals.

[76]*CD* IV/2, 505. See also *CD* IV/1, 307, 558-59.

[77]John Milbank, *Being Reconciled: Ontology and Pardon* (London: Routledge, 2003), 45.

[78]*CD* IV/1, 525; see also 745-46. For similar language about vocation, see *CD* IV/3.2, 512 and 517.

First, we note that Barth considers justification an event with temporality. It is both once and for all and *ongoing*, not stuck in the past but ever present as an accomplished work of Christ. As such, justification is a "definitive movement" rather than a static assertion, which does not imply a dualistic reality or a God in process of becoming God, but *an ongoing history of conflict in which the Victor has already been decided*.[79] Justification is not simply a timeless truth we apprehend and make relevant, it is the time-full gift of One who is Lord *in* and *over* time.[80] As Barth explains,

> There is no moment in his life in which [a person] does not have to look for and await and with outstretched hands request both forgiveness and therefore freedom from his sins. No one can evade the fifth petition of the Lord's Prayer. Its force can never grow less in the Christian life. . . . [One] test of the genuineness of a man's justification as his being in transition is whether the actuality of this petition forces itself increasingly upon him or whether that actuality is lost, whether in this case it has ever been actual, whether, therefore, he does live in this transition which is his justification. If he does live in this transition, he can understand the forgiveness of sins only as the work in which God comes to him as he has absolute need of forgiveness in the light of his past and his present, not as the state in which he for his part goes forward to God. He can have forgiveness of sins only as he receives it from God, as God gives it to him. . . . He has it only as it comes to him in the promise, not otherwise.[81]

At first glance it might seem Barth has shaken the very reliability of one's justification in Christ. However, the impulse of these words is exactly the opposite. In contrast with the assurance found in one's past experience of conversion or repentance, justification is all the more solid for remaining reliant on the God whose promise is a promise.[82]

---

[79]*CD* IV/1, 543-45.

[80]See *CD* III/2, 437-511. See also Carl Reinhold Bråkenhielm, *Forgiveness*, trans. Thor Hall (Minneapolis: Fortress, 1989), 69.

[81]*CD* IV/1, 596.

[82]For Barth, the assurance of faith is the confidence that God will (freely but truly) be true to Godself—and this is in turn grounded on the incarnation and resurrection of Christ. Assurance that rests on an inaccessible "as if" decision in God, or worse yet in the believer, is hardly assurance at all. Ibid., 532; see also 537. Any fear one might have regarding an "unpardonable sin" should buckle under the question whether *any* sin is in itself *pardonable*. On Barth's rendering, all sin is transgression against God and as such is "not tolerated let alone accepted in the death of Jesus Christ." Ibid., 410. See also *CD* IV/2, 232-33.

As such, justification issues forth in our history not as "a futile vacillation or movement in a circle" but as a "constant differentiation" of new from old. The ongoing force of it lies not in a believer's "power of recollection" but in the abiding presence of the One who has reoriented the believer and goes with her in that reorientation.[83] So it is that the believer "lives by the constant prevailing of the promised forgiveness of sins" that is "to be sought and apprehended afresh every moment out of the deepest need."[84] This daily invocation does not imply that justification is unstable or needs renewing, but that the Christian life carries on in the same Spirit as it began.

Having elaborated on justification's temporality, we turn secondly, then, to its *historicity*. For Barth, justification neither ignores nor fossilizes past experience. Those who are freed from sin retain their situatedness. Just as the resurrection is not bound by the history in which it occurs but acts within it in order to act upon it and alter it, so in justification we reckon with an event that does not ignore human sin and enmity but nonetheless refuses to let them be the determining factor going forward. Evangelical preachers have made considerable pedagogical use of the phrase "just as if I'd never sinned," but Barth's account resists such misleading truisms.[85] For all his talk of sin as *das Nichtige*, Barth is clear that "*das Nichtige ist nicht das Nichts.*"[86] In the crucifixion of Jesus we behold sin's reality as an offense God does not simply forget but rejects.[87] Sin is not shrugged off as if it never happened.

It is important to note that in the resurrection of Christ's incarnate flesh we have an affirmation of the continuing historicity of human being. If justification were simply a "nominalistic 'as if'" (a notion Barth thinks is "quite incompatible

---

[83]CD IV/1, 602, 596 and 598. The psalmist's joy is not in forgiveness itself but in the One who forgives. Ibid., 577-80; see also CD IV/2, 531.

[84]CD IV/1, 602, and CD IV/3.2, 531 and 551. See also CD IV/1, 258-59, and ChrL, 94-95.

[85]See Billy Graham, *How to Be Born Again* (Nashville: Thomas Nelson, 1989), 126 and *The Key to Personal Peace* (Nashville: Thomas Nelson, 2003), 49, and Warren W. Wiersbe, *Be Free: Exchange Legalism for True Spirituality*, NT Commentary, Galatians (Colorado Springs: David C. Cook, 1975), 62. Some say it is just "as if we have lived lives of perfect obedience" or "loved God and neighbor perfectly." Erwin W. Lutzer, *How You Can Be Sure That You Will Spend Eternity with God* (Chicago: Moody, 1996), 53-54, and Michael Scott Horton, *Putting Amazing Back into Grace: Embracing the Heart of the Gospel* (Grand Rapids: Baker, 2002), 142. The notion appears in John Milbank, *Theology and Social Theory* (Oxford: Blackwell, 1990), 411, as critiqued in L. Gregory Jones, *Embodying Forgiveness: A Theological Analysis* (Grand Rapids: Eerdmans, 1995), 146. Milbank denounces it, however, in *Being Reconciled*, 29, 36, 43.

[86]KD III/3, 403.

[87]In fact it exists only in that rejection. See CD III/3, 349 and 352-53.

with the truthfulness of God and cannot be of any real help to man") then the persons involved could hardly be said to be the same persons after they had been forgiven.[88] In asserting this Barth does not mean to lock sin at the essence of their identity, but to affirm that they are persons with histories:

> The man who receives forgiveness does not cease to be the man whose past (and his present as it derives from his past) bears the stain of his sins. The act of the divine forgiveness is that God sees and knows this stain infinitely better than the man himself, and abhors it infinitely more than he does even in his deepest penitence—yet He does not take it into consideration. He overlooks it, He covers it, He passes it by. He puts it behind Him.[89]

The language of "overlooking" is here employed for the purposes not of *denial* but of *overcoming*. In justification we have not an "as if" but a "creative work of God" in which the old (which is present but belongs to our past) has been superseded by the new that comes in Christ. In Barth's reckoning, the "divine pardoning is not a weak remission"; rather, it is an "act of divine power and defiance" in which God despises sin, refusing on the basis of the emptied cross and tomb to allow the ensuing history to be determined by it.[90]

When in Jeremiah 31:34 God promises to "remember their sins no more," it is often taken to mean that God forgets sin, but it is worth noting that God is not literally said to be *forgetting*, but to be *remembering no more*. This is not a game of semantics, but an issue wherein an uncertain phrase must be defined with appropriate theological content. To that end, F. B. Huey rightly points out in his commentary that the language of "not remembering" is initially *illustrative* (or even proleptic), and that it is now Christ's forgiveness that defines nonremembering rather than vice versa.[91] Another commentary

---

[88]*CD* IV/1, 517.

[89]Ibid., 597.

[90]Ibid.; see also 517, 542-43 and 598. On these points Barth opposes Albrecht Ritschl and Immanuel Kant, who proceed as if Christ reveals the accessible human ideal that theretofore was simply not clear. See ibid., 381-83, and Barth, *Protestant Theology*, 298.

[91]F. B. Huey Jr., *Jeremiah, Lamentations*, New American Commentary, vol. 16 (Nashville: Broadman & Holman, 1993), 276n37. See also Heb 8:12 and 10:17. Barth is oddly quiet about these passages, but can be seen to push our reading along these lines in §47.1, "Jesus, Lord of Time." *CD* III/2, 437-511. Volf shows himself far more willing to invest the acts of remembrance and nonremembrance with more redemptive weight, even going so far as to define forgiveness and reconciliation within this rubric. See particularly Miroslav Volf, *The End of Memory: Remembering Rightly in a Violent World* (Grand Rapids: Eerdmans, 2006), and J. Alexander Sider, "Memory in the Politics of Forgiveness," in *To See History Doxologically: History and Holiness in John*

explains the result rather well: the point of forgiveness in the new covenant is precisely that "the Lord will not start over again with another" but will give the new covenant to the same old sinner.[92] Barth's construal is highly resonant with these readings. Forgiveness is not dependent upon forgetfulness. In Christ our sins are remembered *not*, or remembered *overcome*. Acting as if we never sinned would be tantamount to acting as if we were not forgiven, which would effectively short-circuit Christ's activity and change what it means to move forward in freedom.[93]

This brings us, third, to justification's *eccentricity*. At this juncture it is too often the case that we think of justification in the rubric of individual sin and salvation, but leave it behind to discuss sanctification and vocation—thus enabling us to speak of personal forgiveness apart from interpersonal reconciliation as well. As indicated, however, for Barth not only is Jesus the Lord of time, but also of space. The personal reality of freedom from sin is a public reality as well. We are not talking here about the social *fallout* of justification, carried out on some other terms, but the social context, or the *reach*, of justification itself. We can illustrate the distinction by looking at the interpersonal corollaries to forgiveness that appear in Miroslav Volf's influential construal in *Exclusion and Embrace*. There Volf refers to forgiveness as "the boundary between exclusion and embrace," helpfully distinguishing forgiveness from the healing and restored communion that it seeks and rightly acknowledging that the latter are contingent upon things that a forgiver cannot (and should not) control. This has much to commend it. However, when Volf says that forgiveness "leaves a distance between people, an empty space of neutrality," he appears to confuse it with the isolation and enmity it overcomes.[94] While distinguishable from the reconciling work that follows, Christian forgiveness does have more positive content than that.

Barth appears to have been more concerned than Volf to draw out the event of forgiveness for its positive content and to trace its continuity with other aspects of reconciliation. Volf leaves a gap between justification and

---

Howard Yoder's Ecclesiology (Grand Rapids: Eerdmans, 2011), 133-55.
[92]Gerald Keown, Pamela J. Scalise and Thomas G. Smothers, *Jeremiah 26-52*,Word Biblical Commentary, vol. 27 (Nashville: Thomas Nelson, 1998), 133.
[93]*CD* IV/3.2, 934, and *CD* IV/2, 569.
[94]Miroslav Volf, *Exclusion and Embrace: A Theological Exploration of Identity, Otherness, and Reconciliation* (Nashville: Abingdon, 1996), 125-26.

sanctification that anthropology or religiosity can rush in and fill, but Barth explains differently. For him, the justified sinner is not only freed from sins but also "free to set out from or continually to begin with" a reordered relation to God characterized by "daily conversion" and all the "interconnexions" it entails.[95] As such, justification is not merely a personal amnesty only vaguely related to interpersonal healing: it is a merciful reorientation that has become the "basic and comprehensive determination of their attitude and action"—including both the personal and interpersonal aspects of their lives.[96] (Volf's account is closer to Barth's when he critiques Friedrich Nietzsche's construal of forgiveness as a superhuman ability to "shrug" off one's "enemies, his misfortunes and even his *misdeeds*" like "worms." Such an account not only puts the onus on victims to simply get over their hurt, but also reinforces a perpetrator's oblivious disregard.)[97] We will say more about Barth and Volf later, but here their comparison highlights the extent to which Barth's account of justification is eccentric, implicating not only the person but the person in his or her social historical context.

As discussed in chapter one, Barth has been supposed by some to have a dehistoricized account of Christian life and community. But it is important to note how adamantly he resists relegating justification to the past and putting it on the backs of believers to apply and maintain its effects in time. Barth reckons forgiveness a gift given once for all in Christ and presented by him every moment as well. Clearly it will be worth our while to weigh the themes of timefullness, situatedness and interpersonal connectedness in Barth's doctrine of justification against common notions of forgiveness as a timeless principle with its telos in individual freedom. This certainly highlights the deficiency of a *therapeutic* rendering of forgiveness that tends to divorce forgiveness from its telos in reconciliation. Our attempt to avoid this deficiency must be careful not to collapse terms like *forgiveness* and *reconciliation* into each other, thereby rendering them relatively meaningless. When Barth says, "We can gather together

---

[95]*CD* IV/3.1, 246-47.

[96]*ChrL*, 23; see also 82. See also *CD* IV/2, 618.

[97]Miroslav Volf, "Forgiveness, Reconciliation, and Justice: A Christian Contribution to a More Peaceful Social Environment," in *Forgiveness and Reconciliation: Religion, Public Policy, and Conflict Transformation*, ed. Raymond G. Helmick and Rodney L. Petersen (Philadelphia: Templeton Foundation Press, 2001), 36-37; see also Friedrich Nietzsche, *On the Genealogy of Morals*, trans. Carol Diethe (Cambridge: Cambridge University Press, 1994), 23-24. Nietzsche's is an inadequate account of justice and an inordinate melding of forgiveness with forgetfulness.

the whole of the promise . . . under the term, the forgiveness of sins," it is not the *conflation* of justification and the whole of salvation; rather, it is a recognition of the factor that mercy plays into every hint of peace on earth.[98] We will explore this further as we proceed.

 Sanctification: Freed for life together (§66). One of the assumptions that ought not to leak into a doctrine of sanctification is the notion that, once justified, believers have the process of sanctification left up to them and their efforts to imitate Christ. Barth's adamancy about this point cannot be missed. "The New Testament," writes Barth, "knows nothing of a Jesus who lived and died for the forgiveness of our sins, to free us as it were retrospectively, but who now waits as though with tied arms for us to act in accordance with the freedom achieved for us."[99] Accounts of sanctification may too often be cross centered without being amply resurrection oriented, thus rendering the sinner forgiven by the work of Christ and then set loose to act, presumably by tapping in to some now-accessible latent goodness. Once justified, if all that remains is to develop spiritual disciplines and community mores to carry the load of Christ's demands, we have something like a moralization of grace, a works without faith. This can lead to a crippling pietism. The more the sinner "succeeds in achieving inner harmony, the less he can be reconciled with God and used by Him," Barth writes, explaining that it is not the "seriousness or consistency" of the saints which sanctifies them, but only "the sanctity of the One who calls them and on whom their gaze is not very well directed."[100]

 In short, for Barth the *imitatio Christi* can only make sense within a *participatio Christi* that reckons that *grace remains grace*.[101] The primary agent in sanctification is the Holy Spirit. This might be taken in a monergistic fashion, but it is more consistent with Barth's theology to understand it not as an expression of *exclusive* divine agency but as a statement about who brings sanctity to bear. Granted this point, however, a remaining criticism is that Barth's polemic lets the *participatio* so inform the *imitatio Christi* as to eclipse it altogether, thus curtailing or canceling the relevance

---

[98]*CD* IV/1, 596; see also 599.

[99]Barth connects this mistake directly to the anemic accounts of atonement mentioned earlier. *CD* IV/2, 516.

[100]Ibid., 525, 528.

[101]At times Barth seems to opt for *participatio* to the exclusion of *imitatio*, but the thrust of his point is that there is an *imitatio Christi* that occurs within *participatio Christi*. See ibid., 516-17, 534, 780.

of such things as character development, spiritual discipline, virtue, tradition and community formation.[102] This critique is felt at the level of ethics and *polis* alike, such that the question is rightfully asked whether, on Barth's construal, anything can be said about how a Christian life or community ought consistently to look.

One might balk at the apparent fickleness of his account, but Barth did not think his ethic so insecure. For him, the house built on sand is the one built on timeless principles and self-sustained virtues; the house built on a firm foundation is that which adheres to the living cornerstone, the resurrected Christ, present to the church by the Holy Spirit.[103] The temptations to either self-contented triumphalism or narcissistic despair are both rejected for faithful living within the ongoing history of a decided conflict. As if anticipating the very language that would one day be used against him, Barth says that the "character" of the Christian life is precisely one of perpetual conversion.[104] If there is any continuity worth speaking about—and it would seem that there is—it is always provided by the One who is yesterday, today and forever. This is an integral part of sanctification's character.

Von Balthasar's counterinsistence, of course, was that divine grace has the potency to create something new—something that, for all its provisional dependence on God, can yet be said to possess sanctity.[105] His question to Barth might be, is Christ competent only to forgive and not to actually re-create? Barth's answer would be, yes, there "is a real alteration of their being," but their action "still stands in need of the forgiveness, the justification, which they cannot achieve of themselves. . . . The change is only relative. For sanctification is not an ultimate, only a penultimate, word. . . . Yet for all its

[102]See for example Stanley Hauerwas, "On Honour: By Way of A Comparison of Karl Barth and Trollope," in *Dispatches from the Front: Theological Engagements with the Secular* (Durham, NC: Duke University Press, 1991), 58-79, and Joseph L. Mangina, "Bearing the Marks of Jesus: The Church in the Economy of Salvation in Barth and Hauerwas," *Scottish Journal of Theology* 52, no. 3 (1999): 269-305.

[103]See CD II/2, 563, 641, and CD IV/2, 9, along with Mt 7:24-27 and 1 Pet 2:4.

[104]CD IV/2, 566; see also 538-45, 587 and 594.

[105]See Hans Urs von Balthasar, *The Theology of Karl Barth: Exposition and Interpretation*, trans. Edward T. Oakes (San Francisco: Ignatius, 1992), 107, 387-88. See also the "graced man" in Hans Küng, *Justification: The Doctrine of Karl Barth and a Catholic Reflection* (Louisville: Westminster John Knox, 2004), 31, 203.

relativity it is a real change."[106] With words like this, it can be argued that Barth retains a place for the maintenance of the positive gains of tradition and the development of good character, but what he resiliently opposes is the frequent and devastating tendency to make more of these gains than is warranted. Even the best actions and ideas of yesterday must be discerned under the continual guidance of Christ and not clutched with the resolve of self-reliance. The idea is to not increasingly trust one's own growing preparedness for obedience but to perpetually trust Jesus to be present, unhindered by circumstance or momentum. Without this the Christian life tends in the name of trend or tradition to "curve in upon itself as self-sufficiency."[107]

Barth has been clear that at no point should justification be thought of as an end in itself—as if the relevance of Christ and his forgiveness can be relegated to a generalized kind of amnesty from sin. When it comes to sanctification, Barth sums it up succinctly: "He sanctifies the unholy by His action with and towards them," giving "them a derivative and limited, but supremely real, share in His own holiness."[108] Where saints are described as "set apart," it should not give the impression of achieved holiness but of repositioning in Christ, or being "set at His side." They are still sinners, but their saintliness rests in the fact that they are "disturbed sinners."[109] Another way to look at this is to ask what Barth means when he depicts the Christian life as an engaged conflict between mutually exclusive selves, the old and the new. If the saint is still the sinner, as Barth describes it, does this not give the old too much credit and render the new life little more than a whiff of the hopeful imagination? It is an important question, but it must first be pointed out that it operates on a different assumption than the one from which Barth is working. For him the "sinful man of yesterday" who got left behind was precisely the one who was locked in the disorientation of self-reliant sloth, so that the new person is caught up by faith in the "superior, dynamic and future" element that comes in Jesus Christ and confronts the old each day.[110]

---

[106]*CD* IV/2, 529-30. One question raised by this quote, which will be left for the next chapter, has to do with what Barth means when he says "they lift up themselves." It might seem to be the self-help of sloth, but it might also be an indication of what would be the rubric of Barth's ethics of reconciliation: invocation.

[107]*CD* IV/1, 249.

[108]*CD* IV/2, 500; see also 501, 504 and 507.

[109]Ibid., 526 and 524; see also 516, 522, 587, 592-93 and 618.

[110]*CD* IV/2, 571, and *CD* IV/3.2, 809.

In his doctrine of sanctification Barth challenges the soul-scrubbing, mor-
alist version of *mortificatio* by locating it in the hopeful "advance" of *vivificatio* that enfolds it.[111] The recommendation is total reliance on Christ to light
the way forward and to make good on what has gone before. Note the concentrated polemic of his presentation: following Jesus "can never be a
question of a routine continuation or repetition of what has hitherto been
our customary practice. It always involves the decision of a new day; the
seizing of a new opportunity which was not present yesterday but is now
given in and with the call of Jesus."[112] On its own this seems to leave us with
a rather minimalistic description of what can be *expected* in sanctification.
However, what must be emphasized against the grain of previous critiques is
the fact that, while Barth hesitates to set up an ethical system or a series of
abiding principles, he does in fact give a considerable (if somewhat ad hoc)
description of the abiding contours of Christian life and community. In addition to his emphatic endorsement of Bonhoeffer's *Discipleship* and his own
exposition of cruciformity in "The Dignity of the Cross," Barth outlined six
"prominent lines" of sanctification in his second part-volume, detailed twelve
"forms of ministry" in the third and had been laying out specifically countercultural paths of action in the posthumously published fourth.[113]

We will here restrain ourselves to some discussion of the "prominent
lines" described in Barth's doctrine of sanctification.[114] Having made it
clear that generalizations cannot stand in for the specific commands of
Christ in each context, Barth nonetheless characterizes Christ's commands
along six revealed trajectories. To begin with, he notes that Jesus' disciples
will (1) renounce "attachment to authority, validity and confidence of
possessions" in favor of his overarching lordship. Additionally, they will
(2) live unenslaved by the "structures of honour" belonging to a world
locked in enmity, and will (3) do so unbound by the structurally insinuated

---

[111]Barth thought Calvin failed to place *mortificatio* properly within *vivificatio*. *CD* IV/2, 574-76;
see also 604.

[112]Ibid., 538.

[113]See ibid., 533-34, 598-613, 548-53, as well as *CD* IV/3.2, 854-901, and *ChrL*, 182-213, 260.

[114]Although Barth was rightly concerned that we "not conceal the living Jesus behind such sche-
mata," neither did he think we should conceal Jesus' life and commission behind an overanxious
allergy to such things. In this project the idea is not to "reproduce" or "copy . . . the outlines,"
but to "envisage the situations" into which we are put by Christ and to adhere to the "main lines"
obedience takes. *CD* IV/2, 536, 553.

false dilemmas of either adherence or revolt. Despite the systems of violence in which they live and interact, disciples of Christ will have a healthy disregard for both the use and the fear of force, neither wielding nor cowering from it, determined as they are by faith and obedience to Jesus Christ. Furthermore, following Christ entails "a radical alteration of the ruling social relationships," such that Christian life is not determined by either (4) familial comforts or (5) pious obligations.[115] All of this leads into the main line of sanctification Barth traces, namely (6) the way of the cross. Barth does not pretend that it can be predicted what form this will always take, but insists that in a world that is yet to be fully relieved of its sinful condition the way of obedience is going to be as cruciform as it was for the Lord.[116]

With these six depictions Barth has curiously depicted the contours of the Christian life mainly in the form of negations—perhaps partly due to the crises faced in his day. Rooted in Barth's Christology, however, it is not difficult to plumb beneath the surface and restate each point positively. In short, Barth describes sanctification in terms of (1) everyday faithfulness to the living Lord Jesus, (2) preference for God's honor, (3) peaceability, (4) deep fellowship, (5) the freedom of obedience and (6) the liberated dignity of a self-giving life.[117] In this, the self-giving love of Christ at the cross judges self-righteous humanity, and his resurrection reveals such sacrificial action not to humanity's denigration but its exaltation.

If meant as ethical injunctions these "prominent lines" are, of course, still fairly nonspecific. That is because, for Barth, sanctification does not unfold in terms of a casuistic, situational ethic based on rules, but as a followership-in-community that expects to hear Christ's command along these prominent lines. No rule—"not even the law of love"—replaces the reign of the resurrected Jesus Christ.[118]

In this, the Spirit who awakens, gathers, quickens and upbuilds also sustains and fills out the commands of Christ in time. As messy as life gets, the "powerful mercy" of Jesus Christ continues to create a new future as we obey.[119] Barth

---

[115]Ibid., 546-51, 564.

[116]See ibid., 552, 598-613.

[117]See *CD* IV/2, 548-53 and 584-613. The cross is not taken up as resignation to fate, but as a "work of the freedom which they are given," wherein they are empowered to love. Ibid., 604.

[118]See ibid., 18 and 179.

[119]Ibid., 192, 223 and 245.

considers this the crux of what Luther stumbled upon in what became the
Reformation, and it comes down to the observation that living by faith rather
than sight is a different *modus operandi* than the one to which we are sinfully
predisposed.[120] Put simply, God does not make superheroes, but participants
in Christ's work of grace. This grace reaches the depths of the person and also
pushes into the experience of reconciliation with other people (as well as all
creation). In sanctification, Barth explains, the Christian "dares to live as one
on whom this judgment has passed, to whom this pardon applies. He dares to
consider all men in the light of the fact that this judgment has been passed on
them, this pardon applies to them."[121] With this we turn to the soteriological
point that is Barth's most unique, which is to include along with justification
and sanctification an account of the vocation which is inseparably entailed.

Vocation: Freed to speak and share (§71). The third part-volume of Barth's
Doctrine of Reconciliation moves from justification and sanctification to vocation, wherein he claims that when God makes the cause of humanity his
own, he graciously also "makes His cause theirs." The believer's call to faith
includes "their personal blessing, experience and endowment," but this "can
have its own power and constancy" only in the context of God's larger
movement—which means that "a proper use of their own freedom is that they
should subject themselves to one another and serve one another in love."[122]
With his emphasis on vocation Barth rallies a doctrinal challenge to the type
of Christianity that sees separateness from the world as an end in itself. The
church's calling out from the world is in fact also a calling to a new relationship
with it. Barth does not pretend to have invented this. In a historical excursus
he suggests that both Luther and Calvin affirmed inclusion in Christ's mission
as part of the *unio cum Christi*, but that this was not extrapolated far enough
in their own work or in that of their Reformation successors.[123]

"It gives a very strange relationship," Barth writes, "if on the one side we
have the selflessness and self-giving of God and Jesus Christ in which the
salvation of the world is effected and revealed, and on the other the satisfaction with which Christians accept this" and then "make use" of it in a

---

[120]See 1 Cor 5:7, and Karl Barth, *The Theology of John Calvin*, trans. Geoffrey W. Bromiley (Grand
    Rapids: Eerdmans, 1995), 89.
[121]*CD* IV/1, 633-34. See *CD* IV/2, 245-47, 316, 319, 809-10 and 814.
[122]*CD* IV/3.2, 574 and 603.
[123]See ibid., 549-54, along with Gal 2:20.

different way.[124] The saving action of God revealed in Jesus Christ cannot be taken to pertain merely to the alteration of one's own situation but has to be received as the alteration of the situation of all. This is not merely a matter of perception and application but is the content of the salvation received. In fact, it is that false freedom of autonomy and that destructive path of self-oriented desire from which humans are saved!

Brought into communion with their Creator and Redeemer, Christians are no longer self-referential. This human participation in Christ's movement is made "actual and definitive . . . in the work of the Holy Spirit," and the grace brought "vertically from above" gains a correspondence "just as real horizontally in their creaturely existence."[125] This is not a works-based salvation. It does not "weaken or question the unconditional givenness" of Christ's accomplishment to say that he makes people witnesses rather than "idle spectators."[126] Freed from sin and freed for life they are freed to speak, serve and share with others. This is not meant to suggest that believers are an extension of Christ's *incarnation*, but of his *action as the living Lord*. Nor does this make them "channels only"—as if they were mere instruments rather than subjective participants in Christ's work. To be a Christian is neither to look to the Savior as a means to an end nor to stand as a customer before a "dispenser," it is to stand before Jesus as a servant before the Lord.[127]

For Barth, the posture envisaged here is not conversion into proselytizers, but solidarity with sinners in a fundamentally shared salvation. In the neighbor a Christian sees Jesus Christ himself, calling to be received as he is loved and served. In Barth's view not only does this explain the rhetoric of Jesus, but also the missionary fervor of Paul: when in Romans 9:3 he says he would rather be cursed to Israel's benefit than enjoy salvation without them, does it make any sense except as the expression of his conviction that the personal nature of salvific blessing is "secondary" to its social component?[128] Taking his cue from Simon and Levi's conversion accounts,

---

[124]*CD* IV/3.2, 567.

[125]Ibid., 492 and 499; see also 490 and 652.

[126]Ibid., 646 and 575; see also 543.

[127]Ibid., 596–97; see also 657. "To speak of a continuation or extension of the incarnation in the Church is not only out of place but blasphemous." Ibid., 729. ("Channels Only" is a popular hymn written by Mary Maxwell and Ada Rose Gibbs.)

[128]So radical is it that Barth calls Paul's expression "almost frightening." Ibid., 591–92; see also 576, 596–97, 657, 778–79. See also *CD* III/2, 210, along with Mt 26:31–46 and Lk 10:29–11:37.

Barth suggests that even a posture of confession can be a self-serving evasion
of Christ if it heeds not the call to "fear not," get up and witness.[129] This is
not an optional appendix to an otherwise individual salvation. On this point
Barth can hardly be more clear:

> [If a person] renounces his ministry of witness, this is not a minor omission
> which he may make in order the more peacefully and surely to enjoy his per-
> sonal experience and assurance of salvation. . . . On the contrary, such renun-
> ciation means quite simply and terribly that he denies and suspends the life of
> Christ in him, his life in Christ, and therefore his vocation. To the extent that
> he really carries through this renunciation, he ceases to be a Christian. And he
> cannot then try to find consolation in his personal experience and assurance
> of salvation. . . . His inner experience and assurance is the glorious fruit of his
> ministry of witness which will not be withheld if he discharges it. But if he does
> not discharge it because he will not accept the other and less glorious fruit of
> affliction, he will lose the very thing which he thinks to preserve in that island
> kingdom of inwardness.[130]

Barth further observes that the only kind of "personal testimony" of conversion found in the Bible is one that is attached to the call to serve God as
a witness and a servant.[131] The crisis of faith simply *is* a call to service. The
crises of service, one might add, are also a call to faith.

In correlation with what we have already seen in Barth's account of justification and sanctification, this crisis, too, is a daily event: to vocation as
much as to salvation the Lord prefers "constantly" to "wake up again."[132]
This does not render one's vocation unstable but addresses the way it is
taken up. Those who are called do not go forward in the strength of their
own conversion experience or perceived vocational success but in obedient
participation with the One who is Lord of all. In this they are not aloof but
alive to present circumstances and particular commissions; they believe
that it is given to them to have a witness that takes place in space and time.
On his way in time from accomplished reconciliation to the goal of full
redemption, in the extremity of his grace, Jesus Christ "does not go alone

[129]*CD* IV/3.2, 590; see Mk 2:13-17 and Lk 5:1-11.
[130]Ibid., 617.
[131]See ibid., 572, 581, 627 and 676-78.
[132]This rather than so-called leaving a person "in peace." *CD* IV/3.2, 512; see 483, 517-18.

but wills to be what He is and do what He does in company with others whom He calls for the purpose, namely, with the despicable folk called Christians."[133] Believers are pilgrims. Their objective alteration is definite but their subjective liberation is incomplete.

The incompleteness of the Christian pilgrimage informs the character of the Christian life, but hardly renders it indefinite or unsure. In "The Liberation of the Christian" (§71.6), Barth gives seven statements expressing the transition of *freedom from* to *freedom for*, particularly as it involves not just the sanctification but the vocation of Christians. As he explains it, the Christian is liberated (1) from isolation in order to live for fellowship, and this entails liberation (2) from the caprice-afflicted autonomy of "freedom of choice" into the actual freedom of serving Christ. It also entails liberation (3) from the dominion of "machinery and gadgets" into the freedom to live with and serve other human beings, characterized by a departure (4) from the demanding posture of a *taker* to that of "pure recipient" engaged in "active waiting" on the Lord. In this, (5) the paralysis of "hopeless confusion" gives way to a hopeful life of action, and (6) the fearful reluctance of moral wavering to the trustful life of obedience to the commands that come from Christ.[134] What this amounts to in the seventh and final statement becomes an anticipation of the rubric under which Barth's ethics of reconciliation would proceed: in all of the above the Christian is liberated (7) "from anxiety to prayer." As such the Christian is not referred to the power of prayer itself—however "pious, fervent or beautiful" it may be—but to the power of the One invoked.[135] This puts the invocation of Christ's promise of grace and mercy at the heart of Christian life and mission.

As it is "led unavoidably from κλῆσις to ἐκκλησία," Barth explains, the church testifies to its own incompletion.[136] Whether it pertains to the church's finitude or its fallenness, however, this incompleteness is not to be understood as the ultimate but the *penultimate* factor in its common life and witness. The ongoing Christian witness is to a mission accomplished in Christ.

With all this in mind, we must take note of the place of forgiveness not only in the message but also the ministry and mission of reconciliation. To

---

[133]Ibid., 542; see also 490, 500, 721 and 813.
[134]Ibid., 664-71.
[135]Ibid., 673.
[136]Ibid., 681.

Barth it is vital that the vocation given in grace is greater than our inability to live up to it. Indeed, "even the worst sin of the Christian cannot alter the totality of what befalls him in the process of his vocation," and should not become an excuse for disengagement with the commission of Christ. Whatever failings, doubts or fears come up in the pursuit of one's vocation, they cannot wreck Christ's ability to utilize the service rendered. Because the "victory over sin" has been "already won," the Christian "may move forward from the forgiveness of all his sins only by . . . continually moving, irrespective of the relationship of his morality to his immorality, to the next action demanded, trusting not in the immanent goodness of his own action but in the revealed goodness of God in Jesus Christ."[137] This speaks volumes about the motivation, empowerment and ongoing character of Christian witness. As is made clear from 1 John 1:9 and 1 John 2:2, the church carries forward undeterred because of faith in the power of forgiveness "not only for ours but also for the sins of the whole world."[138]

The church in Barth's account thus has a "distinctive ethos" in which it lives by this promise: it perceives itself as sharing an ever-renewed participation in divine liberation. Even in the face of "enmity, hatred, cursing and therefore affliction," Christians are not diverted from "their role as witnesses of the kingdom"—and it is precisely this perpetual freedom for action which is the kingdom of heaven on earth.[139] Without rendering interpersonal forgiveness a work that merits salvation, then, we must recognize with Barth that receiving God's forgiveness is tantamount to sharing it. That goes both for the times when we must offer it and the times when we must ask for it. These are theologically and often enough experientially simultaneous.

In this chapter we have cycled through Barth's christological, hamartiological and soteriological sections in order to pick up on important themes in Barth's presentation of forgiveness in *The Doctrine of Reconciliation*. We are now in an excellent position to carry on with the pattern in chapter three by analyzing his sections on ecclesiology and spirituality. It is on this basis that we will then be able in chapters four, five and six to explicate the place and meaning of forgiveness in the church's ministry of reconciliation.

---

[137]Ibid., 508 and 671.
[138]Ibid., 487.
[139]Ibid., 558 and 625; see also 561-63, 593 and 653-54.

3

Forgiveness Shared

THE CHURCH OF CHURCH DOGMATICS *IV*

CONTINUING IN THE BARTHIAN pattern of looking at the same thing from several different angles, we now shift focus more fully from "God with us" to "us with God." With this move from Christology, hamartiology and soteriology to ecclesiology and spirituality, we do not transition focus onto a new primary agent but continue to follow Jesus Christ on the way from his accomplished reconciliation into his revelation in human history. Barth's central point moving forward from the Christ event is that *Jesus lives to share the story*. God willed not only to accomplish cosmic reconciliation in Christ, but to enable participation in space and time on his way to a fully consummated redemption. With the verdict of the Father at the resurrection of the Son, by the Holy Spirit of Jesus Christ there also proceeds into human history the message of new life and mission. This message goes forth not in the power of recollection and rhetoric, but in the ongoing efficacy of the living Lord Jesus Christ in his prophetic office. Even the resurrected Lord had to reveal himself as such to his witnesses![1] For Barth, Jesus' self-revelation at Emmaus, his commission at his ascension and the gift of his Spirit at Pentecost all indicate a transition from the objective accomplishment of Christ to his revelation of that reconciliation in our subjective experience.[2]

---

[1]See *CD* IV/1, 288-92, 355, and *CD* IV/2, 140-44.

[2]"Revelation takes place in and with reconciliation. Indeed, the latter is also revelation. As God acts in it, He also speaks. Reconciliation is not a dark or dumb event, but perspicuous and vocal." What

In this, as it "lives by the fact that Jesus lives," the Christian community is put "continually in that new beginning" wherein its "conflict with God has been turned into the peace of fellowship."[3]

To unpack what this means, in this chapter we will explore what Barth calls the Holy Spirit's gathering, building and sending of the community, as well as the awakening, quickening and enlightening of the persons within it. The goal in this analysis (which will include more detailed focus on some of Barth's excurses) is to see how forgiveness underwrites and finds expression in the communion, reciprocal love and grace-sharing service of those awakened to faith, quickened to love and enlightened to hope. Here we are asking about the character of the community Jesus is making in the world on his way to kingdom come. This will prepare us to delineate ramifications for interpersonal forgiveness and reconciliation in the chapters that follow.

GATHERING AND AWAKENING: FREE FOR COMMUNION (§62–§63)

As Christ is revealed in history there are people who are freed from pride, sloth and falsehood for life in freedom and fellowship. In this they are genuinely freed not simply for an isolated sanctification or a collective appreciation of their personal salvation but for a *communio sanctorum* that is both mutually binding and outwardly expansive. Content from the ecclesiological and spiritual sections of Barth's *Doctrine of Reconciliation* is going to come up again in our closing chapters, but in this section we will narrow our sights on two most important and prominent themes. Building on what has already been explored, we will probe more deeply for their relevance to the task at hand. By analyzing the "gathering" and "awakening" sections of part-volume one, in what immediately follows we will (1) further consider the definitively communal nature of Christian faith and (2) explore the tension between faith and sight as it pertains to the visible character of Christian community in the world.

Selfish piety and blanket forgiveness: Hiding behind justification. As already discussed, Barth sees in justification by faith an eccentric impulse that immediately and perpetually connects the individual to the community of Christ and the kingdom of the Father. The Spirit's act of awakening to

---

comes to us in "Easter knowledge" is not only the awareness but the shared actualization of what God accomplished in Jesus Christ. *CD* IV/3.1, 8, 282-84; see also *CD* IV/1, 268, and *CD* IV/3.2, 503.
[3] *CD* IV/1, 347; see also *CD* IV/2, 309, 363-64.

faith is married to the Spirit's act of gathering into community. Barth goes so far as to say that the church is for each of us "savingly necessary"—not in the sense of mediation or causality but in the sense that "if we hold ourselves aloof from this, we hold ourselves aloof from salvation and the Saviour."[4] Just as the New Testament "does not know of a Jesus Christ who is what He is exclusively for Himself," so it does not know "of a self-enclosed human being confronting this man Jesus."[5]

This last reference sounds similar to a theological implementation of anthropological observations about the socially constructed nature of human being, but Barth treats it more as a derivation from Christ's revelation of the new creation.[6] This does not mean he sees an incompatibility between the order of creation and the order of reconciliation, but precisely the opposite. Because God is the Creator *and* the Reconciler, we can see such truths of creation lit up by Christ.[7] This does not mean that the traffic of self-understanding goes only one way—such that interaction with secular social sciences is a contentious affair that turns faith against reason—but it does mean that the church believes it is given *in Christ* to "know the world for what it is."[8] It may be a warranted exercise to extend personal faith to its social ramifications by appealing to the findings of the social sciences, or to take those findings as illustrative of underdeveloped theological truths. But for the most part Barth is simply expounding on a decidedly theological claim: the privatization of justification robs it of its full Christian import.

This is an important point for us as we proceed. Our theological account of interpersonal forgiveness can expect to find resonance with the social sciences, but should be cautious about making that move too fast. We would be likely to come to different conclusions if we were applying naturally latent "social impulses" before expounding on the specifically eccentric aspects of gospel reception and the new creation in Christ. For his part, Barth's construal aims to be more than an acknowledgment of the social nature of

[4]*CD* IV/2, 621-22; see also 614, and *CD* IV/1, 150-51.

[5]*CD* IV/2, 280-81.

[6]For an account that reads socio-ontology into the atonement with evocative yet less christological results, see Adam Kotsko, *The Politics of Redemption: The Social Logic of Salvation* (London: T&T Clark, 2010).

[7]On one occasion Barth writes, "Just as a man would not be a man in and for himself, in isolation from his fellow-men, so a Christian would not be a Christian in and for himself." *CD* IV/1, 750.

[8]*CD* IV/3.2, 769; see also 771-72.

created humanity. It is stated as a conviction stemming from God's self-revelation in Christ, which has reconciliation reaching individuals as part of God's love for the world. As such the *promeity* (for me) of God is best understood within its *pro nobis* (for us) contours.[9]

We get an indication of the extent of Barth's conviction on this point in §71.4, where he goes on a tirade against what he calls "*sacra egoism*" or "holy selfishness," which centers on "Christian existence" as something "wholly possessive," to the "sanctioning and cultivating of an egocentricity which is only too human for all its sanctity."[10] Put simply, he asks, How can the self-giving love of God produce a self-seeking people? This is not meant as an exposé of the moral failings of Christians—who could withstand such criticism?—but of the notion of salvation that lends support to those failures. Barth begins with the "pious egocentricity" of individuals, extends it to the "collective egocentricity" of churches, and in both cases objects not simply to their failures of compassion but to the soteriological and spiritual construals that validate those self-centered postures.[11] Barth raises serious objections to ecclesiologies that, whether in theory or in practice, present the church in the primary role of servicing the "private good fortune" of saved individuals, such that "the Christian song of praise consists finally only in a many-tongued but monotonous *pro me, pro me*, and similar possessive expressions."[12]

In all of this Barth hears the echoes of Ludwig Feuerbach, who charged that religion is essentially built of pious self-assurances:

> The service performed for me in actual life by another man is performed for me in religion by God. . . . Christ has done for you and given you everything you might seek or desire for yourself, here and in the beyond; this includes forgiveness of sins. . . . The blessed, to be sure, form a group, but it is a group based on no necessity or need for one. Of course, I wish blessedness for others, but only because it is the supreme object for me and I presuppose the same sentiment in others.[13]

---

[9]See *CD* IV/3.2, 653-54, 682, and *CD* IV/1, 644-49.

[10]*CD* IV/3.2, 566-68. Later Barth calls this "corner happiness." *ChrL*, 100. Elsewhere Barth writes, "We need not be fanatically anti-mystical," indeed, "there may be a place for a feeling of enjoyable contemplation of God. But it cannot take the place of that activity [of mission]." *CD* IV/1, 103-4, 106, 741.

[11]*CD* IV/3.2, 568-71.

[12]Ibid., 567.

[13]Ludwig Feuerbach, *The Essence of Faith According to Luther*, trans. M. Cherno (New York: Harper, 1967), 109, 114-15.

Feuerbach saw the apparent sociality of the Christian religion as nothing but
projected self-interest. Without accepting Feuerbach's conclusions, Barth appropriates similarly chastening words, not due to any phenomenological accuracy they may have but due to the discord between what they describe and
what confronts us in Christ. It is not as if Feuerbach put his finger on something Christians had never noticed before. Barth recalls manifestations of the
temptation to self-projection in the Pelagian controversy, in the "sacramen-
talistic and moralistic misunderstandings" of pre-Reformation Catholicism,
and in the Enlightenment-prompted "secularisation" of salvation of the early
nineteenth century.[14] With this he fast-forwards to the twentieth century and
suggests that an overblown reliance on the doctrine of justification to counter
such temptations may ironically be the greatest contemporary threat to its
proper utilization. After all, is there not "a certain narcissism" found in the
overemphasis on justification that puts a "delay" in pursuit of sanctification
and vocation? As Barth would have it, the doctrine of justification "has its
own dignity and necessity to which we do more and not less justice" when
we attach it integrally to other aspects of salvation.[15]

Barth does not consider the prevalence of selfishness among Christians
to be *grounds* for the rejection of the theological primacy of individual salvation, but he does consider the prioritization of private piety more indic-
ative of the *fallen* nature than the one unified to Christ.[16] Church and
mission are not a social add-on to a fundamentally personal faith. In another
place Barth makes this point with what seems at first to be an appeal to
anthropology, saying, "In accordance with creation and by nature humanity
means fellowship." However, in the very next line he writes, "This is equally
true, indeed it is genuinely true, only of the humanity of the Christian. Since
faith is his free human act, he cannot perform it without his neighbours,

---

[14]*CD* IV/1, 523.

[15]*CD* IV/1, 523, 527-28.

[16]Having in the past been rather harsh with Pietism, here Barth does not denounce it but bolsters
his claim by noting the exemplary "centrifugal striving" that broke out among even the most ardent
Pietists, thus illustrating how the Spirit has often gratefully proven truer than the theological foci
of the Spirit filled. See *CD* IV/3.2, 568-71. See also *CD* IV/1, 119; *CD* IV/2, 513; *CD* IV/3.1, 344;
CD IV/3.2, 930 and *ChrL*, 95. For a more phenomenological account that looks from a socially felt
experience of enmity to a critique of individualistic appropriations of justification (based on attention to the Korean concept of han), see Andrew Sung Park, *The Wounded Heart of God: The
Asian Concept of Han and the Christian Doctrine of Sin* (Nashville: Abingdon Press, 1993), 91-96.

without communication with them. . . . To exist privately is to be a robber."[17]
To be clear, when Barth calls Christianity a "public rather than a private
affair" he does not mean to drain it of its personal import but to say that we
become genuine persons precisely under the new direction of the Holy
Spirit wherein we are "integrated into the communion of saints."[18]

It may seem like we are belaboring the point, but the reason for this is that
it is so crucial to the understanding of forgiveness to be put forward. Interpersonally and practically speaking, what do we find at the junction between
"awakening to faith" and "gathering into communion" but the sharing of
Christ's forgiveness? Hopefully it is evident by now that for Barth this is about
more than the static intellectual acknowledgement of one another's indebtedness to God. With every new day of faith in Christ there is a "new gathering"
of the community in the multiplicity of its aspirations and gifts and in the
overcoming of its weaknesses and sins.[19] When Barth wrote that he could not
fathom "the meaning of a supposed Gospel the content of which is exhausted
by the proclamation of the forgiveness of sins and which is to be received by
man in a purely inward and receptive faith," it was not a turning away from
the centrality of forgiveness but an indication of its ongoing dynamism.[20]

Proclamation of forgiveness is not the propaganda of personal reassurance, but the invitation to new life that has not only the *reception* but also
the *extension* of forgiveness perpetually at its core. Believer and community
alike confess not only individual and corporate sin but solidarity with all
sinners in grateful reception of the grace of God. Christians "must always
reassemble and be brought into harmony on this line . . . very definitely
marked out for them in the service of the Gospel."[21] For all that has been
said about an apparent lack of consistent character to Barth's ethic and ecclesiology, it is clearly not so on this point. Thus we ought to further explore
what the church looks like that takes this to heart.

The special visibility of the church. In Barth's understanding a church will
always be a sociologically visible phenomenon—"itself a people like so many
others"—without ever being merely the sum of its observable parts. As a

---

[17]*CD* IV/1, 778.
[18]*CD* IV/2, 522, 596.
[19]See *CD* IV/1, 750-51; *CD* IV/2, 457-58 and *CD* IV/3.2, 653-54.
[20]*CD* IV/3.1, 370.
[21]*CD* IV/3.2, 800-801.

historical spiritual entity a church is "totally and properly both visible and invisible" at once; it "exists in total dependence on its environment and yet also in total freedom in relation to it."[22] A Christian community is fully amenable to description on "the historical and psychological and sociological level" and thus "defenceless against the interpretation" that reduces it to such explanations. As a result, a church should neither recede from its concrete visibility nor cavort to empirical explanations and perpetuations of its existence. Instead it should continue in the "special visibility" with which it is graced.[23]

It behooves us to consider the nature of that special visibility as Barth described it. As we have seen, for Barth the church has "not the being of a state or institution, but the being of an event"; it "*is* when it takes place."[24] At the same time, he claims every church has "a definite situation and position in which they are placed, a definite character which they are given, a definite function which is committed to them, a definite action which they are commissioned to perform."[25] In this a church is "fitted" for its "provisional representation" of Christ on earth as the Lord quickens it by the power of the Holy Spirit—but where it *presumes* itself fitted, it quickly begins to "represent itself" rather than its Lord.[26] This places churches in a bit of a bind: on one hand they cannot remain aloof from the call to represent God in everyday life, and on the other they must remain reserved in their claims to have done so! Faced with these caveats the slothful temptations to either paralysis or presumption become an obvious concern. So what can properly be said about the church's "definite character"? If the church is an event, might we describe it as such *in a particular* way without overstating ourselves?

In §72.3, "The Task of the Community," Barth asserts that the church is reduced to "an unco-ordinated mass" if it forgets the simple point that it is fundamentally the bearer of good news in which the bad news comes to light.[27] What that means, practically speaking, is that the church's visibility centers on its positive confession of faith and the negative confession of sin that is therein—and only therein—entailed. In §62 Barth articulates this

---

[22]*CD* IV/3.2, 722, 726, 734 and 742.
[23]*CD* IV/1, 653-55. See also *CD* IV/3.1, 89-91.
[24]*CD* IV/1, 652.
[25]*CD* IV/3.2, 532.
[26]*CD* IV/2, 622-23.
[27]*CD* IV/3.2, 796-98.

with a characteristically pointed rhetorical question, asking, "Where and
when does it not hang by a knife's edge whether or not there is this remembrance in the community?" Answering it himself, he continues, "If there is
not, the Church not only becomes like the world, but denying its true secret
it becomes especially worldly." Then in a straightforward filling-in of the
content of *credo ecclesiam*, Barth explains, "It is the Church which prays,
'Forgive us our trespasses,' which therefore knows and confesses that it needs
the forgiveness of sins."[28]

It is crucial to note that Barth is *not* recommending a focus on the visibility
of sin but a proper understanding of the church's fundamental point of visibility: the mercy of God. For all that might be made of the church's description
as a sin-confessing community, it is this positive Christ-confessing aspect
that gives it its shape as such. The church's existence in sin and enmity is
neither denied nor made definitive. Thus when it comes to the shape of such
a community's life, one of the things Barth finds central is that churches and
believers confess not only their own sin but also their solidarity with sinners
on the receiving end of Christ's reconciling work.[29]

All of this makes for a revealing window into Barth's view of the distinct
character of the church and the spiritual life of those within it. But how does
the church maintain this confidence and character when its sin is so admit-
tedly prevalent and its mission is in such constant jeopardy?[30] Do they "sin
boldly" and cuddle up to the self-soothing god of best intentions, covered
by a comforting blanket of amnesty?[31] This can only be the conclusion if
one goes forward on an abstract notion of forgiveness as a generalized sentiment. As the freedom for life and love, the forgiveness promised in Christ
is not the stuff of cozy apathy but of compelling liberation.[32] The church
cannot "console itself with the reflection that everything human is imperfect,
or the recollection that its sins are forgiven," Barth writes, adding that the
"grace of sanctification . . . is surely alien to it if it does not try to counteract

---

[28]*CD* IV/1, 658. This is where Barth quotes Luther to the effect that the church is the greatest of
sinners.
[29]See *CD* IV/1, 659, 677; *CD* IV/3.1, 340 and *CD* IV/3.2, 805.
[30]See *CD* IV/3.2, 812.
[31]The rhetoric is Barth's. He says the *sola fide* cannot be "a comfortable kiss [or a 'lazy cushion']
of peace," and denounces a "feather-bed" notion of the assurance of salvation. *CD* IV/2, 506,
638; see also *KD* IV/2, 573.
[32]See *CD* IV/3.2, 815.

the continual menace" of "profanation" which such sins entail.[33] In other words, the church gathered in God's grace goes forward neither with recklessness nor fear. It is not a camaraderie of commiseration but a communion made by God in the grace that remains grace. "In proportion as it will not live by the grace of God, it begins to die."[34]

So the church event entails not just a people's confession of sin but their invocation of God's daily forgiveness. This is not because of a faltering assurance of salvation but precisely because of confidence in the promises of God. Every day the church "is thrown back on His having mercy upon it and making its unholy activity holy." For Barth this does not diminish the church's "indestructibility" but *is* its indestructibility. The church exists *in* and *as* history, not as a relic but as a community existing "on a way" in which it is "always the same" by being "always new."[35] So it is that for Barth to refer to *ecclesia semper reformanda* is to not simply make a claim about the church's unfinished business, but its very dynamic. "Forgive us our trespasses" is the prayer of the church qua church. It is not a groveling reminder of fallibility but a positive confession of the mercy of God.[36]

It should be clear, then, why the church hopes to be a visibly exemplary community but refrains from making its exemplary status a matter of its own concern. In our desire to appropriate this, as we explore the "distinctive ethos" of the church in the remaining chapters, we must resist the temptation to "absolutise" its subjective experience.[37] At the same time, we must be bold to inquire into the particular imperatives of life and fellowship that go into this account of the church's visible core. Notable as much for its frequent neglect as for its poignancy is the fact that in Matthew 18, when Jesus promises to be "there" with two or three who are gathered in his name, it is on the heels of instructions about seeing them reconciled. Jesus' promise is not conditioned upon their reconciling abilities. It is not even a promise of immediate success. On a Barthian reading it is Jesus' promise to be the living head of a body that gathers in his name and joins him in just this way.[38]

---

[33]*CD* IV/2, 709.
[34]Ibid., 666.
[35]*CD* IV/1, 693 and 704.
[36]See ibid., 690.
[37]See *CD* IV/2, 719-26; *CD* IV/3.1, 90-91 and *CD* IV/3.2, 558-63.
[38]See *CD* IV/1, 680, and Mt 18:15-20.

To conclude this section, then, let us make a crucial observation about the topic at hand. *The community gathered by the Holy Spirit's awakening to faith is one that is turned toward mutual forgiveness from the outset, precisely because the forgiveness it receives is not monopolized but shared.* To take matters further, Barth states that the "mutual witness" of such a community "will be genuine and useful to the extent that," on the interpersonal level of its imperfect relationships, "there is a true reflection and imitation of what takes place between God" and humanity. This interpersonal reflection is not to be identified with or set up as a replacement for the divine-human relation it imitates, but for Barth "there is a similarity" wherein "what is done is calculated to give a necessary reminder" of God's love.[39]

So it is that the Christian community is gathered not just in the acknowledgment of one another's divinely forgiven status, but in the confessed imperative to actively forgive one another in Jesus' name as well. The church prays for, believes, receives and shares the forgiveness of sins within the ongoing realization of Christ's reconciliation. Placing this at the core of their visible identity is not to say that their *ability* to bear with one another is the *cause* of their unity or the focus of their witness, but is to say that forbearance, forgiveness and self-giving love are central identification points for the *ecclesia*, constitutive of the worthy walk that corresponds to their unity in Christ.[40] This is not the church's only point of visibility, but it is the dynamic constant. We take this as an impetus to draw out a thick description of the common life of those who profess to be awakened to faith.

BUILDING AND QUICKENING: FREE FOR RECIPROCITY (§67–§68)

When Barth comes to the sections on ecclesiology and the Christian life in his sanctification part-volume he turns directly to the theme of love, noting particularly the priority of mutual edification. As already explained, the person freed in Christ is no longer self-referential. Even the newfound freedoms of the justified believer are submitted to the priority of edification, since "a proper use of their own freedom is that they should subject themselves to one another and serve one another in love (Gal 5:13)."[41] "No such

---

[39] *CD* IV/2, 815-16.
[40] See *CD* IV/1, 244, 659 and 668, along with Eph 4:1-7 and *CD* IV/2, 626, 654.
[41] *CD* IV/3.2, 603; see also 652, and *CD* IV/2, 637. This is a prominent theme in 1 Cor 10–13.

thing [as private edification] is ever envisaged in the New Testament," argues Barth: "I can edify myself only as I edify the community."[42] (For all the attention given to spiritual disciplines in recent decades, surely this suggests attention be given to biblical disciplines of interpersonal relationship.)

This other-focused nature of Christian community springs neither from self-confidence nor self-abasement, but from newfound freedom in Christ and the Holy Spirit's quickening to love. With use of the word *love*, however, we should not presume to have said all there is to say. Particularly when it is most difficult, in the face of personal offense or systemic injustice, the call to love one another is separated from mere sentimentality. The word *love* already suffers the ambiguity of a million uses, but at the collision of interpersonal good intentions and bad results we find a particularly palpable reason to probe for greater specificity. Thus in what follows we will examine the details of Barth's treatment of Christian agape, delineating in two subsections his view of (1) its intended recipients and (2) its intended reciprocity.

In the second part-volume of *The Doctrine of Reconciliation* Barth drives a hard distinction between eros and agape in order to illustrate and articulate a definition of love that is particularly Christian. As he tells it, eros and agape do not touch or overlap but are in "full antithesis." Although he is at this point on somewhat precarious exegetical ground, his point is a theological one. He highlights the "point of departure" (rather than the "point of coincidence") between agape and eros in order to capture the way Christ's love interrupts and reorients what might otherwise have been headed in the wrong direction.[43] Rather than take Barth's rhetoric as an utter denouncement of friendship or erotic love, we would thus be better to say that eros without agape remains on an ultimately destructive path. Eros and philia make horrible *replacements* for agape, but can be sanctified and given their rightful place in the love of Christ. For this reason, when they come into conflict with agape (so defined), agape will not call a "truce."[44]

---

[42]*CD* IV/2, 627.
[43]Ibid., 735-45. See Claude Wiéner, "Love," trans. John J. Kilgallen, in *Dictionary of Biblical Theology*, ed. Xavier Léon-Dufour, trans. Joseph Cahill, 2nd ed. (New York: Seabury Press, 1973), 322-27. Linguistically, the word *agape* on its own does carry all the theological freight assigned to it. However, particularly in the context of its biblical and historical usage, there is still some usefulness in following through on the differentiations Barth delineates by making use of the term.
[44]*CD* IV/2, 462, 736

As Barth's rhetoric means to employ it, agape (or Christian love) in its fullest sense is not self-assertive, possessive, self-serving, self-generated or self-sustaining, but is freely given to others from the new self that is daily re-created by Christ. Such self-giving love is explicitly also not the same as abject self-denial. The giver will have a self to give (as given by God) and will be directed to the love of others (with the hope of being received by them). Although healthy selfhood is closely connected to an orientation to others, the popular notion that one should "give oneself in order to find oneself" is an example of the way that we still color and motivate love with a self-seeking impulse.[45] (Relevant here is also the popular adage that one forgives another in order to set oneself free, but this will be discussed later.) Taking up the Feuerbachian critique that what appears loving can actually be self-serving, Barth asserts that, properly speaking, "we cannot love in order to achieve something."[46] It is precisely in our sinful disorientation that we love as a means to gain love, thus rendering it contractual rather than free. One occasion when this self-motivated love has been seen to sneak into the church education curriculum is when spiritual disciplines relating to service and fellowship are cast within the paradigm of personal growth and leveraged toward it as the ultimate goal.[47] This is not to undermine the importance of spiritual disciplines and is certainly not to judge hidden motives, but there is a personal and ecclesiological chastening to be considered here.

Barth is clear that Christian agape does not arise from heightened world consciousness, sociological insight or self-awareness. Love "falls, as it were, vertically into the lives of those to whom it is given," developing among them as a "seed of new life" that affects their "whole being and thinking and action and inaction." In self-love we may perpetually crash into each other, but God's self-grounded love frees us from this "frenzied activity" for the fellowship of

---

[45]"Agape means self-giving: not the losing of oneself in the other." Ibid., 734, 738 and 745; see also *CD* IV/3.2, 592.

[46]*CD* IV/2, 783; see Feuerbach, *According to Luther*, 95-100. See also J. Alexander Sider, "'Love One Another': Voluntariety Transformed by Dialogical Vulnerability," in *To See History Doxologically: History and Holiness in John Howard Yoder's Ecclesiology* (Grand Rapids: Eerdmans, 2011), 185.

[47]See Richard J. Foster, *Celebration of Discipline: The Path to Spiritual Growth* (San Francisco: Harper & Row, 1978), 1-9, 96-122; Dallas Willard, *The Spirit of the Disciplines: Understanding How God Changes Lives* (San Francisco: Harper Collins, 1988), 104, 182 and John Ortberg, *The Life You've Always Wanted: Spiritual Disciplines for Ordinary People* (Grand Rapids: Zondervan, 2002), 39, 121.

the Holy Spirit.[48] As Caroline Simon puts it, "Actually loving is like coming out of the dark cave in which we hoard and safeguard our unregenerate self."[49] Because love is commanded by Christ and born of the Holy Spirit, we know that it is not self-motivated; it does not stem from a golden-rule platitude or confidence in the illusory equality of a system of exchange. Thus the church must not simply co-opt social strategies for community, as if "sentimental undertones" and cooperative arrangements are inspired and perpetuated by us in order to be "integrated by God."[50] Churches will know the difference between fallen eros and Christian agape most profoundly when push comes to shove and truly self-giving, *forgiving* love is needed most.[51]

It is important to note that even though agape is founded in the eternal self-giving love of the electing God, because a fallen world is the realm in which it comes to us, we do not know Christ's self-giving love apart from his forgiving mercy.[52] In volume one of the *Dogmatics* Barth inserted this as an explanation of that inscrutable line in Jesus' Great Commandment, where we are told to love our neighbors as ourselves: "When I love my neighbour I confess that my self-love is not a good thing, that it is not love at all. . . . The only positive meaning of 'as thyself' is, then, that we are commanded to love our neighbour as those who love themselves, i.e., as those who in reality do not love, as the sinners that we are."[53] On one hand Barth gives such a demanding picture of love that we might despair of ever finding it in the world, but on the other hand he promotes such faith in the mercy of God that we marvel at what God is able to make out of the most dire circumstances and selfishness-riddled philanthropy.[54] Where 1 Peter 4:8 tells us that "love covers

---

[48]*CD* IV/2, 522-23 and 749.

[49]Caroline J. Simon, "What Wondrous Love Is This? Meditations on Barth, Christian Love, and the Future of Christian Ethics," in *For the Sake of the World: Karl Barth and the Future of Ecclesial Theology*, ed. George Hunsinger (Grand Rapids: Eerdmans, 2004), 147; see also Karl Barth, *Ethics* (Edinburgh: T&T Clark, 1981), 457.

[50]*CD* IV/2, 636.

[51]See *CD* IV/1, 107.

[52]Agape has no *need* of the conflict with sin, but prevails within it. *CD* IV/2, 746.

[53]*CD* I/2, 450-52; see also Mt 22:35-40; Mk 12:27-34; Lk 10:25-37.

[54]For example, see Barth's positive treatment of Reformation missions in *CD* IV/3.1, 18-38. For another example see his assessment of the works of Scholz and Nygren in regard to agape itself. Though he thinks the distinctions between loves are more properly explicated by Nygren, Barth finds Nygren's account to be colored by a triumphal note of eros, which leads him to prefer Scholz's overly synthesized account, simply because it is expressed more clearly in the manner of agape. *CD* IV/2, 737-38; see Heinrich Scholz *Eros und Caritas: Die platonische Liebe und die*

a multitude of sins," Barth acknowledges that it refers "in the first instance" to those "sins committed by the neighbour who is to be loved," but he adds that "it applies also to the sins of those who exercise love."[55] In the face of our failures, faith in the grace of Christ compels us to love, even if that love can always be purer. Indeed it will be the love of Christ in it that will purify it.

The church is called to share that which is freely given by Jesus, to love as it is loved and to forgive as it is forgiven. In this the risen Lord enables us to give "with no expectation of a return, in a pure venture, even at the risk of ingratitude" and the "refusal to make a response of love."[56] Christians are used to depicting cruciform love as a pure gift, definitively unconditional. What is perhaps surprising (and certainly telling) about Barth's account of such love is that he nonetheless moves on to describe it as definitively recip-rocal. This leads to our first delineation of agape, which regards a potentially unnerving point: the discernment of its intended recipients.

Everyday agape: Brothers and sisters, neighbors and enemies. Lest this call to self-giving and forgiving love be rendered abstract and trite, we do well to consider carefully the concrete relationships and situations entailed. When Luke's expert in the law asked Jesus who his neighbor was, it appears to have been an evasive question, but Barth thinks Jesus utilized it to cut to the heart of the matter. In volume one of the *Dogmatics* Barth suggests that, by telling a story about an act of love and then identifying the neighbor not as the victim but as "the one who had mercy," Jesus firmly planted the command to "go and do likewise" in the initiative of grace rather than the mere coincidence of location.[57] In volume four Barth takes further cues from 1 Corinthians 13 and adds that Jesus' storytelling appendix to that command indicates a love that takes place in the context of actual relation-ships or else is "deluded" in its claim to be an extension of the love of Christ. There is no room here for retreat into the sentimental platitude that "it is the thought that counts." As Barth explains it, upholding "a universal love of humanity" might be biblically legitimate if it refers to an "attitude of mind," but Christian love "is an act of obedience which . . . takes place somewhere

---

Liebe im Sinne des Christentums (Halle: Max Niemeyer Verlag, 1929), and Anders Nygren, *Agape and Eros*, trans. Philip S. Watson (New York: Harper & Row, 1957).
[55]CD IV/2, 732.
[56]CD IV/2, 745.
[57]CD I/2, 418-19, and Lk 10:37.

in time and space."[58] In light of Jesus' treatment of the legal expert's question, then, we are left to wonder not who our neighbors are but whether we are following Jesus into the event of neighborliness.

This is a reframing of the matter to which we will return, but not before considering the question asked by the expert in the law more carefully. With the pace of travel and the ease of long-distance communication today, his question still has a certain paralyzing ring to it. On any given day there might be countless events of neighborliness that may take place. Flooded by opportunities to show mercy, how does one determine where and when to show compassion today?

Raising just such a question, Slavoj Žižek's *The Neighbor* suggests that a construal of the imperative to love in terms of *proximity* entails an indifference to those who are *distant* that is, in the interconnections of globalization, inevitably unjust. For this reason he argues for the importance of keeping in mind an abstract "Third"—the Neighbor who is not represented in the narrow scenario of one's place and time.[59] Where we fall into the habit of loving only those close to us we might simply be conforming our love to the biased selectivity by which we arrived at that proximity in the first place. Reminiscent of Feuerbach, Žižek claims that religious factors perpetuate this. Our comfortable blindness to background processes of segregation and selectivity, he says, is "a necessary correlate to [belief in] the loving God who selects some," such that our "arbitrary cruelty goes hand in hand with [that] arbitrary selection." In fact, for Žižek, an ethic that favors the convenient neighbor finds its home in "the underside of a ruthless God."[60] In order to put to death such selectivity, the nonpresent "Third" becomes the neighbor to love.

Of course, Žižek's strategy amounts to a mental trick as susceptible to bias and caprice as any other. This is a point he makes himself in his more recent work, *Living in the End Times*. There he comments on how easy it is to network with a nonpresent other precisely in order to avoid what Mladen Dolar calls

---

[58]*CD* IV/2, 816, 806-7 and 802-3. See also *CD* IV/3.2, 617. Evidently Barth did not consider his caution about prescriptive ethics to be a reversion into nondescript Christianity. In fact, he might suggest that the one who reads his *Dogmatics* and finds an ethic wanting in particulars might just be looking for a way to avoid the voice of the living Lord in everyday life.

[59]Slavoj Žižek, *The Neighbor: Three Inquiries in Political Theology* (Chicago: University of Chicago Press, 2005), 183, 185.

[60]Ibid., 189-90. Those familiar with volume two of the *Dogmatics* will recognize this capricious *deus absconditus* as the same one opposed by Barth. See *CD* II/1, 541-42, and *CD* IV/1, 193-94.

"that strange creature next to us whom we are supposed to love, but who causes embarrassment and mortification" by "intruding upon our private space" and "exposing us."[61] It is this "intrusive over-proximity" that tests one's capacity to love; it is the "non-universalizable neighbour" who pierces indifference and occasions the event of love. This may seem to contradict Žižek's prior claim, but in fact it only reiterates it in a different way. He maintains the ability to say that the agape Paul has in view in 1 Corinthians 13 "enjoins us to 'unplug' from the organic community into which we were born" in order to more properly love.[62] On one hand we must look past the next-door neighbor to remember the underrepresented Third, and on the other hand we must look more closely at the sheer Otherness of the person next door. If proximity overdetermines attentiveness, love dislodges regional selfishness and bias; but if proximity underdetermines attentiveness, love disrupts distraction.

The underlying goal in all of this is for love to extend across difference without eradicating difference. This has Žižek clamoring for an antidote to indifference that will heighten the attentiveness of love. His challenge is appropriately jarring, but the directives are daunting and not a little bit abstract. In the end the call is to something like a mixture of humility and imagination. As if often the case, then, the virtue of indiscriminate agape is grounded in epistemological humility and an ideal of equality. For his part, Miroslav Volf recommended that it be a posture or "will to embrace" that guides us here.[63] Søren Kierkegaard suggested that if it seems impossible to love your enemy you should "shut your eyes—and your enemy looks just like your neighbour."[64] In the darkest circumstances of *The Power and the Glory*, Graham Greene's fictional whiskey priest called it "a

---

[61]Slavoj Žižek, *Living in the End Times* (London: Verso, 2011), 2-3 and 122, quoting Dolar from an unpublished paper called "The Art of the Unsaid."

[62]Žižek, *End Times*, 123 and 106.

[63]See Miroslav Volf, *Exclusion and Embrace: A Theological Exploration of Identity, Otherness, and Reconciliation* (Nashville: Abingdon, 1996), 131, 215, 256-58.

[64]Søren Kierkegaard, *Works of Love: Some Christian Reflections in the Form of Discourses*, trans. Howard Hong and Edna Hong (New York: Harper & Brothers, 1962), 79. On the other side of the dialectic, Kierkegaard adds, "At a distance every man recognises his neighbour, and yet it is impossible to see him at a distance." However, he soon retreats again into abstraction, saying that distinctions "hang loosely about the individual" as a "ragged costume in which a supernatural being has disguised itself"—which seems like a hint at the presence of Jesus except Kierkegaard concludes that "there steadily shines in every individual that essential other person, that which is common to all men, the eternal likeness, the equality." Ibid., 89 and 96.

failure of the imagination" to hate someone who has been made in the image of God.[65]

There is some truth in all of this. But is the implication that one must summon the motive to love from within? Is one's imagination not just as likely to project ideology or personal preference onto the other person at the expense of their very otherness? Is it not the case that willpower is what fails us when self-giving love is needed most?

What distinguishes Barth's treatment of concrete, proximal agape from that which recommends it as a posture or principle is the call to faith in the living presence of the commanding Lord Jesus Christ. In the face of difference and sin, Christ's followers are freed by his grace to love and to seek koinonia in this world, notwithstanding the force of either its "clannish warmth" or its enmity.[66] This should not be considered a fickle or purely mystical affair. If one trusts God in the moment then one may have a reasonable amount of trust in one's God-directed past. Rather than flitting to and fro, one might take a neighbor's sustained proximity as an indication of God's persistent call on one's life. The point is that love comes not merely from external circumstance or internal motivation, but the command of Christ.

With Jesus' command to love their enemies Barth reckons that the Christians are given an orientation, within which "the whole friend-foe relationship" is destroyed.[67] This does not mean the denial of friendship or the failure to acknowledge one's foes as foes; rather, it indicates that neighbor love is bound neither by comfort of compatibility nor by resignation to irreconcilable difference, but is bound by hope in a reconciling God. As such it is different from optimism about our shared humanity. Instead it embraces the experience of difference and enmity as something hopelessly contained but no less sustained within the ongoing life of the Christian.[68] For Barth, entrusting reconciliation and peace to Christ, the mediating Third, "abolishes the whole exercise of force"—not in principle, but in practice. Christ calls for neither

---

[65]Graham Greene, *The Power and the Glory* (New York: Penguin Books, 2003), 131.

[66]*CD* IV/2, 550-51. See Lk 14:26 and *CD* IV/3.2, 625.

[67]*CD* IV/2, 550.

[68]As Bernd Wannenwetsch rightly observes, such empathy can equally be hegemonic or colonialist in its impulses, veiling a tendency to "transpose oneself into the other" so that "the other's difference all too easily gets lost along the way." Bernd Wannenwetsch, *Political Worship: Ethics for Christian Citizens*, trans. Margaret Kohl (Oxford: Oxford University Press, 2004), 328. See *CD* IV/1, 364, and *CD* IV/2, 457.

self-love nor the love of death, but for a love for life in Christ that, compelled by faith in his resurrection, takes the form of a willingness to die.[69]

This is not to suggest a principle of so-called unconditional love. For all that it admirably recommends, such a platitude makes love an individually possessed ideal, complete as soon as it is offered. To complement this, it is crucial to note that Christian love, fully understood, hopes to be other-receiving and reciprocal. In fact it is to the detriment of agape if its telos in koinonia is ignored or abstracted. As Stephen Post points out, if Søren Kierkegaard could exalt love for the dead as the height of agape because of its persistence in the face of impossible return, it shows a notion of self-giving love which exaggerates self-denial and overly diminishes the koinonia which agape seeks.[70] This is a common shortcoming in accounts of "unconditional" love and forgiveness, about which Barth is not silent. For him it is important to note that love has a christologically grounded telos of reciprocity. To get a further sense of his emphasis on this point, in the last part of this section we will look at his claim that Christian love is, properly speaking, an act that "takes place between Christians."[71]

The inherent mutuality of agape. In §68.3, "The Act of Love," Barth suggests that there is a reciprocity so unique to the Christian community that it is only here that agape truly takes place. Properly speaking, Barth explains, love "can flourish only on this soil. As it cannot be practised by all, it cannot be meaningfully addressed to all." Challenging those who would see "Christian love as a human virtue," Barth rather provocatively asserts that "fellow-man can be loved only in the form of the other Christian who is brought into a definite relationship to the Christian by the love of God and of Jesus Christ." If there is a worry about exclusivity here, Barth is more likely to call it a concern about incompleteness. Every person is "called to enter" and "may, of course, belong to this community," he explains, but on "this

---

[69]*CD* IV/2, 550 and 602-4. The last line paraphrases Chesterton, who called courage "a strong desire to live taking the form of a readiness to die." G. K. Chesterton, *Orthodoxy* (London: Hodder & Stoughton, 1996), 134.

[70]See Stephen G. Post, *A Theory of Agape: On the Meaning of Christian Love* (Cranbury, NJ: Associated University Presses, 1990), 12, 31-32, and Kierkegaard, *Works of Love*, 37, 317-29. For his part, Post proposes a "pattern of mutuality" and a principle of "non-coerciveness" shaped more by natural theology than salvation history. See Post, *Theory of Agape*, 17, 32, 25, 21, 25, 50, 81-83, 97-100, 106, 111, 114.

[71]*CD* IV/2, 805.

side [of] the end of all things with the coming again of Christ, faith is not a matter for everyone," thus not all belong.[72] The worry seems to remain, however, that Barth is recommending a kind of social contract wherein love is held out until common faith can be confirmed. But this is to forget that all persons are to be considered would-be Christians in this regard. The point is not to withhold acts of love, but to recognize that Christian love is not shared except in common faith.

This interpretation of Barth's statements might need some defending. Does Barth not seem to suggest that only professing Christians can commit acts of self-giving love, or that they should only love other Christians? Indeed, Gene Outka thinks Barth was confused and inconsistent on this point. By suggesting that proper "objects of agape are confined to co-believers," Barth makes it sound as if the enemy and the outsider to this community *cannot* be loved.[73] Barth's rhetoric does get muddled at this point, but the charge of internal inconsistency ought to at least alert us to the possibility that Barth means to qualify himself. In this regard, a close analysis reveals that Barth does not think agape is *confined* to the Christian community. Barth is not outlining a practical restriction but making a theological point, which is that it is ultimately in the community of Christ that agape finds (what Outka calls) its "shared meaning" and "intelligibility."[74] In §28, "The Being of God as the One who Loves in Freedom," Barth explained that God's love is "not conditioned by any reciprocity" on the part of his creatures.[75] In §68 Barth is saying that human love can only be given as such within the love and freedom of God, wherein its designed reciprocity is held in trust.

Does this vision of love have the inevitable effect of bolstering the strategy which reserves a show of love until signs are that it will be satisfactorily reciprocated? (This question is highly relevant to the practice of forgiveness as well.) In regard to believers, Barth maintains that the "sign of baptism" simply "has to be taken with positive seriousness."[76] It is all the sign anyone

---

[72]Ibid., 804.

[73]Gene Outka, *Agape: An Ethical Analysis* (New Haven, CT: Yale University Press, 1976), 255; see also 210.

[74]Outka notes that Barth "does not wish to find a meaning of love already functioning in a non-theological context and merely modify it for theological purposes." Ibid., 212, 239-40.

[75]*CD* II/1, 278.

[76]*CD* IV/2, 807.

needs to reach out in the hope of experiencing communion. In regard to those who have not come under this sign, Barth explains,

> But this positive fact does not involve the negative one that we must in no case love the fellow-men whom we do not know or think we know as our neighbours in this specific concrete sense. Baptism and visible fellowship in confession are for us an inclusive sign, but they are not for this reason *a limine* an exclusive sign. . . . In the last instance it is not we who have to decide whether or not this other man loves God.[77]

On one level this denouncement of discriminate love (and of triumphalist or cloistered ecclesiocentrism) might be based simply on the observance of our finite knowledge and our displacement as judges. On another level it is to be read as a positive confession of the reconciliation of the world to God, so that "the love of Christ urges us on" and we "regard no one from a [merely] human point of view" (2 Cor 5:14, 16).[78]

It is on the latter basis that Barth considers neighbor- and enemy-love sustainable within an account that sees Christian love as definitively confessional and reciprocal. As he puts it,

> I have to be prepared and continually ready to receive new light beyond what I now think I know, always making new discoveries, and thus finding it possible and necessary to love to-morrow where to-day it seems out of the question to do so because I do not yet perceive the relationship in which the other stands to me. Hence the restriction of Christian love to the circle of brothers known to me cannot be theoretical and definitive, but only practical and provisional. . . . I anticipate in my love to the brother of to-day what I shall be bound to do in relation to the brother of to-morrow. In the narrower love I am always reaching out to the wider. And since I cannot know of any man that he will not prove to be my brother to-morrow, I cannot withhold from any of my fellows an attitude of openness, of expectation, of good hope and therefore of readiness for love.[79]

In these citations it is clear that Barth does not intend for Christian love to be exclusive, but for Christians to recognize the telos in mutual fellowship. If this puts us back into the realm of a recommended attitude or posture, then it is

---

[77]*CD* IV/2, 807.
[78]See *CD* IV/1, 105-6.
[79]*CD* IV/2, 808.

in good company with Paul's exhortations to have "the same mind" as Jesus (Phil 2:5) and to take a new-creation "point of view" (2 Cor 5:16-17), as long as the impetus for such love is not in the mind and heart of the believer alone.

To suggest that Christ's self-giving love finds its home in a reconciled community is not to confine it to the walls of the church but is to clarify the telos and the vitality of its ministry and mission. Barth's approach to this is resonant with what Alexander Sider appropriates from Milbank: "An economy of gift that foregrounds reciprocity . . . highlights the way in which the voluntary character of the church cannot be a species of contractualism" but must operate from the "assumption of plenitude."[80] In the abundance of God's love, Christian communion is not insular but expansive. Christian love is given freely—even though it finds fullness only in reciprocal communion. Christians are called to be indiscriminately friendly, but in Barth's view "what the New Testament calls 'love' is in fact other and more than this friendliness." As a created good, friendliness is still but an "anticipation" of Christian love; as such it is the "position of readiness" Christians take "even in relationships in which its realisation is at the moment impossible."[81] Where some might paint friendliness as the pinnacle of a church's aspirations, Barth sees it as a penultimate imperative next to the ministry of reconciliation.

Caroline J. Simon explains this distinction by drawing a contrast between Barth and Andre Trocme:

> For Trocme the essence of Christian witness had its foremost application in how outsiders were treated; the love of the parishioners for one another was rooted in their joint adventure of aiding those outside their circle that needed their help. For Barth the order of emphasis is the reverse: the foremost obligation is toward the *insider*; outsiders are aided by the witness of mutual love insiders share for one another and are given help as potential or nascent insiders.[82]

This is certainly helpful, but it runs the risk of too strongly emphasizing the line between "insiders" and "outsiders." Attention must thus be paid to Simon's final line, which grapples with the force of Barth's belief in the

---

[80]Sider, "Love One Another," 188; see also John Milbank, "The Midwinter Sacrifice," in *The Blackwell Companion to Post-Modern Theology*, ed. Graham Ward (Oxford: Blackwell, 2002), 124. See CD IV/1, 103.

[81]*CD* IV/2, 809.

[82]Simon, "What Wondrous Love," 152, 154.

objective universality of Christ's reconciling work. To put a point on it: as an act of faith and hope, love is extended to any and all as Christ commands. This rests not on internal motive or external signs of reciprocity—although it will be attentive to the latter because of its concern not to force itself upon the other. The ramifications of this for our account of forgiveness are significant, and will become clearer as we proceed in chapters four and five. But before moving on we must take up one more point.

Given the inherent reciprocity of Christian love, Caroline Simon rightly presses the point that for Barth the church's koinonia is essential to its witness. In other words, a church proclaims the gospel not only by loving its neighbors but also by being a community where people reconcile with each other. "Liberation for God is one thing," Barth explains, but it is another thing to witness "the liberation of the members of this people for one another." Without this, "even the most profound words . . . cannot alter in the very slightest the fact . . . that they are not fulfilling their reciprocal obligation." A church that proclaims but does not practice this interpersonal liberation may be internally "deluded" and publicly misleading, such that "as far as they are concerned the life of the community is arrested and thrown into confusion, and its mission in the world is compromised."[83]

This makes a great deal of sense, but the difficulty is articulating how Christian love seeks reciprocated fellowship while also extending itself without "strings" attached. Cognizant of Feuerbach's charge that the religious deploy a concept of God that self-servingly shields them from real interaction with others, Barth reiterates that Christian love must seek koinonia without withholding until the koinonia feels satisfactory.[84] As John Webster explains, "To love the other as a latent Christian is not to do violence to his or her integrity; still less is it to set up barriers to compassion. It is nothing other than a matter of affirming the other's teleology, to treat the other as what he or she already is in Christ. My neighbour is 'ordered' to be the witness to me of Christ's mercy."[85] The wording here is significant. Recognizing Christ's love as the conditioning factor, one enters into acts of love without even presuming to be the primary witness. In any given encounter

---

[83]CD IV/2, 810 and 816.
[84]See Feuerbach, *According to Luther*, 109.
[85]John Webster, "Response" to "What Wondrous Love Is This?" in Hunsinger, *For the Sake*, 163-64.

it may just as well turn out that the neighbor is the one who does the bulk of the witnessing. No matter the circumstances for asking, "Who is my neighbor?" the question is always best asked of Christ.

Furthermore, alongside his exhortations to view others as prospective Christians regardless of their confessional status, Barth makes a crucial distinction between recognizing love's telos in communion and subsuming it beneath the machinations of an idealized vision of community. This is important to keep in mind if the argument thus far is accepted, and the quality of a church's fellowship is taken to be part of its witness. This does not mean that the church is "a heterogeneous collection of individuals" united by a lack of conflict or by an excellence at cooperation.[86] Overzealous attempts to establish an appearance or experience of unity will inevitably settle for a self-made delusion rather than receive such communion in faith as a gift of God in Christ. As a counterpoint to this Barth's missional ecclesiology might be summed up as follows: *the church testifies to Christ's new creation as its members receive and share the forgiving love of the Savior in the throes of reconciliation's realization in a still-broken world.* Apart from this they are hardly a church. Apart from this their mission is suspect. As Barth states, their "witness will be genuine and useful to the extent that between man and man, with all the imperfection of what one man can be and do for another, there is a true reflection and imitation of what takes place between God and man."[87]

This section has been painstaking in its focus on this because it is crucial to define Christian forgiveness within an understanding of Christian love. One cannot be understood without the other. Love is the definitive reality within which forgiveness is understood but, this side of the fall into sin, forgiveness is the timely reality within which that love is made known. This means that love is witnessed and known in the midst of and not apart from our experiences of difference and sin, imperfection and conflict. Indeed, if encounters with difficult neighbors are few and far between, it could be a signal to a church that it has buffered itself within a congenial demographic, clung to a false peace of conflict avoidance and called it Christian community. Jesus may visit such churches in the form of different and difficult others not only out of solidarity with the "least of these" but also out of a

---

[86]*CD* IV/2, 635.
[87]Ibid., 815-16; see 778-79.

merciful desire to interrupt the church's self-love and rescue it from its collective narcissism (Mt 25:40, 45).[88]

Although one-way expressions of love are not the ultimate goal, it must be
reiterated that, in an as-yet unreconciled human experience, it will often be
unreciprocated love that bears the greatest witness to the self-giving love of
Christ. This continues to be the place where agape most dramatically confronts the world: when the enemy pierces the Christian community with
hatred and is loved in return.[89] Contrary to the assumptions of many a contemporary apologist, in 1 Peter 3:15-16 it is persecution that begs the question
of hope so strongly that Christians must be ready to give a reason for it.

All of this should lead us to ask, along with Clifford Green, "how the
Christian community, in its own life and practice, can better become *itself* a
socio-political parable of the gospel, an enacted parable of God's reign and
realm."[90] This will be the focus of chapters four, five and six. It should be
clear by now that, whatever we say about *how* this path of life proceeds, all
roads lead through forgiveness. As Barth expresses it in one place, "Our
particular theme at this point must be the human weakness of the communion of saints on earth; more importantly, its preservation in spite of this
weakness."[91] In the turbulence of sin and enmity, one "becomes free for
existence in an active relationship with the other" by the power of the Spirit
as "a matter of faith in the remission of sins," such that there is no way
forward but "living by forgiveness."[92] When Barth says that "each one receives the consolation of the Gospel and passes it on to others," it is not
meant as a piece of propaganda to cover up moral failings, but quite the

---

[88]See *CD* IV/3.2, 855-56.
[89]*CD* IV/2, 805.
[90]Clifford Green, "Freedom for Humanity: Karl Barth and the Politics of the New World Order," in
Hunsinger, *For the Sake*, 105. As Hauerwas and Willimon put it, "The church is the visible, political
enactment of our language of God by a people who can name their sin and accept God's forgiveness
and are thereby enabled to speak the truth in love." Stanley Hauerwas and William H. Willimon,
*Resident Aliens: A Provocative Assessment of Culture and Ministry for People Who Know That Something
Is Wrong* (Nashville: Abingdon Press, 1989), 171. Outka thinks Barth is keen to provide such description, since his three forms of witness include not just "explicit declaration" and "attitude" but
also "psycho-social existence" as "a sign of the promised help of God." Outka, *Agape*, 248-49; see
also *CD* I/2, 444, and *CD* IV/2, 626.
[91]This is my slightly clarified translation of *KD* IV/2, 747; see *CD* IV/2, 661.
[92]"The one to whom much is forgiven (Lk 7:47f.) can love much, whereas little is forgiven to the
one who loves little." *CD* IV/2, 818.

opposite.[93] It is the indication of a central ecclesial dynamic to which we ought to pay attention. Here we see clear ramifications for the place and meaning of forgiveness in the Christian community. It is precisely by entering into the ministry of reconciliation that church members have a message to speak and a mission to extend.

SENDING AND ENLIGHTENING: FREE FOR THE WORLD (§72–§73)

So much of Barth's ecclesial ethic hinges on this that we must risk belaboring the point for one more section before we build on it in the chapters to come. To further explicate Barth's integration of vocation with justification and sanctification, in this section we turn to the incorporation of "sending" with the "gathering" and "up-building" of the community, and of hope with faith and love. By the time readers come to the third part-volume of Barth's *Doctrine of Reconciliation*, his focus on vocation ought not to surprise them. But it is hard to resist the impression that Barth appears either to have been bursting at the seams to put things more explicitly or to have begun to realize the ramifications of what he has been saying. As we have already observed, for Barth the reception of Christ's mercy is no mere private phenomenon, separable from the option of a corresponding vocation.[94] Where this is forsaken the church is found to be a "source of disillusionment"; but "when what is given to it passes through its hands it does not go hungry but is itself fed."[95]

Barth's construal aims not to conflate or dichotomize the internal and external affairs of the church but to render them in order. Prioritization of mission does not imply neglect of internal ministry any more than the latter implies neglect of the former. The church's inner life finds its character in the motions of its mission, and vice versa. If the missionary task is relegated to the level of a postlude to an otherwise independently conceived common life, both the task and the community tend to take on a life of their own, prone to adopt means of propagation that only loosely correspond to the gospel message itself. Barth's conceptual framework does not offer immunity from such temptations, but it can help to put right the misconceptions that

---

[93]Ibid., 636.

[94]Further to this point, in Psalm 51 Barth observes that the experience of God's forgiveness brings with it the reception of a commission. *CD* IV/1, 580; see Ps 51:10-17 and *CD* IV/3.2, 567, 571-74, 681 and 883.

[95]*CD* IV/3.2, 778.

feed it. If the church is a city on a hill, it is because it is a community continually guided from enmity to peace, not because it is a company of angels
or superheroes. The promise that "Hades will not prevail against it" (Mt
16:18) remains a promise and not a possession, such that the church should
not at any time presume itself to have prevailed (especially not based on
fickle indicators of success).[96] Indeed if it patronizes its neighbors and acts
"too sure of itself," in Barth's view the church "falsifies its task."[97]

What the church "owes the world" is the gospel: "It cannot give in the world
a direct portrayal of Jesus Christ," since "it is itself only a human society
moving like all others to His manifestation." However, "in the form in which
it exists" the church gives itself and the world both a "reminder" and a "promise"
of Christ's establishment of the kingdom of God. It does so by showing "that
there is already on earth an order which is based on that great alteration of the
human situation and directed towards its manifestation."[98] Attention to this
"order" will preoccupy us in the next two chapters. Here we press the point that,
despite the pressure to be a buttress for self-help religion, a central mark of the
church's witness is the confession, forgiveness and mutual care that take place
in the work of the Spirit.[99] In this final section of chapter three we thus zero
in further on Barth's missional ecclesiology, which is articulated most strik-
ingly in his two-page excursus on "binding and loosing."

Binding or loosing: The community for the world. The "keys of the
kingdom" and "binding and loosing" sayings of Jesus found in Matthew 16
and 18 have been interpreted to support everything from papal authority to
the interpretive responsibility of each in the priesthood of believers.
Readings of these passages are usually concerned with moral discernment
and ecclesial authority, as interpreted via the blending of Jesus' teachings
with later rabbinic use of the phrase.[100] For his part, Barth implies rejection
of this rabbinical reading when he takes note of the later extracanonical

---

[96]*CD* IV/2, 648.
[97]*CD* IV/3.2, 827, 829; see also 794.
[98]*CD* IV/2, 721; see also *CD* IV/3.2, 803-5, 808, 813-16.
[99]See *CD* IV/3.2, 786-94.
[100]See Donald A. Hagner, *Matthew 14–28*, Word Biblical Commentary (Dallas: Word, 1993), 473.
   The less common rabbinic usage renders it "to impose and remove the ban" of a person from an
   assembly. Friedrich Büchsel, "δέω (λύω)," in *Theological Dictionary of the New Testament*, ed.
   Gerhard Kittel (Grand Rapids: Eerdmans, 1964), 2:60-61.

literature and links his reading of Matthew to John 20:23 instead.[101] When he addresses this along with the Great Commission toward the end of volume four, Barth is tellingly in the midst of an attempt to specify the variegated forms of a church's ministry. For him as for others, Jesus' instructions sit at the front edge of the church's practical orders and functions. In distinction from others, however, by interpreting Matthew 16:19 and 18:18 ("whatever you bind on earth will be bound in heaven, and whatever you loose on earth will be loosed in heaven") in light of John 20:23 ("If you forgive the sins of any, they are forgiven them; if you retain the sins of any, they are retained"), Barth concludes that if the ministry of the community "is in order and its work is well done" it will be characterized *not* by binding but by loosing, or forgiving, alone.[102]

Exegetically speaking, while his interpretation is by no means in the majority, Barth may be right to steer attention away from the language of the synagogue. Recorded usage of the "binding and loosing" phrase in rabbinical midrash comes a couple centuries after the time of Christ and likely several decades after the writing of the Gospels.[103] It is possible that an oral tradition of such terminology may have been around when Christ gave Peter and the disciples what he appears to have thought was a self-explanatory charge, but evidence to support this notion is inconclusive.[104] For Barth to interpret this saying via other Gospel sayings rather than postcanonical evidence is credible

---

[101]See *CD* IV/3.2, 860-62, along with Mt 16:13-20; 18:15-35; Jn 20:23.

[102]Judging from their "solemn connexion with the founding of the community," Barth takes it that Jesus' instructions establish the main "function of the community in and in relation to the world." *CD* IV/3.2, 861.

[103]Jacob Neusner, *Introduction to Rabbinic Literature* (New York: Doubleday, 1994), xxii.

[104]It is just as probable, if not more, that it was the rabbis later picking up this language to use it their own way. For arguments in favor of a rabbinical interpretation, see Raymond F. Collins, "Binding and Loosing," in *Anchor Bible Dictionary*, ed. David Noel Freedman (New York: Doubleday, 1992), 1:744, and Thomas Cahill, *Desire of the Everlasting Hills: The World Before and After Jesus* (New York: Doubleday, 1999), 135. For arguments against a rabbinic rendering, see Enns, "Biblical Interpretation: Jewish" and Jacob Neusner, "Rabbinic Literature: Mishnah and Tosefta," in *Dictionary of New Testament Background*, ed. Craig A. Evans and Stanley E. Porter (Downers Grove, IL: InterVarsity Press, 2000), 161, 896. It is interesting to note that the rabbinical exercise of binding and loosing may have sprung largely from the loss of faith in prophets and the loss of the priesthood, so that responsibility was thrust upon "the properly constituted majority of the learned" to discern the guidance of God. See J. Duncan and M. Derrett, "Binding and Loosing (Matt 16:19; 18:18; John 29:23)," *Journal of Biblical Literature* 102, no. 1 (1983): 113. If Jesus *was* setting a similar process in motion, in light of Joel 2:28; Acts 2:17; Rev 1:4-6, we would have to say it was for other reasons.

and may arguably be a surer hermeneutical move.[105] The plausibility of the connection is not *lexical* but *grammatical* and *thematic*. The *words* used in John and Matthew are not etymologically tied, but the *phrases* share the same formulaic pattern, are each found in the context of *commissioning* and each imply a seemingly unqualified heavenly blessing of earthly action. If we follows Barth's reading for these reasons, we see the ground he is able to cover by letting the interpretive traffic between the passages go both ways.[106]

As is seen in this lengthy but important excerpt, Barth finds in Jesus' charge to the church not two options, but one:

> If everything is in order and its work is well done, there must be a great opening, permitting and releasing, i.e., the promise and reception of the forgiveness of sins. If its work is not done or done badly, then contrary to its task the community closes the kingdom of heaven and excludes men from it instead of pointing them to the door which is open for all. It holds where it should release. The remission which is the content of its witness is kept from men. Was it and is it not a strangely perverted mode of interpretation to think that the community may actually be commissioned to choose this negative alternative, using some standard (but which?) either to open on the one side or to close on the other, either to proclaim forgiveness or to withhold it, and thinking that this dual action is even given heavenly sanction?[107]

Equating this with hypocritical neglect or pharisaical corruption of the church's ministry, Barth suggests that

> the point of the sayings is that what takes place or does not take place between the community and the world or the community and its own members, its opening or shutting, its forgiving or non-forgiving, i.e., its obedience or disobedience, its action *per fas* or *per nefas*, has more than earthly significance. In one way or the other heaven is at stake in what it does or fails to do on earth.

---

[105]Whether John 20:23 provides the proper interpretive lens is debatable, but such a reading is neither unheard of nor unwarranted. The connection is made in Duncan and Derrett, "Binding and Loosing," but is there simply assumed and not defended. Yoder comes to similar conclusions as Barth's. See John Howard Yoder, "Binding and Loosing," *The Royal Priesthood: Essays Ecclesiological and Ecumenical* (Grand Rapids: Eerdmans, 1994), 327-29, and *For the Nations: Essays Evangelical and Public* (Grand Rapids: Eerdmans, 1997), 43.

[106]Barth does treat "binding" (δήσῃς) and "loosing" (λύσῃς) and "retaining" (κρατῆτε) and "forgiving" (ἀφῆτε) as conceptual synonyms, but is less interested to trace lexical associations than he is to expound on their resonance when taken together. *CD* IV/3.2, 861.

[107]Ibid.

By its work God Himself is either glorified or compromised and shamed in His work. God Himself rejoices or weeps.[108]

In this context Barth goes so far as to label the imperative to forgiveness "lawful," explaining that—while God is not "bound" by the church's forgiving or not forgiving—God in his free self-determination "shares most intimately in it." Thus Jesus is heard to underscore "the infinite relevance, the sacred and inestimable responsibility, the promise yet also the violability of the one ministry and witness to which the community is engaged."[109] It is hard to imagine how Barth could more squarely locate interpersonal forgiveness at the beating heart of the church's life.

Of course, if the recommendation here is toward a kind of "blanket" forgiveness or a posture of live-and-let-live tolerance, we would have reason to question how this is even unique, let alone compelling. Moreover, if Barth's interpretation renders moot the exhortation for churches to discern right from wrong, we might have reason for moral despair. However, thick descriptions of Barth's ethics and his theology of forgiveness show that Barth intends neither of these things.

Many commentators on the binding and loosing passages see in them the empowering of church leaders to make decisions, moral or creedal or otherwise, but Barth does not think Jesus is pointing out the reality of ethical and theological dilemmas and endorsing the church as carte-blanche authority.[110] This does not preclude a discussion of ecclesial authorities based on other passages of Scripture; the point is that *here* Jesus is primarily detailing the life dynamic of the church wherein disciples are oriented and mobilized to seek truth together. When *this* is in place, the church can exercise moral discernment and accountability in the community with its essential act in order.

This is not out of line with what Barth has said before. Barth has been clear in his conviction that the fallen creature could not know God—let alone his or her createdness or fallenness—except in the light of the

---

[108]*CD* IV/3.2, 861-62.

[109]Ibid., 862.

[110]See R.T. France, *The Gospel of Matthew*, New International Commentary on the New Testament (Grand Rapids: Eerdmans, 2007), 627, and Fritz Rieneker, *A Linguistic Key to the Greek New Testament*, ed. Cleon L. Rogers Jr., vol. 1, *Matthew Through Acts* (Grand Rapids: Zondervan, 1976), 49.

atonement.[111] Indeed if for Augustine knowledge comes by the love of God, we have seen that for Barth it comes more specifically as we are reconciled with God in Christ.[112] Until Christ's return there remains an element of incompleteness to our knowing, but in the meantime, "to know Him is identical with knowing the power of His resurrection (Phil 3:10)," which means it is lodged in the ongoing prophetic ministry of Christ as he is present by the Holy Spirit.[113] "Our being in Him is our justification, and therefore the forgiveness of our sins, even that of our cognition. More than that, it is our sanctification, and therefore the renewal of our life, and therefore of our cognition." In other words, in the received forgiveness of Jesus Christ is found not only the power for *beginning* the Christian life but also for "the conclusions that have to be drawn afresh each day."[114]

In Matthew's Gospel, Peter is the *confessor of Christ* before he is the binder or looser—but strangely enough on that occasion he is restricted from telling others what he has confessed. In John 20 it is *after the resurrection* that the forgiven and reinstated Peter is loosed upon the world with the community to feed Jesus' lambs and to fully be fishers of people.[115] Thus, whereas Miroslav Volf's *Exclusion and Embrace* recommends a dialogical posture of embrace even at cost to oneself and calls it the "epistemological side of faith in the crucified," Barth's *Doctrine of Reconciliation* takes it one further and invokes the forgiveness of God on the enterprise, reckoning it the epistemological side of faith in the risen Lord.[116] The point is that, for Barth, the proper home for seeking truth is Christian communion, not because its people *possess* absolute knowledge and thereby enlighten others, but because Christ *reorients* people to live and grow and learn together in a common grace. For Barth the keys of the kingdom are the freedom in Christ to simultaneously share participation in his message, ministry and mission of reconciliation (2 Cor 5:18-20).

---

[111]See *CD* III/1, 27, 34, 40, and *CD* IV/1, 45.
[112]This is not a pejorative contrast, but highlights Barth's elaboration. See Augustine, *De Trinitate*, VIII.10.
[113]*CD* IV/1, 299; see also 77 and 301.
[114]*CD* IV/2, 288 and 307-8; see also 289.
[115]See Craig S. Keener, *A Commentary on the Gospel of Matthew* (Grand Rapids: Eerdmans, 1999), 430.
[116]Volf, *Exclusion and Embrace*, 214.

For thorough readers of the *Church Dogmatics* this may come as no surprise, but the payoff is never clearer than in the final volume's depiction of the community Jesus sends into the world. By holding together Matthew 18 and John 20, Barth is able to observe that it is in the midst of forgiving as they are forgiven that believers come to know God, seek his will together and present a witness to the world. Integral to Barth's understanding of the church's "infinite relevance" and "sacred responsibility," then, is the notion that by failing to confess and forgive sin the church is holding back Christian knowledge of God not only from others but from itself.[117] If we refuse to forgive we put up interference to heaven's transmission. Like the screaming pitch of a microphone brought too close to the speakers—stinging the ears with a loop living off its own feedback—is the sound of the church drowning out God's voice in its efforts to perpetuate his kingdom self-righteously and unmercifully.

As we wrap this chapter up to a conclusion, we can set ourselves up for the chapters to come by highlighting the resonance between Barth and a few others on the meaning of Matthew 18. In their recent analysis of the passage, Ched Myers and Elaine Enns rightly point out that if Jesus' "community conferencing" instructions (vv. 15-22) are read apart from his prior challenge to "social stratification" (vv. 1-5) and his hyperbolic exhortation to avoid wrongdoing (vv. 6-10), then we lose sight of Jesus' main focus, which is mutual accountability in the priesthood of believers.[118] When we miss this we run the risk of putting too much emphasis on church leadership, who appear in Jesus' instructions as facilitators of difficult cases rather than an essentially hierarchical apparatus. There may be other grounds for establishing church governance structures, but this passage is about the ministry of reconciliation that takes place in the reign of Christ, not an institutional power construct. The ministry of reconciliation does not exist to serve the maintenance of leadership structures; leadership exists (among other things) to serve the ministry of reconciliation.

Myers and Enns resonate further with Barth's account when they draw out the link between the reconciling instructions of Jesus with his subsequent parable of the unmerciful servant. Referring to Amos Wilder's depiction of

---

[117]*CD* IV/3.2, 862.

[118]Ched Myers and Elaine Enns, *Ambassadors of Reconciliation*, vol. 1, *New Testament Reflections on Restorative Justice and Peacemaking* (Maryknoll, NY: Orbis Books, 2009), 56, 65-66.

Jesus' parables as a "war of myths," they interpret it rather provocatively as a
satirical judgment on the "retributive justice liturgy" that prevails upon each
of the parable's characters.[119] Because the king shows himself "unwilling . . .
to forgive more than once," Myers and Enns maintain that he is not intended
by Jesus as an allegorical stand-in for God, but as an indication of the extent
to which the king is himself deeply mired in Lamech's "logic of retribution."
Caught up in that logic, the parable's king utilizes the common practice of
"predatory lending" in order to keep slaves in his debt. The other servants
operate under the same competitive logic when they turn the unmerciful
servant in, such that *all* the characters are depicted as condemning themselves—along with Lamech and everyone after him—to the "collective death
sentence of our own design."[120] Particularly given Peter's question and Jesus'
answer about how often to forgive, Myers and Enns conclude that the parables' audience is meant to hear in the final verse of the chapter not an *ap-
proval* of any of the story's characters but a *warning* that "God will not save
us from the consequences" of leaving Lamech's "spiral of vengeance" uninter-
rupted. Similar to Barth, they conclude that for the church it is either Lamech
or Christ, bind or loose, "lock down" or "liberate."[121] This is the fork in the
road that lies before us every day.

In the final chapter of *The Christian Experience of Forgiveness*, H. R. Mackintosh reflects on John 20:23 and makes connections and conclusions similar
to Barth's, suggesting that it is "only too likely that the pitilessness of man will
hide the pity of God." For Mackintosh (as for Barth), "the experience of receiving God's pardon involves the consciousness that we form part of a pardoned company," which "means that we are content to share and share alike
with them, for in the Kingdom of God none can be saved in isolation."[122] In a
similar vein, John Howard Yoder's essay "The New Humanity as Pulpit and
Paradigm" concludes that the "very existence" of this "new peoplehood" would
need "no apologetic bridge" to the rest of the world if it lived its "common life
in the light of Christ's lordship" as these texts suggest.[123] For Yoder (as for Barth),

---

[119] Ibid., 81.

[120] Ibid., 79 and 71-72; see also Gen 4:24.

[121] Ibid., 80; see also 71.

[122] H. R. Mackintosh, *The Christian Experience of Forgiveness*, 2nd ed. (London: Nisbet, 1934), 284.

[123] Yoder, *For the Nations*, 41 and 27. For Yoder this is not built from a supposed natural common
ground. Secular egalitarianism and pluralistic tolerance are inadequately grounded. The "new

the order of the faith community constitutes a public offer to the entire society. It is not that first we set about being a proper church and then in a later move go about deciding to care prophetically for the rest of the world. To participate in the transforming process of becoming the faith community *is itself* to speak the prophetic word, *is itself* the beginning of the transformation of the cosmos.[124]

The church stands before the world as a community of disturbed sinners continually gathered and built up in the mercy of Christ. This is why in his focus on twelve specific, persistent forms of church ministry, Barth says that if all goes well there will go forward "the promise and reception of the forgiveness of sins."[125]

Hope and promise: A peace that summons understanding. As we have seen, Barth is painfully aware of the failures and mistakes made in the course of the church's mission—but he nonetheless maintains that it should carry on undaunted, taking confidence in the mercy in Christ.[126] It is one thing when the errors of the church remain a matter of relatively harmless interpersonal misunderstandings, but is it not another thing altogether when collateral damage is known to arise? In his differentiation between evangelism to the near and mission to the unreached, Barth shows his awareness that there is a lot of clean-up to be done in those cases where the witness to Christ has been diluted or spoiled beyond recognition.[127] However, he does suggest that a bad witness is better than no witness at all. Is Barth thus to be chastised for naiveté? Or does this question itself put too much faith in the *quality* of witness?

If Barth seems flippant he may be in good company with Paul's apparent lack of concern about motives and rivalries as long as "Christ is proclaimed" (Phil 1:15-18). We would be remiss if we took that as an excuse for recklessness. In Paul's case it seems an expression of undaunted faith. In Barth's

---

humanity" created by the Spirit of Christ *supports* but is not *built from* a "principle" of equality. Ibid., 44-45.

[124]Ibid., 27-28, emphasis in original. Barth might quarrel over the phrase "is itself" (since churches and their activities definitively do not make sense in themselves), but there is little doubt that he too thinks the church a witness in its modus operandi as much as in the verbalization of its message.

[125]CD IV/3.2, 860-61.

[126]See CD IV/2, 674.

[127]Barth classifies evangelism as ministry to the nominal or misinformed who only know the gospel via "hearsay knowledge" or contact with a mostly "sleeping Church." CD IV/3.2, 872-73; see also *ChrL*, 122.

case, similar expressions of confidence in the gospel seems to stem from its inclusion of the call to *semper reformanda*. Without this call to perpetual reformation—which an all-too-perfect proselytizer obscures—Barth prods us to ask whether the gospel has even been properly proclaimed. After all, in Barth's view the goal is "not to convert heathen in the sense of bringing them to a personal enjoyment of their salvation" but to invite individuals to "the life of the community as a whole authentically lived" in the grace of Christ.[128] On the cusp of his ethics of reconciliation Barth turns to the theme of hope and concludes that, no matter the doubtfulness of the church's efforts, it has a sure foundation in Jesus' resurrection promise to be present as it humbly but boldly proceeds. That the church hopes *in faith* implies precisely that it will express that hope not only in its own repentance, but in a corresponding pursuit of kingdom come despite an otherwise hopeless situation. Although they cannot predict or manufacture occasions of the kingdom's coming, believers can be sure that as they engage one another in the mutual liberation of interpersonal reconciliation they will experience the earthly-historical presence of Christ on earth.[129]

Since Christian revelation is neither *merely noetic* nor *inarticulately practical*, it will be worth it to reflect on the biblically commanded practices that are called for in a missional ecclesiology of this kind. Hopefully this chapter has shown that Barth took Jesus' commands to baptize, to break bread, to offer hospitality and to seek reconciliation as a call for the church to be a social embodiment of the reign of God.[130] Even if this social embodiment is not to be *prescribed* or *presumed*, it is nonetheless to be *sought* and *expected* that "the peace of God which passeth understanding should be experienced, tasted and felt as an event" in the fellowship of Christ.[131] Having completed this section-by-section analysis of Barth's *Doctrine of Reconciliation*, the next chapter aims to bring into greater clarity not only the definition of forgiveness that has emerged, but also the community dynamics that have been seen to surround it.

---

[128]*CD* IV/3.2, 878; see 558-63.
[129]See ibid., 861-62, 904 and 934, along with Mt 18:15-20.
[130]See Inagrace Dietterich, "Missional Community: Cultivating Communities of the Holy Spirit," in *Missional Church: A Vision for the Sending of the Church in North America*, ed. Darrell L. Guder (Grand Rapids: Eerdmans, 1998), 153-80.
[131]*CD* IV/3.2, 764.

4

Forgive Us

The Meaning of Christian Forgiveness

BARTH IS CLEAR THAT A general idea of love should not form our understanding either of the God who is love or of the virtue that is said to be a fruit of the Spirit. The same can be said of forgiveness. While it expects to be ultimately commensurate with human experience, the concept of Christian forgiveness aimed at in these pages is not merely an anthropological understanding of what forgiveness effects. The mercy God introduces to the world in Christ and asks believers to share is wholly new. While some might argue that love is latent in human nature and waiting to be perfected by grace, the argument here is that forgiveness is not to some degree already possible apart from Jesus. There may occur many Spirit-infused manifestations of forgiveness in the world apart from an articulated Christian faith but, properly understood, forgiveness is a gift that runs shallow when it does not have a wellspring in the merciful extension of God's free and everlasting love.[1]

Steeped in sin, as Christ has shown us to be, we hit a dead end when we look to resource interpersonal forgiveness with our own compassion or desire for reconciliation. Founded in the overflow of God's love and grounded in the actuality of the Christ event, interpersonal forgiveness has a basis outside itself that is not aloof and fickle but free and sure. This is the

[1]CD IV/1, 203.

reality reckoned true in faith. Forgiveness is more solidly motivated and guided in Christ than if it relies on a forgiver's own understanding, resources and goals. To understand forgiveness as such, however, it must be embedded in the whole ministry of reconciliation that *has taken place* in Christ and *is taking place* as he is present in the world by his Spirit. This is the rationale that transitions previous chapters into those that follow.

In this chapter we examine the place and meaning of Christian forgiveness by not just defining it but also extrapolating the way it is expressed with other aspects of Christ's ministry of reconciliation. A central argument is that Christian forgiveness needs to be differentiated from anthropological analogies and its provisional forms in the world. However, to build to a theological definition via a process of elimination would hardly be any better than a flat identification of forgiveness with its provisional phenomena. That said, since we have already gone to great lengths to establish Barth's christological approach to interpersonal forgiveness, in the first part of this chapter we will nonetheless clear the ground for that more constructive conclusion by distinguishing particularly Christian forgiveness from some philosophical and socio-scientific approaches to the matter.

FORGIVENESS IN THE WORLD: FORGERIES AND PARABLES

From Jesus we learn that God is a forgiving God who asks and enables us to forgive one another. Following Barth's lead, our aim is to describe how forgiveness is particularly Christian. In this we must be careful not to give merely an apophatic account of its particularity. Often it is the case that a theology of forgiveness will work its way to a definition by securing itself against descriptions of what forgiveness is *not*. Given the absence of an explicit definition in *The Doctrine of Reconciliation*, something similar might also be ventured based on Barth's own denials and distinctions in this regard. As Barth might argue, however, such a construal could easily be reactionary rather than reflective upon revelation, thereby ceasing to be properly *theological*. Practically speaking, a negation-based definition might also hamper our ability to recognize provisional manifestations of forgiveness in the world that are the Spirit's work in the ups and downs of reconciliation. If these are ruled out in principle ahead of time, it may short-circuit the entailments of Christian life and witness in the world, leading us to disengage with any imperfect action despite the fact that it may be a work of the Spirit anticipating fuller expression in Christ.

As explained in regard to the special visibility of the church, we should expect that what takes place in Christian forgiveness and reconciliation will be a human phenomenon that is both within the scope of intelligibility and yet not wholly reducible to an intelligible explanation of the event itself apart from faith in Christ.[2] As Barth warned against isolating and appropriating the power of faith itself, so too should we be wary of divorcing forgiveness from its reference point in Christ, neglecting its constant character as grace.[3] At the same time, we should also expect to find Spirit-led occurrences of forgiveness in the world without having to declare such phenomena the exclusive property of the church. Forgiveness between persons is going to be frequently manifest in some provisional way, and we would be foolhardy to completely dismiss initial forms of it as we aim to define it in its fullest Christian sense. As our look at falsehood and sloth has already suggested, in the world there will be as many forgeries of forgiveness as there are of peace and love, but we must not be so hasty to negate these that we miss events of prefigured gospel living brought about by the Holy Spirit in the world. Indeed, there may be many such events lit up by the revelation of Christ with which the Spirit is summoning us to engage. Pastorally speaking, there will often be more harm in putting out a candle before the flame has had time to catch than in engaging with analogous acts outside the Christian community, trusting God to bring truth and love to light.

To say this is not to suggest, with Rodney Petersen, that there is a "universal significance" in the practices of forgiveness found in other cultures, traditions and religions that must simply be mined for an "unacknowledged" but "common point of reference in Jesus Christ."[4] Despite the fact that he utilizes Barth's account of Christian parables, Petersen's account lends to the notion of a latent point of contact in humanity—something

---

[2]See *CD* IV/2, 616-17.

[3]*CD* IV/1, 627.

[4]Rodney L. Petersen, "Theology of Forgiveness: Terminology, Rhetoric, and the Dialectic of Interfaith Relationships," in *Forgiveness and Reconciliation: Religion, Public Policy, and Conflict Transformation*, ed. Raymond G. Helmick and Rodney L. Petersen (Philadelphia: Templeton Foundation Press, 2001), 22.

Barth adamantly sought to avoid.[5] Preferable to this is the employment of
Barth found in Gregory Jones's *Embodying Forgiveness*:

> We ought to be wary of descriptions and practices that emerge from the world,
> for it is all too easy to substitute the simulacra of forgiveness . . . for the authentic
> judgment of grace, which reconciles and makes new. Even so, we ought to be on
> the lookout for signs of Easter, celebrating authentic forgiveness and reconcili-
> ation wherever it is found and practiced, even as we recognize that the source
> and sustaining power of that authenticity is the Spirit of the crucified and risen
> Jesus. Barth strengthens his claim by suggesting that Christians are more likely
> to find signs of authentic forgiveness and reconciliation in the world precisely to
> the extent that we embody it ourselves. . . . Unfortunately, the converse would
> also seem to be equally true. . . . Barth insists that Christians may be forced to
> recognize "with shame" that the secular realm has often attested certain aspects
> of the truth "far better, more quickly and more consistently" than the Church
> seems to have done.[6]

These are excellent appropriations of Barth. Jones is particularly on the mark
when he highlights aspects of the secular ethos—such as "the warm readiness to understand and forgive" or the expression of "simple solidarity"—
that may be used by the Holy Spirit to awaken those churches that are caught
up in active sloth, buttressed by a claim to be flatly countercultural.[7]

That the secular realm in itself has inadequate ground for its Christlike
actions does not diminish the fact that it might be exemplary in various
ways. In such an event, any church concerned to witness would do better to
confess, repent and engage than to take a defensive posture and miss the
provision of grace with which it is summoned to take part.

This irenic, pastoral approach does not detract from but *accentuates* the
need for theological acuteness. Attentiveness to the guidance of the Spirit
works hand in hand with readiness to give biblically informed reasons for
one's actions and hope in Christ. The difference between Petersen and

---

[5]See *CD* IV/3.1, 122, and *CD* IV/3.2, 686. See also Barth's *Nein* to natural theology in Emil Brunner
and Karl Barth, *Natural Theology: Comprising "Nature and Grace" by Professor Dr. Emil Brunner and
the Reply "No!" by Dr. Karl Barth*, trans. and ed. Peter Fraenkel (Eugene, OR: Wipf and Stock
Publishers, 2002).

[6]L. Gregory Jones, *Embodying Forgiveness: A Theological Analysis* (Grand Rapids: Eerdmans, 1995),
221-22; see also *CD* IV/3.1, 122, 124.

[7]See Jones, *Embodying Forgiveness*, 222, and *CD* IV/3.1, 125.

Jones in this regard may best be illustrated by distinguishing Christian forgiveness from the recent proliferation of psychological, philosophical and political approaches to forgiveness with which it will intertwine but be too often confused. With a constructive vision of Christian forgiveness in view, we begin by highlighting some of the perils of therapeutic and utilitarian forgiveness, ensuring that we pause to take hold of positive perceptions as well.

The lordless powers of therapeutic amnesty. Published in 1984, Lewis Smedes's *Forgive and Forget* instigated much exploration of the therapeutic value of forgiveness among psychologists in the decades that followed. In it Smedes depicted forgiveness against the backdrop of several "nice things forgiving is not"—including such things as forgetting, excusing, "smothering conflict," accepting and tolerating—before reappropriating it for its many advantages to personal health and interpersonal relations.[8] While the book rightly denounced the temptation to ignore wrongdoing for the sake of mere congeniality or "inner peace," in its effort to promote learned skills of forgiveness it drifted from some of its own best impulses.[9]

With an anemic account of freedom and some unwarranted presumptions about the ability to properly discern the nature of past hurts and future improvements, Smedes touted the crucial task of thinking *past* "the person who needs to be forgiven" in order to "perform spiritual surgery inside," developing "the magic eyes that can heal" and set forgiver and forgiven free.[10] So it was that Smedes evoked a cavalcade of luminous psychological and sociological explorations of this basic Christian theme, but also foreshadowed the ways Christian forgiveness would subsequently surrender to the rubric and practices of psychological therapy and sociological maneuvering. In confluence with trends of individualism and consumerism, forgiveness has increasingly been marketed in church and world as a therapeutic means to the ultimate end of maximized personal health and spirituality.[11]

---

[8] See Lewis B. Smedes, *Forgive and Forget: Healing the Hurts We Don't Deserve* (New York: Harper & Row, 1984), 38-49; see also 95-113, 32-35, 66-68. With its calls for understanding and perseverance Smedes's book remains an accessible, if simplistic, challenge beyond cheap grace and reconciliation avoidance.

[9] Ibid., 31-32.

[10] Ibid., 27.

[11] See this point in John Swinton, *Raging with Compassion: Pastoral Responses to the Problem of Evil* (Grand Rapids: Eerdmans, 2007), 160.

A keen awareness of the therapeutic misuse of forgiveness has come from within the psychological and social scientific fields themselves. In a book full of "cautionary views of forgiveness in psychotherapy," Bill Puka points out that the imperative of forgiveness can in fact serve to perpetuate exploitation, distract from proper responsiveness and substantiate existent hegemonies—such that alternatives to forgiveness ought be commended with equal measure.[12] Further problematizing matters, Carl Bråkenhielm observes that forgiveness can be little more than an "expression of a lack of respect for oneself" or of an "inflated psychological self-consciousness," thus amounting essentially to a premature "withdrawal of moral criticism."[13] On the other hand, he also finds a nugget of truth in the pre-Christian objections of the Roman poet Pubilius Syrus, who observed that expressions of forgiveness were often lorded over others in order to effectively uphold the social roles of the benevolent dictator and ever-penitent debtor.[14]

For his part, Barth perceptively pointed out that forgiveness can be little more than an exercise in self-congratulation:

> There is a refined satisfaction which I can procure for myself by making perhaps a show of the deepest sympathy, by actually experiencing it in the guise and feeling of the greatest readiness to forgive, but by seeing that I am set by contrast in a much better light myself, that I am equipped and incited to a much more worthy representation of that which is good, and that I am thus confirmed and strengthened and exalted and assured in my own excellence. . . . How much of the impulse of private and common Christian action would fail at once if deprived of its basis and nourishment in this "rejoicing!" But love finds no nourishment here.[15]

In Barth's hamartiology one sees social scientific problematizations of forgiveness lit up as a phenomenological diagnosis of the pathology of sloth. Self-serving slothful action can be found both in self-help and philanthropic forms. For all that might be commended in societal attempts at forgiveness

---

[12]These alternatives include a safe expression of anger, a reasonable compensation and an accountable impetus to "move forward" in any given scenario. Bill Puka, "Forgoing Forgiveness," in *Before Forgiving: Cautionary Views of Forgiveness in Psychotherapy*, ed. Sharon Lamb and Jeffrie G. Murphy (Oxford: Oxford University Press, 2002), 151, 138-47.

[13]Carl Reinhold Bråkenhielm, *Forgiveness*, trans. Thor Hall (Minneapolis: Fortress, 1989), 7, 10, 12, 16.

[14]Ibid., 4.

[15]*CD* IV/2, 834.

and reconciliation, we still have to ask what is lost when self-perpetuated patterns of apology and amnesty become, to borrow a phrase from Derrida, "a process of Christianisation which has no more need for the Christian church."[16] Within the church, too, we have to ask what is lost when forgiveness and reconciliation has no need for the living Lord.

Often it is the case, of course, that a problematized picture of forgiveness is still to be preferred to the alternatives of vengeance and festering resentment. Observations of a misused forgiveness emerged even among one of the most lauded attempts at societal healing in recent history: South Africa's Truth and Reconciliation Commission.[17] For instance, in the course of those proceedings Thomas Brudholm reported occasions of a subtle pressure he called "forgiveness boosterism" wherein expressions of forgiveness were prompted from victims' families in order to vindicate the use of amnesty as a "reconciliation instrument" toward a greater cause.[18] Antjie Krog's firsthand account likewise reported a variety of inadequacies and abuses in the reconciliatory proceedings, and nonetheless concluded that the Commission was still the "lesser of two evils."[19] Criticisms like theirs need to be heeded in order to sharpen moral understanding and practice, but do not necessarily render the entire proceedings inappropriate.

There is a great possibility for error in even the best attempts at grace, so much so that if a real grace does not undergird it all, the situation would be hopeless. Interestingly, apart from faith a Christ figure of sorts often serves as a compelling moral impetus or a placeholder for hope in this regard. No stranger to the tragic violence of the twentieth century or to the inevitable errors entailed in the work of societal restoration, despite its misuses and abuses, Hannah Arendt promoted the practices of forgiving and promise making as worthy alternatives to the machinations of reactionism.[20] Naming

---

[16]Jacques Derrida, *On Cosmopolitanism and Forgiveness*, trans. Mark Dooley and Michael Hughes (London: Routledge, 2001), 31.

[17]See Desmond Mpilo Tutu, *No Future Without Forgiveness* (New York: Doubleday, 1999).

[18]Thomas Brudholm, *Resentment's Virtue: Jean Améry and the Refusal to Forgive* (Philadelphia: Temple University Press, 2008), 34, 52.

[19]Antjie Krog, *Country of My Skull: Guilt, Sorrow, and the Limits of Forgiveness in the New South Africa* (Toronto: Times Books, 1998), 142. For a sociologist's arrival at similar conclusions, see Pumla Gobodo-Madikizela, *A Human Being Died That Night: A South African Woman Confronts the Legacy of Apartheid* (New York: Mariner Books, 2004), 133.

[20]Hannah Arendt, *The Human Condition* (Chicago: University of Chicago Press, 1998), 236-47. Kant also appropriated divine forgiveness for its moral usefulness. See Immanuel Kant, "Conflict

Jesus the "discoverer of the role of forgiveness in the realm of human affairs," Arendt declared his religious context unnecessary to the utilization of this human faculty in societal affairs.[21] After scrutinizing societal phenomena such as the "victimage mechanism" and "scapegoating," René Girard similarly recommended Jesus' subversive strategy of siding with the victim, because it breaks "the spiral of violence . . . by yielding to it despite his evident guiltlessness, and so through forgiveness opens the way to reconciliation."[22]

What should not be missed is the fact that—in the case of both its personally therapeutic and its societally helpful appropriations—forgiveness is often wrongly taken up as a means to an end to which it is related only loosely. It was instrumental appropriations such as this that played into Ludwig Feuerbach's criticism of Christianity, wherein he called Martin Luther's doctrine of justification by faith little more than a projection of human wishes, thus questioning both the personal and interpersonal utilizations of divine forgiveness.[23] Having already discussed Barth's reply to this we may yet take Feuerbach's challenge as an exposure of some inadequate variations on the Christian theme. Is forgiveness simply the name we give to our supposed ability to rise from the ashes of corruption and ignorance and self-transcend our circumstances?[24] Is forgiveness an instrument we use to put the past behind us and reconcile ourselves to a supposedly grander scheme?[25]

Such incisive questions can be paralyzing. Indeed, having considered the ease with which forgiveness can be wrongly "confounded" with "excuse, regret, amnesty, [and] prescription"—or wielded in service of what the

---

of the Faculties," in *Religion and Rational Theology*, trans. and ed. A. Wood and G. di Giovanni (Cambridge: Cambridge University Press, 1996), 271.

[21] Arendt, *Human Condition*, 237-39.

[22] See Petersen, "Theology of Forgiveness," 10-11. This is Petersen's Christianized version of Girard's thesis, which interpreted forgiveness in terms of a self-sacrificial exposure of ignorance. See René Girard, *The Scapegoat* (Baltimore: Johns Hopkins University Press, 1986), 100-24, 211-12, and *Things Hidden Since the Foundation of the World* (Stanford, CA: Stanford University Press, 1987), 154.

[23] See Ludwig Feuerbach, *The Essence of Faith According to Luther*, trans. M. Cherno (New York: Harper, 1967), 95-100, 109, 114-15. Barth addresses Feuerbach directly in *CD* IV/3.1, 72-86.

[24] Barth calls this the "anthropologizing of theology." Karl Barth, *The Theology of Schleiermacher: Lectures at Gottingen, Winter Semester of 1923/24*, ed. Dietrich Ritschl, trans. Geoffrey W. Bromiley (Edinburgh: T&T Clark, 1982), 269; see also Friedrich Schleiermacher, *On Religion: Speeches to Its Cultured Despisers*, trans. Richard Crouter (Cambridge: Cambridge University Press, 1988), 219 and 202.

[25] We detect this in Kant, *Conflict of the Faculties*, 278, and G. W. F. Hegel, "The Consummate Religion," in *Lectures on the Philosophy of Religion: One-Volume Edition; The Lectures of 1827*, ed. P. C. Hodgson (Berkeley: University of California Press, 1988), 474-75.

powers that be call "normality"—when the dust settles and Derrida aims at a positive account of forgiveness he relegates it to an ideal so "pure" it seems impossible.[26] Ironically, it is often the case that these phenomenological and philosophical approaches to forgiveness, in the attempt to make themselves accessible, end up highlighting the extent to which forgiveness is a Spirit-created miracle only fully sensible in the light of faith in Christ.

Of course, it is precisely when a miracle is needed that people rush to fill the need themselves. Curiously, when Aaron Lazare compares the inordinate attention given to forgiveness rather than apology in recent decades he proposes the explanation that forgiveness is simply easier to manage alone.[27] An apology runs the risk of correction, whereas forgiveness can be done quietly. Or so it is commonly supposed. Contrary to popular opinion, C. S. Lewis rightly clarified that "excusing" a wrong is tantamount to declaring "there is nothing to forgive," thus rendering it "almost the opposite" of forgiveness.[28] Derrida poses the same problem perfectly when he asks, Who will "judge or arbitrate" forgiveness and reconciliation, when we are left to "accuse ourselves"?[29] Barth was well attuned to the prevalence with which a person "regards himself as free to . . . be his own reconciler, renouncing any other forgiveness than that which he lavishes on himself."[30] "We are all in process of dying from this office of judge which we have arrogated to ourselves," he wrote, and this is seen in our hastiness to excuse others as much as to "pronounce ourselves innocent" out of turn.[31]

As discussed earlier, Barth looked to the cross and saw Christ in our place not only as *judged* but as *judge*, so that justification by faith should never be a prop for self-justification.[32] Here it is important to note that self-judgment and self-forgiveness are flip sides of the same coin: rejection of Jesus as Lord. Slothful usurpations of divine forgiveness are tantamount to an avoidance of

---

[26]See Derrida, *On Cosmopolitanism*, 27, 31-32, 40. See also Nick Smith, *I Was Wrong: The Meanings of Apologies* (Cambridge: Cambridge University Press, 2008), 133, and Joram Graf Haber, *Forgiveness: A Philosophical Study* (Boston: Rowman & Littlefield Publishers, 1991), 11-27.

[27]Aaron Lazare, *On Apology* (New York: Oxford University Press, 2004), 229; see also 85-106.

[28]C. S. Lewis, "On Forgiveness," in *The Weight of Glory and Other Addresses* (New York: Collier Books, 1980), 129.

[29]Derrida, *On Cosmopolitanism*, 29.

[30]*CD* IV/3.1, 243-44.

[31]*CD* IV/1, 232-33.

[32]See *CD* IV/1, 616; *CD* IV/2, 284-85 and *ChrL*, 72.

God's grace for a world of our own making. In *Discipleship*—a book Barth explicitly recommends before embarking on his own account—Bonhoeffer's now-famous denunciation of "cheap grace" described this as the reckoning of "forgiveness of sins as a general truth" and the "denial of God's living word."[33] Cheap grace, he explained, "is preaching forgiveness without repentance; it is baptism without the discipline of community; it is the Lord's Supper without confession of sin; it is absolution without personal confession."[34]

Highlighting these connections, Gregory Jones rightly observes that a "cheap, 'therapeutic' forgiveness" will inevitably "end up incurring other, more deadly costs."[35] This goes for both personal and social dimensions. Falsehood in either is sure to affect the other. A privately therapeutic choice to forgive may be socially devastating not only because it reneges on societal accountability and the confrontation of falsehood, but also because it is liable to misdiagnose the enmity and exacerbate the potential of inadvertently perpetuating it. On the other hand, a gesture of amnesty on behalf of a well-intentioned social majority may be ruinous to individuals because it asks them to forgo their well-being for the sake of what is deemed to be expedient social progress by the powers that be.

Here the radicality of Barth's aforementioned criteria (discussed in chapter three) for discerning Christian reconciliation comes into focus: "The power of the resurrection of Jesus Christ may be known by the fact that at one and the same time and in one and the same movement it impels us to peace with God *and* our fellows *and* ourselves."[36] As Wannenwetsch notes, it is because God *assumed* that which he wished to *redeem* that we believe reconciliation will engage each of these dimensions, refusing to brush over the historical realities and contingencies of hurt and disappointment.[37] While it is true that we always find ourselves in an anticipatory and provisional manifestation of fully consummated redemption, it is precisely this conviction that frees us to patiently seek the Spirit's work in each of these

---

[33]Dietrich Bonhoeffer, *Discipleship*, ed. Geffrey B. Kelly and John D. Godsey, trans. Barbara Green and Reinhard Krauss, Dietrich Bonhoeffer Works 4 (Minneapolis: Fortress, 2001), 43; see also CD IV/2, 533-34.

[34]Bonhoeffer, *Discipleship*, 44

[35]Jones, *Embodying Forgiveness*, 6-7.

[36]CD IV/2, 315, emphasis added.

[37]Bernd Wannenwetsch, *Political Worship: Ethics for Christian Citizens*, trans. Margaret Kohl (Oxford: Oxford University Press, 2004), 311.

three dimensions, and to further inspect those movements which recommend themselves in favor of one angle over the other.

Following through on this conviction may not be easy. In fact, Barth warns
that things may go most smoothly for the church that "has been fitted into the
system of human self-justification."[38] At this point, it will be helpful to articulate a differentiation between Barth's account and that of Jones's *Embodying
Forgiveness*. Aptly observing the complexities of forgiveness, Jones recommends honing the *craft* of forgiveness and forming community *habits* that
support its processes. In an important sense this is commendable. What is
inadequately expressed in Jones's account, however, is the fact that a focus on
honing *skills* and *habits* will be inclined to redirect and professionalize what
must on the very terms of the issue remain a dynamic process of invocation
and obedience under the lordship of Christ. John Webster rightly registers the
caution that "talk of crafting forgiveness may run counter to its sheerly unas-
sailable character as the gift and work of God." Any account of "reconciling
practices" and "learned habits of peacemaking," Webster argues, needs "to talk
of the church as the creature of the Word, in order to retain the fundamental
asymmetry between divine and human action."[39] This need not result in a
reticence to outline such practices, but it does indicate the inherently receptive
manner in which they must be practiced.

Barth was not wholly opposed to the promotion of some practices over
others. Indeed, he was interested to frame the gains of human wisdom within
a properly Christian ethic. In *The Theology of Schleiermacher* he expressed
thankfulness that "God has equipped the human soul with the gift of *forgetfulness* on the one side and *discernment* on the other."[40] The implication is
that human experience contains actions, skills and habits that are identifiably
better than others. In light of Barth's *Doctrine of Reconciliation*, however, a
rejoinder must be added to the effect that skills and habits not be profession-
alized or turned into principles. Such things are *provisionally useful* within a
life of invocation and confession. Barth makes this clear when he addresses
the physical and social sciences as "products of a human self-understanding"

---

[38]CD IV/1, 642.
[39]John Webster, *Word and Church: Essays in Christian Dogmatics* (Edinburgh: T&T Clark, 2001),
227-28.
[40]Barth, *Theology of Schleiermacher*, 127.

that require a person to "first be radically disturbed and interrupted in the work of self-analysis by receiving the Gospel of God" before seeing the extent to which the "self-analysis . . . was [or was not] on the right track."[41] When it comes to our part in Christ's reconciling work, to take that work upon ourselves is to undermine it. This does not mean one should ignore therapeutic and socially beneficial aspects of forgiveness in reaction against reductive accounts and misuses. The superiority of Jesus' mercy—even in the midst of our misappropriations—frees us for hopeful engagement rather than cloistered dismay.[42] But neither should one pretend that all approximations are indeed what Jesus was signifying when he commanded his disciples to forgive. In fact, they may be evasions of the call of Christ.

Having observed the forgiveness forgeries of therapeutically or philanthropically motivated self-judgment and amnesty, we turn now to another distinction that needs to be made before a positive account is given. This may strike close to home for the church today: it involves the tendentious relationship between forgiving and forgetting.

Resentment and nonremembrance: The "as is" and the "as if." As noted, a good deal of socio-scientific analysis begins to raise objections when it sees forgiveness utilized to downplay wrongdoing, suppress truth or condone behaving *as if nothing happened*. One of the ways to counter this tendency is to insist that forgiveness not be allowed to curtail our ability to assess a situation *as it stands*. We will now explore this tension between the "as if" and the "as is" by considering the promotion of nonremembrance on one hand and healthy resentment on the other.

In *Resentment's Virtue* Jean Améry famously offered an account of resentment that, as Thomas Brudholm puts it, "uncouple[s] the concept of *ressentiment* from a specific act of particularly disagreeable emotions including spite, malice, and envy." Based on this, Brudholm positively depicts resentment as a moral resource for the community that helps it to avoid the perpetuation of wrongdoing and to promote "deeply ethical concerns about dignity and humanity, moral acknowledgement and repair."[43] This is not dissimilar to the propositions of eighteenth-century English bishop Joseph

---

[41]*CD* IV/3.2, 803.
[42]See *CD* IV/2, 422, 525, 623, and *CD* IV/3.1, 464.
[43]Brudholm, *Resentment's Virtue*, 173-74.

Butler in his sermons "Upon Resentment" and "On Forgiveness of Injuries"—
considered by some to have been one of the earliest modern articulations of
the value of a properly conditioned resentment.[44] In these influential sermons
Butler highlighted the natural human reaction of resentment for its provisional goodness as well as its openness to abuse, thus commending it to
Christians only inasmuch as it is combined with and governed by the truth
and compassion of Jesus Christ.[45]

For his part (and rather typically for the twenty-first century), Jeffrie
Murphy rallies in support of striking a balance between compassion and
"vindictive passions," the latter of which he says are not wholly negative, but
are related to the values of "self-respect, self-defense, and respect for the
moral order."[46] After all, would it not be an insult to victims, and a total
surrender to evil, to suppress the memory of guilt and wrongdoing? In reflection on the Holocaust, Vladimir Jankélévitch put this question sharply:

> The sentiment that we experience is not called rancor but horror—insur-
> mountable horror over what happened, horror of the fanatics who perpe-
> trated this thing, of the passive who accepted it, and the indifferent who have
> already forgotten it. This is our "resentment" [*ressentiment*]. For *ressentiment*
> can also be the renewed and intensely lived feeling of the inexpiable thing; it
> protests against a moral amnesty that is nothing but shameful amnesia; it
> maintains the sacred flame of disquiet and faith to invisible things. Forget-
> fulness here would be a grave insult to those who died in the camps and
> whose ashes are forever mixed in the earth. It would be a lapse of seriousness
> and dignity, a shameful frivolity.[47]

The heat of this objection is spurred not only by the memory of victims and
the lasting effects of loss, but also by the rhetoric of pardon that appears
hurried to rebuild society at the further expense of those who have been
wronged. A failure of resentment is seen as a further aggravation of past
victimhood and a potential perpetuation of the conditions that first enabled

---

[44]Jeffrie G. Murphy, *Getting Even: Forgiveness and Its Limits* (Oxford: Oxford University Press, 2003),
12, 19.

[45]See Joseph Butler, "Sermon VIII. Upon Resentment" and "Sermon IX. Upon Forgiveness of Injuries," in *Fifteen Sermons Preached at the Rolls Chapel* (Cambridge: Hilliard and Brown, 1827), 68-83.

[46]Murphy, *Getting Even*, 19, 38; see also 17-18, 71-72.

[47]Vladimir Jankélévitch, "Should We Pardon Them?" trans. Ann Hobart, *Critical Inquiry* 22, no. 3
(Spring 1996): 572.

the objectionable events. Brudholm suggests that when we make forgiveness the "order of the day" because we "tire of the angry and accusing voices of survivors," we become complicit in a form of damage control that can hardly be called reconciliation.[48]

If we are exchanging responsibility for amnesty and truth for false peace then many of these objections are clearly warranted. Such calls for a properly conditioned resentment should remind us that Christ's work of forgiveness and reconciliation dealt with the "as is" of creaturely reality rather than gesturing from the privileged safety of what would otherwise have remained for us an idealized "as if." As John Milbank warns, if a "secular performance of forgiveness poses as an illusory *eschaton*," far be it from Christians to perpetuate the deception.[49]

A deeper problem is both exposed and exacerbated by these social analyses, however. It revolves around the question of how to accurately diagnose the *is* and to overcome in favor of the *ought*. This is where we turn our attention to the other side of the tension, from the relative merits of resentment to those of nonremembrance.

Perhaps the best argument for a relationship between forgiving and nonremembering has recently been given by Miroslav Volf in his books *Exclusion and Embrace* and *The End of Memory*, wherein he promotes a posture of embrace toward others that is buoyed by hope in an ultimate nonremembrance of sin and its effects, finalized by God himself.[50] Volf pointedly addresses the fact that forgiveness concerns the past and explores how it is distinguished from the convenient forms of forgetfulness that arguments for proper resentment have pushed us to avoid. In *The End of Memory* he explicitly appropriates Elie Wiesel's belief in the "redeeming power of memory," on the one hand acknowledging that memory can perpetuate suffering, while on the other hand maintaining that memory rightly integrated "into a

---

[48]Brudholm, *Resentment's Virtue*, 175; see also Brandon Hamber and Richard Wilson, "Symbolic Closure Through Memory, Reparation and Revenge in Post-Conflict Societies," *Journal of Human Rights* 1, no. 1 (March 2002): 45.

[49]John Milbank, *Being Reconciled: Ontology and Pardon* (London: Routledge, 2003), 59.

[50]See Miroslav Volf, *Exclusion and Embrace* (Nashville: Abingdon, 1996), 128-40, and *The End of Memory: Remembering Rightly in a Violent World* (Grand Rapids: Eerdmans, 2006), 123, 191, 202. For an earlier analysis, see Jon Coutts, "Once for All and New Every Morning: Forgiveness in the Theology of Miroslav Volf and Karl Barth" (paper, Oxford Research Archive, 2010), http://ora.ox.ac.uk/objects/ora:5258.

broader pattern of one's life story" can still be "a means to salvation" and healing.[51] Skirting the boundaries between harmful resentment and careless forgetfulness, Volf's provision of a gospel context for human memory, combined with his rubric of "remembering rightly," helpfully locates forgiveness within the complexities of Christ's unfinished work of reconciliation.

The practical and phenomenological weight of Volf's construal does cause problems, however, particularly as the gestures toward memory management curtail the helpfulness of his account of *forgiveness*.[52] A few of these problems merit our attention, especially since they stand in contrast with Barth's emphasis on the historicity and time-fullness of Christ's presence. Noting these will give us more incisive insight into the contribution Barth makes to the practical theology of forgiveness and reconciliation.

The central problem in Volf's account has to do with his near surrender of the rubric of reconciliation to that of psycho-social phenomena. Consider the way he articulates his view of final reconciliation: "Only nonremembering can end the lament over suffering which no thought can think away and no action undo."[53] Within this trajectory a number of concerns are entwined, the first of which is well articulated by Jon Horne, who suggests that "Miroslav Volf's theory of non-remembrance stands in need of Christological qualification" and asks, "Since evil pervades every facet of life would we not need to *not remember every* facet of life for Volf's argument to work?"[54] With the Eucharist in view, LeRon Shults and Steven Sandage are right to add that "forgiveness not only remembers but also anticipates."[55] Volf does hesitate to equate divine nonremembrance with human forgetfulness, but the point remains that his is a soteriology that is itself undermined by an insufficiently christological hamartiology. Does not the subtitle of Volf's book—*Remembering Rightly in a Violent World*—betray a fundamental ontological statement

---

[51]See Volf, *End of Memory*, 19-21, 27-28, citing Elie Wiesel, *From the Kingdom of Memory: Reminiscences* (New York: Summit, 1990), 201, and "Ethics and Memory," in *Ernst Reuter Vorlesungs im Wissenschaftskolleg zu Berlin* (Berlin: Walter de Gruyter, 1977), 14-15.

[52]In Volf's construal, three crucial steps accompany forgiveness: remembering truthfully, remembering therapeutically and learning from the past. See Volf, *End of Memory*, 93, 123, 191, 202.

[53]Volf, *Exclusion and Embrace*, 135, see 294, 131.

[54]Jon Horne, "A Reservation About Miroslav Volf's Theory of Non-remembrance," *Theology* 114, no. 5 (September/October 2011): 323-24.

[55]F. LeRon Shults and Steven J. Sandage, *The Face of Forgiveness: Searching for Wholeness and Salvation* (Grand Rapids: Baker Academic, 2003), 219.

about reality that bases itself in violence rather than the peace of God? If
forgiveness hinges on the nonremembrance of sin then at the cross Christ
essentially bows to horrors greater and more definitive than himself, which
he can only overcome by ultimately brushing from recollection.

Horne cites Hauerwas to take the objection further: "The problem with
Volf's non-remembering is . . . what it implies about God's life. Consummation
comes too close to a false eternity. God's eternity is . . . not the simple contradiction of time. . . . We can trust memories to be transformed by forgiveness
and reconciliation."[56] As Alexander Sider observes, "Any account of redemption that does not involve our negative memories of past violence and
our histories of loss is inadequate. . . . If Volf is right about forgetting, it turns
out that Augustine was wrong: the God who created us without us will, after
all, save us without us, too."[57] Alternatively, Sider suggests Yoder's "doxological
vision of history," wherein "cross and resurrection . . . are the 'first principles'
for making judgments about the meaning of history," freeing us not to forsake
but to "use memory to survey past events and make sense of them in light of
cross and resurrection."[58] The language is not Barth's, but it resonates.

In light of what we already discussed in chapter two regarding Jeremiah
31:34 and the *remembering-not* of sin by God, it might thus be preferable to
heed Müller-Fernandez's reference to forgiveness as an act of "deep remembering" wherein there is "an effort to transfigure past pains in order to construct vital and forward looking societies."[59] Such language is misleading,
however. Barth would warn against putting "transfiguration" in our own
hands, since it takes us a step removed from the *participatio Christi* in which
the *imitatio* remains a point of grace. This misleading notion is rather pronounced in Volf's *The End of Memory*:

> When we forgive those who have wronged us, we make our own God's miracle
> of forgiveness. Echoing God's unfathomable graciousness, we decouple the

---

[56]Stanley Hauerwas, "Why Time Cannot and Should Not Heal the Wounds of History but Time
Has Been and Can Be Redeemed," *Scottish Journal of Theology* 53 (2000): 42-43, as cited in Horne,
"A Reservation," 326. See also Ray S. Anderson, *The Shape of Practical Theology: Empowering
Ministry with Theological Praxis* (Downers Grove, IL: InterVarsity Press, 2001), 303.

[57]J. Alexander Sider, *To See History Doxologically: History and Holiness in John Howard Yoder's
Ecclesiology* (Grand Rapids: Eerdmans, 2011), 157.

[58]Ibid., 136; see also 159.

[59]Geiko Müller-Fahrenholz, *The Art of Forgiveness: Theological Reflections on Healing and Reconciliation* (Geneva, Switzerland: World Council of Churches, 1997), 49-59.

> deed from the doer, the offense from the offender. We blot out the offense so
> it no longer mars the offender. That is why the non-remembrance of wrongs
> suffered appropriately crowns forgiveness.[60]

If this were merely a rhetorical flourish gesturing to the final mystery of
divine redemption it might not be such a concern, but it betrays an over-
reliance on psycho-social strategies in order to incorporate divine forgiveness and reconciliation in human affairs—thus divesting it of its status
as a miracle precisely in the attempt to "make it our own."

As Sider observes, not only has Volf's emphasis on the "will to embrace"
fallen back into the very "liberal notion of freedom Volf criticizes as insufficient," but it also lends to the idea that we can presume "radical discontinuity
with the past" from which to put "handles on history."[61] John Milbank is right
that it would take a certain "sense of moral superiority" to think we can "gaze,
passively, at a violent past" without "analogically or even literally *doing violence* to the past" ourselves.[62] This is where the proponents of qualified resentment and provisional nonremembrance—the "as is" and the "as if"—both
run into the same problems. There may be strategies for managing our memories to the promotion of healing, but it is far too easy to self-servingly prefer
a lack of complexity, to side with the powers that be or to engender a form of
denial wherever it supports harbored bitternesses or favored utopias.[63]

An excellent illustration of this comes from the field of memory research
itself, wherein psychologist Daniel Schacter describes what he calls "the seven
sins of memory," including "transience, absent-mindedness, blocking, mis-
attribution, suggestibility, bias, and persistence."[64] What is remarkable about
Schacter's analysis of these mental errors is that he is able to give a compelling
account of how each might also be seen as "adaptive strengths" for the promotion of human life and social relations: for example, "blocking" certain
memories serves the cause of mental efficiency, and "bias" or "persistence"

---

[60]Volf, *End of Memory*, 208; see 142-43. A caveat about forgiveness being *God's* work is often given,
but it stands in tension with depictions of forgiveness as a "fine art" and a craft to be honed. See
also Miroslav Volf, *Free of Charge: Giving and Forgiving in a Culture Stripped of Grace* (Grand
Rapids: Zondervan, 2006), 120, 177, 202, 215.

[61]Sider, *To See History*, 149-50, 152-53; see Volf, *End of Memory*, 128.

[62]Milbank, *Being Reconciled*, 29, 36.

[63]See Volf, *End of Memory*, 45-46, 49-51.

[64]Daniel Schacter, *How the Mind Forgets and Remembers* (London: Souvenir Press, 2001), 1-6.

serves the cause of personal safety.[65] For our purposes, what this illustrates is
that the decision to call an event of remembrance either a sin or strength still
entirely depends on the means by which one discerns helpful from unhelpful,
truth from falsehood and good from bad. In that case, even if there are func-
tional analogies between psychological strategies related to memory and the
Christian practice of forgiveness, it is decidedly the christological that must
illumine and redirect the anthropological (rather than vice versa). Furthermore, lest such an ethic be based on individualistically applied principles,
the Christian community's *participatio Christi* must enfold its *imitatio Christi*.

With this we thus return to our exploration of what it meant for Jesus to
teach forgiveness to his disciples in the context of a daily prayer, and to place
it within the vital ministry of the church.[66] With the dilemma that has been
posed between resentment and nonremembrance, it behooves us to clarify
that even though hope in a final resurrection alters our view of the "as is," it
certainly *does not* necessitate acting as if there are no residual effects of sin to
be dealt with in real time. As Gobodo-Madikizela observes in regard to the
post-Holocaust reflections of Hannah Arendt, we can empathize with the
feeling that there are "radically evil" acts for which "no yardstick exists by
which we can measure what it means to forgive them," but if we give evil such
a radical designation it undermines our ability to see it for its real horror,
which is its closeness to home.[67] Where apathy has arisen, attention to the
horror of tragedy may rightly and surely startle us out of it. But Milbank is
right that by "rendering [a past tragedy] outside all comprehension whatsoever" we paradoxically end up "granting it a demonic status equivalent to
divinity" in a manner which "absolutizes" and "perpetuates its terror."[68] In
this way the godly sorrow of repentance can be seen to be more profound
than the worldly sorrow of despair, for it confesses a good that overcomes sin
rather than a mirage behind which sin can be made to disappear.

So it is that Christian forgiveness hinges on faith in the earthly historical
reality of Jesus Christ and not an abstract moral projection or psychological
strategy used to cope with radical evil.[69] Christian faith is in neither

---

[65]See ibid., 1-6, 187-96.
[66]See Mt 6:5-15; 18; Jn 20:19.
[67]Gobodo-Madikizela, *A Human Being*, 123-24; see Arendt, *Human Condition*, 241.
[68]Milbank, *Being Reconciled*, 54-55.
[69]Desmond Morris's term is put to use in Bråkenhielm, *Forgiveness*, 15-18, 20, 27.

resentment or nonremembrance, but a living Reconciler and Lord. The goal of this section has not been to delineate a definition of forgiveness either according to a negation of its forgeries or an appropriation of its parables in worldly experience. Instead, the goal has been to problematize such approaches, relaying the complex if hidden relationship between forgiveness and other contingencies, and pointing to the unique ways that a Christian account of forgiveness begs to be embedded in a ministry of reconciliation undertaken under the lordship of Jesus Christ. With these distinctions in place, it is important that we turn our attention now to a positive account of what Christian forgiveness means.

ONLY GOD CAN FORGIVE: THE DIVINE AND THE INTERPERSONAL

When in Mark 2:7 we see the teachers of the law asking "who can forgive sins but God alone?" we know that the issue is Jesus' divinity and not the question of whether we can forgive one another our interpersonal sins. However, the event provides food for thought. Hannah Arendt saw it as Jesus' assertion that forgiveness is *a human faculty*, enacted by way of his contradiction of the religious leaders' assertion of the divine prerogative.[70] In her case a correspondent denial of Jesus' divinity underlies her point, but Christians also tend toward the notion that forgiveness is a natural moral faculty picked up and put to use by Jesus Christ.[71] In our analysis of Barth we have come to expect an affirmation of reflections of forgiveness in human experience tempered by an adamant insistence that Jesus is not the *discoverer* but the *creator* and *catalyst* of forgiveness in the world. On one hand, when Barth considers biblical exhortations to forgive "just as the Lord has forgiven you" (Col 3:13), he takes it to be the presentation of a "distinctive pattern (usually indicated by the adverb καθώς) of which Jesus Christ is the original and which the members of His community have to copy by mutual love."[72] On the other hand, as we have seen, Barth is against cutting the *imitatio Christi* loose from the *participatio* because it transforms the Christian life "into intellectual, moral and religious riches which each

---

[70] Arendt, *Human Condition*, 239.

[71] This notion is seen in Volf's work, for example, when he puts all his emphasis on imitating a pattern and then turns to anthropology to explore how this is done. See Miroslav Volf, "Theology for a Way of Life," in *Practicing Theology: Beliefs and Practices in Christian Life*, ed. Miroslav Volf and Dorothy Bass (Grand Rapids: Eerdmans, 2001), 254.

[72] See *CD* IV/2, 821-22, along with Jn 13:34; Rom 15:7; Col 3:12; Eph 5:2, 25.

[person] can begin to handle as if he had himself created them, as if they were at his disposal, as if he could claim them as his own possession and power and glory."[73] Since "liberation for God . . . is followed at once by the liberation of the members of this people for one another," with Barth we are forced to explore how Jesus *does not deny that it is only God who can forgive, but brings divine forgiveness into human affairs nonetheless.*[74]

If we are looking for a self-sure, self-authenticated line from the vertical to the horizontal, the divine-human to the interpersonal, we search in vain.[75] As it is expressed so well by Bonhoeffer,

> [Jesus] stands not only between me and God, he also stands between me and the world, between me and other people and things. . . . So people called by Jesus learn that they had lived an illusion in their relationship to the world. The illusion is immediacy. . . . All our attempts to bridge the chasm that separates us from others, or to overcome the unbridgeable distance, the otherness or strangeness of another person, by means of natural or psychic connections are doomed to fail. No human way leads from person to person. The most loving sensitivity, the most thoughtful psychology, the most natural openness do not really reach the other person—there are no psychic immediacies. Christ stands between them. The way to one's neighbor leads only through Christ.[76]

There is no mention of sin or enmity in this paragraph, but Bonhoeffer's point rings even truer when our sinful condition is revealed within the reconciling action of God in Jesus Christ. Self-giving love may be the God-ordained constant, but when *self-giving* requires *forgiving* the world of relationships has clearly become more strained. Given that this strain stems from a break with the God who is love itself, the situation is, on its own, hopeless. If experience alone tells us that lasting and loving relationships are difficult to maintain, the incarnation and death of the Son of God reveal that, without divine intervention, they are impossible. As expressed by Paul, however, the resurrection of Jesus changes everything:

> From now on, therefore, we regard no one from a human point of view; even though we once knew Christ from a human point of view, we know him no

---

[73]*CD* IV/2, 826.
[74]Ibid., 810; see also *ChrL*, 251.
[75]See *CD* IV/4, 204.
[76]Bonhoeffer, *Discipleship*, 93-96.

longer in that way. So if anyone is in Christ, there is a new creation: everything old has passed away; see, everything has become new! All this is from God, who reconciled us to himself through Christ, and has given us the ministry of reconciliation; that is, in Christ God was reconciling the world to himself, not counting their trespasses against them, and entrusting the message of reconciliation to us. (2 Cor 5:16-19)

As we have seen, what Barth believes is that "all this is from God" on a daily basis as Jesus goes with us in time.[77] Forgiveness is not offered from a personal storehouse of goodwill; rather, we forgive as we are forgiven and, in fact, are forgiven as we forgive.

Because a corresponding fellowship is entailed in the reception of forgiveness, the implications for the place and meaning of interpersonal forgiveness are especially vital, if not wholly unique. According to Barth's understanding, this is not a matter of continually reminding ourselves of our forgiven state, but of confessing sin daily to the One who is Judge and Forgiver not only in history past but also in the course of it. Barth finds great significance in the fact that the third article of the Apostles' Creed places the communion of saints and the forgiveness of sins together as predicates of a confession of faith in the Holy Spirit.[78] In this dynamic relation of interpersonal and divine forgiveness there are thus three positive claims that need clarifying before we proceed to unravel a thick description of forgiveness within the broader context of Christ's ministry of reconciliation. In particular, we must (1) define the way that forgiveness relates to the past and its residual effects, (2) distinguish the act of forgiveness from a learned skill or human faculty and (3) address the question whether interpersonal forgiveness is unconditional.

Forgiveness redefines the past (but does not erase it). We begin with the historicity, or time-fullness, of Christian forgiveness; or, more specifically, the relationship it gives with our past. We have already questioned the notion that forgiveness must cancel or rewrite memories in order to be effective. In this regard John Milbank rightly argues that "if we seek forgiveness in purely human terms . . . the *aporias* of forgiveness and time will indeed stand, offering us no possibility of forgiveness whatsoever."[79] In his

---

[77]*CD* IV/1, 575.
[78]See ibid., 577 and 652-55.
[79]Milbank, *Being Reconciled*, 56.

earlier book on the Lord's Prayer, on one page alone Barth promoted interpersonal forgiveness by calling it a "small thing" in comparison with divine
forgiveness, reckoning it "infinitely lighter," "not so serious," a "small impulse," a "very small freedom" and a "little matter."[80] The sentiment is not
wholly inaccurate, but it does sacrifice theological complexity for the sake
of a homiletic exhortation (which, it must be said, comes across as trite and
pastorally insensitive). It also comes across as a *dismissal* of past sins rather
than an articulation of their having been overcome in Christ.

If this were Barth's prevailing rhetoric in the *Dogmatics* it would be highly
detrimental—but our concern is later alleviated when Barth spells out the
relation of forgiveness to the past:

> To-day, already impelled by the Spirit, he is still in the flesh of yesterday. He
> is already the new man, but he is still the old. Only in part? Only to a limited
> extent? Only in respect of certain relics? . . . It was an unfortunate delusion if
> this remnant was regarded as fortunately smaller in relation to something
> other and better. On the contrary, if we are just a little honest with ourselves
> (as we will be in serious conversion), we cannot conceal the fact that it is again
> the whole man with whom we have to do in this residuum. . . . Thus in the
> to-day of repentance we have not only to do with the presence of certain re-
> grettable traces of his being and action of yesterday. No, the one who is under
> the determination and in the process of becoming a totally new man is in his
> totality the old man of yesterday.[81]

This is much more refined than Barth's earlier treatment of the Lord's Prayer,
wherein he spoke against the "habit of always casting our eyes on our own
sin, instead of looking up to" the Lord who "hast severed us from this past."[82]
The either/or implied in his prior rhetoric is replaced with an explicit claim
that Spirit-led forgivers and forgiven alike can honestly confront the residuals of sin without being defined by them.

As Lois Malcolm observes, "We find ourselves enmeshed in a residue of
personal and corporate guilt that contaminates us in deep, often uncon-
scious ways."[83] Suppression and denial of these contaminations would

---

[80]See Karl Barth, *Prayer*, 2nd ed. (Louisville: Westminster John Knox Press, 2002), 55.
[81]*CD* IV/2, 571.
[82]Barth, *Prayer*, 56.
[83]Lois Malcolm, "Forgiveness as New Creation: Christ and the Moral Life Revisited," in *Christol-
    ogy and Ethics*, ed. LeRon Shults and Brent Waters (Grand Rapids: Eerdmans, 2010), 120.

hardly be an outworking of Christ's healing and compassion. In reflection
on the lives and prayers of David and Moses, Barth suggests that forgiveness
does not erase the historicity of the sinner or exempt the forgiven from the
loving discipline of God.[84] Christian forgiveness does *not* entail the necessary suppression or revision of memories, let alone a determination to
ignore the shrapnel from past explosions of sin. What forgiveness does is
entrust these things entirely to God and proceed in the freedom of faith. In
freedom from guilt and sin there is also the freedom to see what our sin has
brought about and to have it dealt with in the avenues newly opened up by
the Spirit of the reconciling God. The residual effects of past sin are still
there to be dealt with, but are reoriented to the accomplished reconciliation
and provisional healing of Christ. The old "relics" are there, but are not definitive anymore.[85] "We are free to move forward," Barth explains; excuses
have been taken away and there is "no more future as sinners."[86]

With Barth we see Christ's forgiveness in terms of an ever-inbreaking new
creation. It displaces our sinful disorientation and redirects the exacerba-
tions of enmity into the freedom work of a peace that passes understanding.
Forgiveness does not entail the promotion of a blissful neglect of truth, responsibility, self-respect or justice. The forgiver is freed for resilient truth
seeking and courageous peacemaking in the Spirit's reorientation to faith,
hope and self-giving love. In a fallen world this new life is taken up as a cross
but not a fate. It is a life of reliance on God in the midst of enmity, not a life
of servitude to sin and its pathologies in the name of banal tolerance. There
is hope for victims (or repentant offenders) who do not feel they have the
strength for forgiveness and reconciliation: it does not depend on their skill
or moral fortitude but the promised presence of the resurrected Lord. A
believer "can now live only by the remission of sins, but may do so quite
unconditionally . . . [and] quite unafraid."[87] Occasions for cross bearing are
not self-sought or sadistic, but particularized callings both given and provided for in the freedom of the Holy Spirit.[88] In the imperative to forgive,

---

[84]See *CD* IV/2, 465, 482-83, 635.

[85]*CD* IV/3.2, 664.

[86]*CD* IV/2, 569, 773; see also *ChrL*, 78-79. Barth writes this after saying that forgiveness is not
simply acting as if nothing happened.

[87]*CD* IV/3.1, 246-47; see also 340-41; *CD* IV/2, 604 and *CD* IV/3.2, 517-18.

[88]See *CD* IV/2, 607-12.

believers are not deterred from but freed for the discernment of such par-
ticularizations. This is why our final section will embed forgiveness within
a depiction of the reconciling activities to which it is related.

   Forgiveness is a grace (not a skill). Before we get there, however, we come
to our second positive claim, which has to do with distinguishing (but not
divorcing) Christian forgiveness from a learned skill or a human faculty. It
should be no surprise for us to conclude that, for Barth, forgiveness is not a
"power" that "we make our own," a "fine art" or a "skill" that we can hone, or
a "logic of grace" that we can appropriate.[89] An act of forgiveness is not a
"self-grounded and self-motivating" occurrence, as if there is a "Christian
spirit" that can stand in for the Holy Spirit.[90] Surely it is right that we will find
ourselves sometimes more and sometimes less naturally equipped for the
forgiving and reconciling acts that need doing; and surely it is wise to seek
agility and adeptness in the ministry of reconciliation, giving preference to
those personal and corporate habits that invoke the grace of Christ. Indeed,
considerable discussion of good habits and skills may thus enter under the
category of wisdom, insofar as wisdom remains primarily and decisively submitted to the ongoing invocation of the Lord's daily guidance and strength.

   Lois Malcolm is closest to the truth when she speaks of forgiveness in terms
of new creation.[91] Over and above both our incapacitations and complexities
on one hand and our finely honed practices and habits on the other, Christian
forgiveness remains a miracle of God that is to be participated in by faith. This
construal need not render us paralyzed before the specter of an inaccessible
forgiveness; rather, it opens us up to engage with the Spirit's activity in the
world, based on the accomplishment and promise of Christ. The participation
opened up is not a divine sublation of the human being's will or activity, but
"a true reflection" of God's grace that takes place between persons "within the
limits and with all the frailty of human action."[92] "What can take place on this
level," Barth is careful to say, "can be only a reflection of what takes place on

---

[89]See examples of such expressions in Volf, *End of Memory*, 208-9, and *Free of Charge*, 120, 196,
   202, 215; Johann Christoph Arnold, *Why Forgive?* (Rifton, NY: Plough Publishing House, 2009),
   183-84; Jones, *Embodying Forgiveness*, 127, 193, 196; and Stanley Hauerwas, *Dispatches from the
   Front: Theological Engagements with the Secular* (Durham, NC: Duke University Press, 1991), 88.
[90]*CD* IV/3.2, 498.
[91]See Malcolm, "New Creation," 101, 110, 123.
[92]*CD* IV/2, 815-16.

the vertical level, between God and [persons]. It can be only a copy of it in a reciprocal human action."[93] Divine forgiveness will have an "earthly and historical form" that is *intelligible at* "the historical and psychological and sociological level" even as it is *irreducible* to the level of *humanity alone.*[94]

Because interpersonal forgiveness follows a history lived by Jesus and not a timeless truth or a principle of anthropology, the ensuing ethic must retain the frame of reference within which we follow God. We can glean an insight into this by looking into Jesus' declaration, found in Luke 7:47, that one who "has been forgiven little loves little" (NIV). The saying is often assumed to mean that *one's capacity to forgive others is directly correlated with the measure of forgiveness one happens to have needed*—but in context we see that Jesus is not implying that the woman worshiping at his feet is a greater sinner than the Pharisee, nor that she will be a more gracious and loving person because of the degree of her sin or contrition.

When Barth discusses the passage he retains the language of cause and effect and applies it to love *toward God* rather than toward others.[95] One's love for God is relative to one's recognition of one's indebtedness to God. If we apply this to interpersonal relations, then, it may help to imagine the woman as she gets up from her act of worship and faces either the Pharisees or the disciples. In that event, the woman might be more likely than the Pharisee to forgive and love others, but it would be out of character for Barth to attribute this to her level of empathy or her lowly state. Indeed, for him, she would love and forgive simply because "each one receives the consolation of the Gospel and passes it on to others."[96] It is not her *capacity* to forgive under consideration in the Lukan text, but the veracity of her faith and her confession of Christ as all in all. The one thing that might keep her from sharing grace with the Pharisee would be if she perceived (along with him) that he was somehow removed from that need himself. *So it is not the*

---

[93]See *CD* IV/1, 724 and *CD* IV/2, 189-90, 522, 815.

[94]*CD* IV/1, 655; see also 657-58. This is why Gregory Jones can rightly speak of Christian forgiveness as more than a "general human capacity and desire" and yet still outline "practices of forgiveness and reconciliation" to be prayerfully fostered. Jones, *Embodying Forgiveness*, 9; see also 192, 211-17. On these points Jones borrows helpfully from Margaret Paton, "Can God Forgive?" *Modern Theology* 4, no. 3 (April, 1988): 230, and Marilyn McCord Adams, "Forgiveness: A Christian Model," *Faith and Philosophy* 8 (July 1991): 294.

[95]See *CD* IV/2, 818.

[96]Ibid., 636, quoting O. Michel without citation.

extent of her sin but her appreciation for the all-sufficiency of Jesus that makes the difference. It is the one who perceives little need for forgiveness who will be on the outside looking in at the shared love and grace of a Christian community. True reciprocity of grace and love in Christ will be present where forgiveness is accepted from Christ as a *shared reality*. As the woman might have discovered in the face of the unbelieving Pharisee, self-giving and for-giving love will often go unrequited in the world. However, this will not keep her or the church either from freely extending it or from believing that love, definitively speaking, is meant to be reciprocal.[97]

Forgiveness is free (not "unconditional"). With this we come to our third positive claim about Christian forgiveness: namely, the notion that it is both *freely given* and *contextually conditioned*. By now it should be clear that, for Barth, living in the freedom of Christ means we freely forgive as we are freely forgiven, and are freely forgiven as we freely forgive. In fact, there is no freedom apart from the sharing of the earthly historical presence and power of the merciful God. Anything else is an illusory freedom. With this freedom, for-giveness is not self-selectively shared from an imagined vantage point of objec-tivity, nor dispensed from a place of stoic superiority.[98] As believers live among neighbors and enemies, then, the question is not *whether or not* they will forgive, but *what this will involve*. In fact, the way Jesus commands forgiveness in and after teaching the disciples to pray, it sounds to our ears as if we may not even be forgiven by the Father *unless* we forgive others. Many resolutions have been offered to this conundrum. Anthony Bash rightly asks how the "divine forgiveness is an unimaginably lavish gift to the undeserving" if it is "made contingent on the degree to which one person forgives another," and thus pro-poses that the hints of contingency in Jesus' statement apply not to the gift of divine forgiveness but to our *experience* of it.[99] John Owen explains it a bit dif-ferently: "Our forgiveness of others will not procure forgiveness for ourselves; but our not forgiving others proves that we ourselves are not forgiven."[100]

These offer some helpful perspective, but they remain wrapped up in the logic of merited grace and assurance, potentially lending to a construal in

---

[97]Ibid., 636.
[98]See *CD* IV/3.1, 243-44.
[99]Anthony Bash, *Forgiveness and Christian Ethics* (Cambridge: Cambridge University Press, 2007), 100.
[100]John Owen, *The Forgiveness of Sins* (Grand Rapids: Baker, 1977), 209.

which the struggling victim of wrongdoing is to be blamed for a lack of grace precisely at the point of its greatest need. As we have seen, Barth does not wish to cast doubt on the reality of divine forgiveness. At the same time, he undermines the psychological obsession with assurance of salvation in order to redirect toward confident participation in the ministry of reconciliation already provided in Christ. Simply put, Barth suggests that one who prays the Lord's Prayer cannot do so in isolation—and so it goes for the lines regarding forgiveness as well. One's "personal blessing, experience and endowment," he says, "can have its own power and constancy only in this relationship" with God's larger movement.[101] Thus in one breath Barth shuns the notion that divine forgiveness is *conditional* and opens up the question whether an "embedded" account of forgiveness (such as the one offered here) can really claim to be *unconditional*. Charles Griswold put it pointedly: "A gift that comes with *quid pro quo* strings attached is no gift"—which suggests that if forgiveness contains an "expectation of reciprocity" then its status as a free gift is in jeopardy.[102]

This poses a considerable challenge to the depiction of forgiveness and reconciliation under construction in these pages. One possible response might be the one employed by Volf, who separates the "will to embrace" from the embrace itself, naming the first "unconditional and indiscriminate" and identifying the second as a free gift that unravels within a complexity of contingencies.[103] There is much to be said for this construal, but in the final analysis it too can be found lacking. It is preferable to retain the term *forgiveness* and to point out how its hopes are manifest in—but not reliant on—related activities. In this we are aided by the trajectory of a distinction made by Griswold, who differentiates *expectation* from *hope* and comes to a conclusion rather resonant with Barth's theology. Griswold asserts that "forgiveness cannot be 'unconditional'" because it entails "conditions that define what would count as forgiveness"—but it *can* be understood as "elective" without meaning that it is merely "arbitrary."[104] Indeed, with Barth we understand that there is a defined freedom from whence forgiveness

<hr>

[101]*CD* IV/3.2, 574; see also 566-71, 678, and *CD* IV/2, 442, 512, 565-66, 609-13.
[102]Charles Griswold, *Forgiveness: A Philosophical Exploration* (Cambridge: Cambridge University Press, 2007), 63.
[103]Miroslav Volf, "Forgiveness, Reconciliation, and Justice: A Christian Contribution to a More Peaceful Social Environment," in Helmick and Petersen, *Forgiveness and Reconciliation*, 42-43.
[104]Griswold, *Forgiveness*, 63, 67, 69.

comes, and it is a definition that is provided by neither the victim nor the offender. It can therefore be shared without manipulation, even as it hopes for reciprocity. Forgiveness is free and prior, even if there remains an expression of forgiveness that is only fully realized when it has been mutually engaged and genuinely received. Thus we are in agreement with Gregory Jones, who effectively argued against the abstract designator *unconditional* because it obscures the truth that forgiveness, while freely given, is for its fullness of reciprocity conditional upon repentance.[105]

One might still say that Christians forgive *unconditionally*—that is, in keeping with the way grace freely comes to them—as long as they are able to also say that Christ's grace is invoked to *condition* the lives of those who share and receive it. Note carefully how Barth defines forgiveness in the first part-volume as "a releasing of man from a legal relationship fatal to him, from an intolerable commitment which he has accepted, from an imprisonment in which he finds himself."[106] This he describes as a "necessity" born of God's free self-determination in Christ that comes to us "not partially but totally, not conditionally but unconditionally, not provisionally but definitively."[107]

When Barth says that divine forgiveness is not partial but total, we understand that between persons in time it works itself out in the day-to-day contingencies of life without doubt as to the totality of its relevance and establishment in Christ. When he says it is not conditional but unconditional we understand that it is freely given, freely conditioning the Christian life accordingly. When he says it is not provisional but definitive we understand that it is in keeping with who God is and what has been accomplished in Christ—even if it is realized now in a substantial but provisional way compared to when it will be fully revealed. Barth expressed this in his earlier reflections on the Apostles' Creed, where he wrote that all things are "determined and conditioned by the fact that forgiveness of sins is gifted to man, and received by him as a gift. . . . The forgiveness of sins or justification of the sinner by faith is *the* gift of the Holy Spirit . . . [and] the common denominator, so to speak, upon which everything that can seriously be called Christian life must be set."[108] When Barth

---

[105]See Jones, *Embodying Forgiveness*, 19, 121.
[106]*CD* IV/1, 256.
[107]*CD* IV/1, 256; see also 596.
[108]Karl Barth, *Credo* (London: Hodder & Stoughton, 1936), 153.

wrote *Church Dogmatics* he did not turn from these notions but described them in further detail. His intertwining of forgiveness with everything else in the Christian life should not dilute but highlight the intricacies of each aspect of Christ's reconciling ministry, and in the process make clear how forgiveness retains its character as both *free* and *freeing*.

If we return to Mark 2:7, where Jesus neither confirms nor denies that only God can forgive, we do well to note what Barth makes of it in this regard. Calling it the only New Testament example "in which there is a prior reference to the sin of the one who is healed," Barth points out that "even here there is no demand for repentance, but the sin is annulled unrequested and without examination, in view of the faith, not of the man himself, but of those who had brought him to Jesus." In his view the aim of the passage is not to recommend a vicarious repentance or to uphold the prerequisite of repentance, but to show that the basis of reconciliation is Christ's "pure, free proclamation" of mercy, "and not a psychologico-moral encouragement" to instigate the grace of God.[109] Forgiving is free self-giving in the face of sin. Just as the atonement is the extent to which Jesus goes in his eternally determined love toward humanity, so occasions of Christian forgiveness are a fallen-world extension of the self-giving love that grounds them.

As it takes place in the same motion as agape, forgiveness is given not in the sense of "losing oneself in the other" or making a contractual exchange, but of giving "to the other with no expectation of a return, in a pure venture, even at the risk of ingratitude, of [the] refusal to make a response of love, which would be a denial of [that person's] humanity."[110] For Barth the atonement is unlimited; thus the human has no right to limit or manage the sharing of forgiveness.[111] We do not *create* communion with our forgiving ways; Christ's love is a creative love that "causes those who are loved by Him to love."[112] This love engenders forgiveness on the interpersonal level that undermines both our sense of entitlement and our systems of exchange. While "we must not arrogate to ourselves that which can be given and received only as a free gift," Barth wrote, "we are surely commanded the more

---

[109]*CD* IV/2, 223.
[110]Ibid., 745.
[111]See *CD* IV/1, 630. As argued, if atonement is limited this may still be the case, but for different reasons.
[112]*CD* IV/2, 776; see also 777.

definitely to hope and pray . . . in spite of everything . . . that in accordance with His mercy which is 'new every morning' He 'will not cast off for ever.'"[113] With all this in view it needs to be maintained that there is a reciprocity to forgiveness that is only fully known when the wrongdoer has made a full confession to the forgiver, but that forgiveness is not prescriptively reserved until this occurs, even as it hopes and endeavors toward reconciliation.

In refinement of Anselm's position we saw Barth stress that Christ's forgiveness is not merely a declaration of innocence but a once-and-for-all event that includes Christ's descent into the thick of that history wherein his mercy triumphs over judgment.[114] LeRon Shults and Steven Sandage are right to point out that interpersonal forgiveness is always expressed in "cultural constructs related to social scripts about the healing and repair of interpersonal conflict."[115] Therein lies its special visibility as an aspect of churchly life. The visibility remains *special*, however, in that it is only known *for what it is* by faith in Christ. As a part of Christ's work in the world, Barth says, "this history will at least call for notice, and, whether understood and noticed or not, it will certainly not be without relevance and significance for the history of this world around and for human history generally. It will thus be a history which itself makes history."[116] To discern their way through this history, believers invoke the Lord for direction within a fellowship of mutual submission and accountability, submitted to the Spirit and the Scriptures and living in the rhythms of the sacraments and the Lord's Prayer.

We can see Barth trying to hold together both the freedom and the effectiveness of interpersonal forgiveness when he asks, "Is there any event more serious or incisive or effective than that in which God forgives man all his sins? And does not the recognition of the divine decision in this event depend upon the fact that it is understood as pure and free forgiveness?"[117] Clearly Barth does not think the freedom of forgiveness undermines its connectedness to reconciliatory imperatives. In fact, when forgiveness is received "here and now with unconditional certainty and unlimited fullness . . . the whole content enters the present of man. Where and when man trusts the promise . . . he

---

[113]*CD* IV/3.1, 477-78, quoting Lam 3:23, 31 (KJV). See also *ChrL*, 80-83.
[114]See *CD* IV/1, 486-87.
[115]Shults and Sandage, *Face of Forgiveness*, 23.
[116]*CD* IV/3.2, 500.
[117]*CD* IV/1, 487.

receives forgiveness, the divine pardon, and the freedom of a new and the only true capacity."[118] The question, then, is not *whether* we forgive, but *why we think we cannot.* The question is not *whether* to forgive, but *what it entails.*

THE PRAXIS OF GRACE: THE PLACE AND MEANING OF CHRISTIAN FORGIVENESS

With the assertion that interpersonal forgiveness has its meaning in relation to other acts and imperatives in Christ's ministry of reconciliation, the question becomes one of tracing the connections in that regard. As we do so, our picture of the central meaning of forgiveness will become clearer. As noted in our discussion of Barth's rejection of an *ordo salutis*, we know that he would not have been interested in *prescribing* an order of reconciliation. However, we also know that Barth did not rule out its provisional explanatory usefulness entirely, and in fact gave us plenty of fodder for highlighting the complex array of possibilities in the interpersonal ministry of reconciliation, as long as we refrain from tracing them out into a psycho-social method or sequence. Shults and Sandage are right: "Forgiveness is not a singular step in an individualistic *ordo salutis*, but a dynamic following of the *way* of salvation in Jesus Christ"—thus we need to "explore how the overlapping and interlacing of Christology and anthropology may shed light on the experience of redemptive forgiveness."[119] Begging to differ with their implication that anthropology shares a revelatory status separable from Christology, we join them in the effort to see forgiveness in its relation to other biblically exhorted reconciling activities. Indeed, it is Barth's resilience on this point that provides a good explanation why no section of his *Dogmatics* is dedicated to defining forgiveness in isolation. In what follows, then, we look to understand the place and meaning of Christian forgiveness by seeing it in its relation to other things. First it behooves us to render account of what those things might be—an endeavor that will be aided by the path our discussion of Barth's *Doctrine of Reconciliation* has taken thus far.

---

[118]We see the perceived need to embed forgiveness within an array of related imperatives when Barth continues, "The phrase 'the forgiveness of sins' is well adapted to sum up all that has to be said in this connexion. But it is better not to try to sum it all up in this phrase." Ibid., 598.

[119]Shults and Sandage, *Face of Forgiveness*, 171.

Outlining the ministry of reconciliation. One who looks for an order of reconciliation can find plenty of input from psychological and sociological fields. Many attempts have been made to articulate the processes of accountability and restoration that surround the impetus to forgive. As one example, take Carl Bråkenhielm's philosophical approach. Bråkenhielm describes the "multi-dimensionality" of political forgiveness in terms of (1) selective forgetfulness, (2) establishment of empathy, (3) acknowledgement of harm, (4) the will to improve, (5) the will to avoid rancor and hatred, (6) the joint effort to be free of a "destructive lifestyle," (7) remission of punishment, (8) freedom from guilt, (9) the creation of confidence and trust and (10) the rebuilding of fellowship.[120] As another example, take the approach found in Beverly Flanagan's clinical sociology. Flanagan called forgiveness "the accomplishment of mastery over a wound," describing it rather individualistically as a journey with six phases, ranging from naming, claiming and blaming to "balancing the scales," "choosing to forgive" and seeking "a new self."[121] Notably, for all the helpfulness of these delineations (and many others), one of the running themes is that the impulse of reconciliation hinges on the willpower of an individual to conquer their situation.

One of the more insightful and appropriately elaborate models comes from the work of Olga Botcharava, whose practical theology workshops produced an enlightening contrast between "seven steps toward revenge" and "seven steps toward reconciliation."[122] Although her comparison of the two orders begins with the instance of "aggression" rather than setting itself in the context of God's grace and peace, it helpfully shows how the cycle of revenge always ends up back at "aggression" (by rechristening it "justified"), and suggests that when "forgiveness is at the core of the model" the dynamic is set on a new axis. Interestingly, for Botcharova the first departure point from the cycle of vengeance is the moment of properly expressed grief, which she suggests enables one to "re-humanize the enemy" and to risk forgiveness

---

[120]Bråkenhielm, *Forgiveness*, 52-55.

[121]Beverly Flanagan, *Forgiving the Unforgivable: Overcoming the Bitter Legacy of Intimate Wounds* (New York: Wiley Publishing, 1992), 71-170, 138-39. Curiously, the fourth phase seems to reduce the fifth to a mere assent to justice.

[122]Olga Botcharova, "Implementation of Track Two Diplomacy: Developing a Model of Forgiveness," in Helmick and Petersen, *Forgiveness and Reconciliation*, 281, 288.

rather than nurse a hopeless version of history.[123] This dovetails well with Barth's invocation-based construal, particularly if we open up room for lamentation in the life of confession. In Botcharova's model, however, it should not escape our attention that the acknowledgment of cohumanity is the basic impetus for forgiveness, which leaves unclear the basis for discerning not only the offense but also the character and rationale of the new "joint history" to be written.[124] Despite its insight, for our purposes it is insufficiently connected to the particular redemptive path of Christ's mercy.

If we were to gather up the various imperatives in these philosophical and psycho-sociological accounts under more biblical terminology we might be on the best track with John Dawson's "model for reconciliation," which correlates forgiveness with four hoped-for events: confession, repentance, reconciliation and restitution.[125] However, Dawson does not elaborate at length or trace out interconnections with forgiveness as we will be attempting here. The two most compelling theological accounts with which we have interacted—by Gregory Jones and Miroslav Volf—gesture toward a model of reconciliation without attempting a detailed outline.[126]

If Scripture offers anything like a model or order of reconciliation, it is in what Ched Myers and Elaine Enns call the "community conferencing" instructions of Jesus in Matthew 18:15-20. As Myers and Enns so crucially observe, these instructions are situated between a challenge to social orders (vv. 1-5) and an exhortation to mutual accountability (vv. 6-14) on one side and a challenge to Lamech's system of retribution (vv. 21-22) exhorting to free and perpetual forgiveness (vv. 23-35) on the other.[127] In that context, the first

[123]Ibid., 288 and 293.
[124]Ibid., 287-91.
[125]John Dawson, "Hatred's End: A Christian Proposal to Peacemaking in a New Century," in Helmick and Petersen, *Forgiveness and Reconciliation*, 226. Note how this lines up with a Human Development Study Group's condensation of twenty "psychological variables" into four phases, working from the "uncovering" and "decision phase" toward the "work" and "deepening phase." See Robert D. Enright, Suzanne Freedman and Julio Rique, "The Psychology of Interpersonal Forgiveness," in *Exploring Forgiveness*, ed. Robert D. Enright and Joanna North (Madison: University of Wisconsin Press, 1998), 53. Compare also the four steps of decision, discussion, detoxification and devotion in Everett L. Worthington Jr., *Forgiveness and Reconciliation: Theory and Application* (New York: Taylor & Francis Group, 2006), 11, 170-75, 198-218.
[126]See Volf, *End of Memory*, 151, 208, and Jones, *Embodying Forgiveness*, 182-83.
[127]See Ched Myers and Elaine Enns, *Ambassadors of Reconciliation*, vol. 1, *New Testament Reflections on Restorative Justice and Peacemaking* (Maryknoll, NY: Orbis Books, 2009), 56; see also 49-81.

word Jesus gives—"If"—becomes a rather loaded one (v. 15). Not only does
this imply some kind of prior discernment of sin by the offended party, but
also the passing of time and the implication of forbearance leading up to and
accompanying the discretionary process of confrontation. The last words of
that verse are similarly significant: "winning over" a brother or sister should
not be read in terms of personal competition but as an indication of confrontation's telos in a restored mutuality of fellowship with the Father.

In the binding and loosing saying that follows, the reference to participation in heaven's work gives us a sense of the ground on which this reconciliatory procedure operates, so that when Jesus promises to be present with
those gathered in his name, the implication is that it refers to the *process* and
not merely the *result*. It is this promise that provides the foundation for the
ministry of reconciliation, and it stands in contrast to those accounts that
launch from the premises of a violent world (Volf) or an act of aggression
(Botcharova). Resonant with our reading, Myers and Enns see the centrality
of Peter in the narrative as a gesture not toward his office or authority but to
his confession of Christ, thus bringing us to focus less on the necessity of
priestly, professional or legal mediation and more on the call for believers
to speak truth in love in a confessing community.[128]

Within this understanding of Matthew 18—toward which we are compelled not only by Barth's telling excursus on "binding or loosing" but also
by the resonance with his emerging ethics of reconciliation—we are prepared to embark on a consideration of forgiveness that understands it within
the general constructs of Jesus' exhortation. Having scoured the psycho-
sociological literature on this score and gathered it under the aforementioned categories of John Dawson, we will take up the gains of the above
analysis by expanding those categories in order to capture all the nuances
of Jesus' instructions. To do this we will utilize the teaching of David
Guretzki, whose practical theology of reconciliation embeds forgiveness

---

[128]See ibid., 69. In their next volume, Myers and Enns gather up "a continuum of peacemaking
strategies" for truth and justice rather than a schematic of reconciliatory imperatives. This does
not contradict what we are attempting here; in fact it is hoped that this book provides a theological paradigm amenable to their excellent work. Indeed, were we to attempt even more detail
regarding missional engagement with the community, it would be difficult to improve upon
what they have already written. See Elaine Enns and Ched Myers, *Ambassadors of Reconciliation*,
vol. 2, *Diverse Christian Practices of Restorative Justice and Peacemaking* (Maryknoll, NY: Orbis
Books, 2009), 15-21.

along with six other reconciling activities taken up by those who follow Jesus—namely, forbearance, gracious confrontation, confession, repentance, correction and restoration.[129] What commends this list is not necessarily its innovation but the simplicity with which it captures key biblical themes and imperatives of grace—all to the illumination of not only the social-scientific literature but the prominent impulses of *The Doctrine of Reconciliation* we are aiming to appropriate.

Forgiveness among other things. In light of our use of Matthew 18, it is interesting to note Barth's treatment of it in part-volume one, where he writes, "The promise of the Lord that where two or three are gathered together in His name He is there in the midst (Mt 18:20) will be true of this Church in spite of the doubtful nature of its separate existence."[130] When he returns to it in part-volume two, Barth asks, "What does this mean? Does it mean only that He comes and is present as a third or fourth? Does it not mean rather that He is present and at work in the gathering together of the two or three, as the centre which constitutes this circle?"[131] Relating this to the similar promise found in Jesus' Great Commission, Barth inquires further,

> Does it mean that He is there as an interested spectator who occasionally gives friendly help? Does it not mean rather that when and as they act in accordance with His orders in the time which hastens to the end He is present every day to sustain and protect and save in His mercy, to accompany them in His omnipotent *concursus*, to rule them by His will which alone is holy—Himself the primary and proper Subject at work with and amongst them?[132]

To unravel this, we heed the explanation of Alexander Sider, who says that "forgiveness and reconciliation are a process that *takes* and *makes* time" as persons have their situation taken up in the "ongoing conversation" of Jesus. Between persons, "forgiveness names the possibility of and desire to continue conversing with the one who has offended, without assuming that one can predict in advance the shape that conversation will take"—and this is

---

[129]This is a slight adaptation of his wording. Quick to explain that his model is not a prescribed sequence, Guretzki places forgiveness on a circle of reconciliation that contains these other actions (as well as the offense itself). David Guretzki, "Life in the Mess: A Theology of Forgiveness and Reconciliation" (lectures, Briercrest Seminary, Caronport, SK, October 1–5, 2007).
[130]*CD* IV/1, 680.
[131]*CD* IV/2, 658.
[132]Ibid.

not a reversion to "radical situationalism" but a confession of the One who defines the way forward.[133]

Resonant with this, Anthony Bash rejects the idea that forgiveness is a "discrete phenomenon" and proposes that it "comprises a variety of different responses to wrongdoing."[134] Building on a similar notion, Vincent Waldron and Douglas Kelley observe that, even though "theologians and social scientists have portrayed forgiveness as an interpersonal process," to this point "they have been slow to consider forgiveness as a communicative construct."[135] This is an evocative point. Rather than turn to the logic of grammar or sociology to unravel this construct, however, we are looking to the Word living and active, paying special attention to the reconciliation-encompassing exhortations found in the apostolic witness of Scripture. Against the tendency to corner forgiveness in the past and relegate reconciliation to the future, we want to see how forgiveness checks and informs every nook and cranny of the ongoing ministry of reconciliation. Thus we must look at how it is embedded with other imperatives that come to us in Christ's reconciling activity. We begin with an analysis of the relationship between forgiveness and forbearance.

---

[133]Sider, *To See History*, 158. Similar arguments are made in Anderson, *Shape of Practical Theology*, 304-10.

[134]Bash, *Forgiveness and Christian Ethics*, 177.

[135]Vincent R. Waldron and Douglas L. Kelley, *Communicating Forgiveness* (Los Angeles: Sage Publications, 2008), 18.

5

As We Forgive

FORGIVENESS IN THE MINISTRY OF RECONCILIATION

TO EACH THEIR OWN? FORGIVENESS AND FORBEARANCE

As seen in Barth's descriptions of "false fellowship," there is a kind of societal tolerance characterized by "mere proximity" that claims a kinship with the notions of forgiveness but is merely a veil for what is, when its preconditions break down, "finally hostility."[1] "Alliances and pacts and unions" may be successfully established "under the dominion of the idea of toleration, provided there is sufficient good will" toward the "attainment of political and social and moral and practical tactical ends," but Barth perceives that these are not constitutive of the communion that makes a church. In his view, a "doctrine of toleration" may well be appropriated for "good reasons or bad" in social settings, but as a *doctrine* it belongs to "congenial deities" who service our self-justification. Ironically, the assertion of such doctrine often manifests itself in the form of intolerance for a crucified God.[2] Rather insidiously, however, the calls for tolerance in post-Christendom tend to invoke a banal deity in Jesus' clothes who poses "monotonously as 'love'" for the sake of conflict avoidance.[3] John Howard Yoder finds this especially evident in the egalitarianism of supposed "equal opportunity" found in "Jeffersonian deist

---

[1] *CD* IV/3.1, 470.
[2] *CD* IV/1, 676-78; see also *CD* IV/2, 406-7, 664, and *ChrL*, 84.
[3] *CD* IV/1, 490.

humanism."[4] For all the relative good this has brought about, it is a far cry from the new humanity of mutual submission that corresponds to faith in the reconciling Christ.

Philosophical support for such a "doctrine of tolerance" is not uncommon. Klaus Brinkmann notes a Hegelian form of it in the "reconciling Yea" that views conflict as a necessary inevitability that is surmounted by the "spirit" of reconciliation whenever "two I's let go their antithetical *existence*" and "forgive each other" their collective guilt.[5] Richard Findler observes a Nietzschean form of it in the idea that "guilt is not necessary and can be overcome" if we turn it back on itself and render it a nonfactor.[6] Within these trajectories, however, the notion of forgiveness employed pertains more to the surmounting of *indecipherable perplexities of difference* and less to the confrontation and overcoming of *discernible wrong*. Societies built on tolerance—caricatured in expressions like "live and let live"—do not do justice to the ethos that is needed if there are wrongs being done.

Cultures that value tolerance often depend on hegemonically perpetuated codes of honor wherein the appearance of conflict and disunity can be avoided as long as the code goes unchallenged and, as much as possible, unspoken. This is never more clear than when those who try authentically to seek confrontation amidst the flotsam and jetsam of hurt and offense find themselves edged out by the loudest voices, caricatured and marginalized, and thus reach a level of frustration that leads them to either revolutionary violence or stoic retreat. According to Barth, "the theory and practice of what we call tolerance" appears to be the perennial "general lassitude to which men surrender for a time, only to break out again sooner or later in new dogmatisms and acts of judgment and conflicts and mutually caused troubles and well-intentioned wrongs."[7] In the meantime there is a blanket of tolerance thrown over the public discourse that claims no need for faith but that rests on belief in an "imaginary god"; namely, the

---

[4]John H. Yoder, *For the Nations: Essays Evangelical and Public* (Grand Rapids: Eerdmans, 1997), 33-45.
[5]Klaus Brinkmann, "Hegel on Forgiveness," in *Hegel's Phenomenology of Spirit*, ed. Alfred Denker and Michael Vater (New York: Humanity Books, 2003), 251, citing G. W. F. Hegel, *The Phenomenology of Spirit*, trans. A.V. Miller (New York and Oxford: Oxford University Press, 1977), 409.
[6]Richard S. Findler, "Reconciliation Versus Reversal: Hegel and Nietzsche on Overcoming Sin or Ontological Guilt," in Denker and Vater, *Hegel's Phenomenology*, 310-11.
[7]*CD* IV/1, 447; see also *CD* IV/2, 399, 420 and 548-49.

majority's capability for "self-communing."[8] With pathologies like this in mind Barth was willing to suggest that "the most terrible weapon of intolerance" may actually end up being "toleration," since it perpetuates evil and stockpiles enmity behind "sheer indifference" while hostility mounts under the cover of false peace.[9] This explains why he calls division in the church a troubling scandal and yet prefers it to an "artificial suppression of the mutual difficulties."[10]

One of the common methods of motivating forgiveness in recent discourse has been to call upon cultural concepts and processes such as South African *ubuntu*, Ghandi's *satyagraha* or the general practice of empathy or "thoughtfulness"—all of which rely to some degree on some form of faith in the common ground or goodness of humanity.[11] Charles Griswold rightly counters that even though a "recognition of shared humanity by the injured party is a necessary step on the way to forgiveness" it is nonetheless an insufficient impetus for such a thing—"pity and forgiveness are mutually exclusive."[12] As Barth says, the commonality of a wrongdoing may lead us to believe that "we can readily find forgiveness" for it, but little is gained from the confession, "We are all of us human."[13] An experienced sense of empathy may of course aid one's readiness to forgive wrongdoing, but it is not a sufficient basis. In fact, Bernd Wannenwetsch observes that empathy can equally be hegemonic or colonialist in its impulses, veiling a tendency to "transpose oneself into the other" so that "the other's difference all too easily gets lost along the way."[14]

Christian forgiveness is simply different from the recollection of cohumanity or the relativization of guilt. At times it may appear to coincide with these forms of tolerance, but its Christian character will emerge when

---

[8]*CD* IV/1, 364; see 372.

[9]*CD* IV/2, 664.

[10]*CD* IV/1, 676, 678.

[11]See Desmond Mpilo Tutu, *No Future Without Forgiveness* (New York: Doubleday, 1999), 31. See also Iain S. Maclean, "No Future Without Forgiveness, by Desmond Tutu," *Missiology* 31 (October 2003): 505, and Anthony da Silva, "Through Nonviolence to Truth: Gandhi's Vision of Reconciliation," in *Forgiveness and Reconciliation: Religion, Public Policy, and Conflict Transformation*, ed. Raymond G. Helmick and Rodney L. Petersen (Philadelphia: Templeton Foundation Press, 2001), 202-4.

[12]Charles Griswold, *Forgiveness: A Philosophical Exploration* (Cambridge: Cambridge University Press, 2007), 79, 81; see also 66.

[13]*CD* IV/2, 457; see also *CD* IV/1, 364.

[14]Bernd Wannenwetsch, *Political Worship: Ethics for Christian Citizens*, trans. Margaret Kohl (Oxford: Oxford University Press, 2004), 328.

one bears with another's sin in hopes of a shared experience of forgiveness on which such "bearing forward" is based. Unlike tolerance, then, in Christian forbearance, as in forgiveness, the call is not to a "weak overlooking and pardoning of human wrong. Such an idea has nothing whatever to do with the truth of the grace and mercy of God."[15] As Barth explains it, the Christian is "deprived of all authorisation" to establish any "equipoise" with the conditions of enmity; transgression "is not tolerated let alone accepted in the death of Jesus Christ," but "can only be forgiven to man."[16]

In many circumstances forgiveness and forbearance may appear synonymous, not because they are the same, but because forgiveness will entail forbearance in various contexts at the Spirit's lead. When we encounter the exhortation to "bear with one another" in Colossians 3:13, we see it joined to the call to forgive "just as the Lord has forgiven you." We have a view to Barth's view of this when he considers the question whether one can ask forgiveness on another's behalf, and points to 1 Samuel 25:28, suggesting an openness to the phenomenon, even if it may not be normative. On closer inspection, however, we see that Abigail did not ask David for forgiveness so much as for forbearance. What she asked was that Nabal be granted a gracious reprieve for the sake of hoped-for confession and repentance. The fact that David grants it is motivated by his kingship of Yahweh's people more than his personal inclinations, which is itself a prefiguration of the promise of the Messiah.[17] Inclined to look for particularities rather than "general moral exhortations to unity, peace and neighborly love," Barth guides us to recognize David's forgiveness more specifically as the restraint of his vengeance in light of his knowledge of God.[18] It would be wrong to say David's act is *not* forgiveness, but it would also be wise to refrain from equating it with forgiveness in its totality or fullest definition. It is better to observe that in the face of unconfessed sin Christian forgiveness will manifest itself in particular acts of forbearance that may yet be manifest in more direct and reciprocated ways. Forbearance is a

---

[15]CD IV/1, 563.

[16]CD IV/2, 574, and CD IV/1, 410; see also CD IV/2, 400-401.

[17]See CD IV/2, 430-31, and 1 Sam 25. We will not deal with the question of vicarious forgiveness directly, except to agree with Milbank that to presume to forgive on behalf of another can be a form of complicity with the wrong that was done, a cooperation in the silence on which it depends in order to thrive. See John Milbank, *Being Reconciled: Ontology and Pardon* (London: Routledge, 2003), 50-51.

[18]CD IV/3.2, 858.

specific action, and it is faith in a living Lord that enables forgiveness to *act* within the *particularities* of reality in such a way. A church that turns to a principle of general tolerance to stay together has made itself inappropriately invisible as a church and forfeited its own unique existence by inoculating the gospel with something timeless (and irrelevant) in its stead.[19]

We can further explore the distinction between not only tolerance and forbearance but also forbearance and forgiveness via Barth's distinction between "love" and "friendliness," wherein he explains that "the latter is a kind of anticipation of" the former:

> [Friendliness] is the position of readiness of the Christian as he looks and moves to the neighbour or brother of to-morrow in each of his fellows, even including the "enemy" of the people and the community. Those who themselves exist in this context of the history of salvation . . . must be ready and on the way to love for all, even in relationships in which its realisation is at the moment impossible.[20]

Such love is "longsuffering" because it is "self-giving" in spite of sin, "because as such it is a reflection of the love of God, which has to do with men who are wholly bad but according to 2 Cor. 5:19 does not impute or reckon their trespasses to them."[21] Disconnected from a full-bodied ministry of reconciliation, this might well be seen to endorse an ambiguous posture of tolerance or benign forgetfulness, but it is clear from the context that Barth sees it as a provisional precursor to loving engagement rather than a preclusion of confrontation or remembrance of any kind.

Christian forbearance differs from tolerance because of the particular content of its hope. If divorced from this hope, "the divine Yes has become curiously like the Yes which man is always about to say to himself," thereby "facilitating, supporting and even furthering man's evasion and escape from its message in perhaps the most respectable and unchallengeable form." As such, tolerance can be a "most effective" buffer between people and the God who would otherwise brace them for transformation: "The most cunning of all the strategems which the resisting element in man can use in self-defence

---

[19]See *CD* IV/4, 197, 204, and *CD* IV/3.2, 816.
[20]*CD* IV/2, 809.
[21]Ibid., 832. Barth in this context says love "does not compile a dossier about" the other, but the difference between this and a readiness to speak truth in love will be explained presently.

against the Word of grace is simply to immunise, to tame and harness."[22] In contrast to this, forbearance trusts God and freely forgives, even as it looks to him for truth, justice and reconciliation. It is the manifestation of forgiveness that is called for when the "if" of Matthew 18 is in question, when a confrontation is still on its way to resolution, when an offender is not available or when an offender is not predisposed to enter the reconciliation process on common ground. As the incarnate Son of God works out his accomplished reconciliation in time, forbearance is the form forgiveness takes when hope is all one has.

In some ways it can be helpful, even if finally inadequate, to differentiate forbearance and forgiveness according to a sequential or an internal/external distinction. Indeed, manifold attempts to articulate such a thing could be leveraged in support. Everett Worthington differentiates between intrapersonal (internalized) and interpersonal (expressed) forgiveness.[23] Baumeister, Exline and Sommer differentiate "silent forgiveness" from "full forgiveness," suggesting we not confuse silence with inaction.[24] Anthony Bash speaks in terms of a move from "thin" to "thick" forgiveness.[25] Stephen Williams identifies forgiveness that precedes repentance as "a disposition of the heart" that "awaits it."[26] Nigel Biggar describes "forgiveness-as-compassion" as a "unilateral and unconditional . . . inner reining-in of resentment" and "forgiveness-as-absolution" as a "properly reciprocal and conditional" response to repentance.[27] Finally, and perhaps most helpfully, Solomon Schimmel differentiates between private and interpersonal forgiveness, which leads him to work out "four possible combinations" of the two: forgiveness could be (1) private but not interpersonal, (2) interpersonal but not private, (3) both

---

[22]*CD* IV/3.1, 259.

[23]Everett L. Worthington Jr., *Forgiveness and Reconciliation: Theory and Application* (New York: Taylor & Francis Group, 2006), 18-20, 175.

[24]R. F. Baumeister, J. J. Exline and K. L. Sommer, "The Victim Role, Grudge Theory, and Two Dimensions of Forgiveness," in *Dimensions of Forgiveness: Psychological Research and Theological Speculations*, ed. E. L. Worthington Jr. (Philadelphia: The Templeton Foundation Press, 1998), 79-104.

[25]Anthony Bash utilizes the depictions of R. A. Sharpe in this regard. See Anthony Bash, "Forgiveness: A Re-appraisal," *Studies in Christian Ethics* 24, no. 2 (May 2011): 143, and R. A. Sharpe, *Forgiveness: How Forgiveness Endangers Morality* (Exeter, UK: Imprint Academic, 2007), 63-65.

[26]Stephen N. Williams, "What Christians Believe About Forgiveness," *Studies in Christian Ethics* 24, no. 2 (May 2011): 153.

[27]Nigel Biggar, "Melting the Icepacks of Enmity: Forgiveness and Reconciliation in Northern Ireland," *Studies in Christian Ethics* 24, no. 2 (May 2011): 203.

or (4) neither.[28] In this construal, we would certainly consider the third combination as the ideal, but situations abound in which it would be foolhardy to refuse to consider anything forgiveness that did not (yet) live up to it.

The problem with framing forbearance and forgiveness sequentially is that it fails to consider the residuals of sin that will continue to need forbearance even after an expression of forgiveness has been offered and accepted. It also suppresses the truth that forgiveness is not only responsive but free and prior as well. The problem with framing forbearance and forgiveness according to internalization and externalization is that it obscures the fact that forbearance can just as easily entail external acts. Indeed, forbearance may be the active form forgiveness takes when the wrong that was done has yet to be fully discerned for the truth of what exactly occurred. Leaving room for this time of forbearance may save forgiveness from too hastily becoming a kind of self-judgment or premature and private acquittal.[29] Forbearance can also be the form forgiveness takes when confession and repentance have occurred, but there are baby steps being taken in the follow-up restoration of the relationship. Negatively, of course, forbearance could also be manipulated by an offender to prolong a situation of oppression or abuse, and this would be a poor substitute for the judgment of grace that is called for by forgiveness in Christ. The point is that for all the helpful delineations given above, we are best to say that forbearance is the form that forgiveness takes when it is freely internalized and faithfully enacted on the still-hopeful side of confrontation, confession and further reconciliation. It is not to be confused with full reconciliation, but as the forbearing person waits on Christ, "a fine skin begins to grow over all these wounds, open and painful though they still are. They are not yet healed. But it is the sign and beginning of their healing."[30]

Rooted as it is in the freedom of Christ's gift of forgiveness, forbearance is neither coercively manipulative nor helplessly passive. It is a hopeful act of trust in God. In Ephesians 4 Barth is sure to point out that "bearing with [ἀνέχομαι] one another in love" falls under the exhortation to walk worthy

[28]Solomon Schimmel, *Wounds Not Healed by Time: The Power of Repentance and Forgiveness* (Oxford: Oxford University Press, 2002), 43-44.
[29]See Geoffrey Scarre, "Political Reconciliation, Forgiveness and Grace," *Studies in Christian Ethics* 24, no. 2 (May 2011): 181-82.
[30]CD IV/2, 314.

of one's call.[31] Disciples *correspond to* rather than *create* the unity provided in Jesus Christ. They are called to neither tolerance nor violence. Whether directly communicated or wordlessly offered, forbearance will often be given sacrificially—even at considerable cost to oneself—but it may also be given in the process of finding protection from further mistreatment. Bearing with another person does not necessitate submission to repeated abuse. As a matter of fact, it may be the best form of forbearance to seek just mediation from a fair third party despite one's (potentially warranted) desire to see evil avenged. It is often when there is no such third party in sight that conflicts ends up perched on the shoulders of isolated individuals to carry alone, thus perpetuating their victimhood. Such are the conditions of false peace, of a merely tolerant society. In the Christian community of self-giving love, when those doing all the giving find themselves in a position of sub-servience to takers they have a place to ask for truer fellowship, to ask to be received and respected as others. To ask for this is not to renege on the free forgiveness shared, but to point to the ministry of Christ's reconciliation within which that forgiveness finds its meaning. Therefore, forbearing grace does not preclude but enables and informs a certain kind of confrontation. To this topic we now turn.

THE JUDGMENT OF GRACE: FORGIVENESS AND CONFRONTATION

Common sense tells us that "one cannot forgive an innocent person," but one would not know it from the way forgiveness is commonly practiced.[32] The notion of unconditional forgiveness may lend to this. Often forgiveness is construed in such a way as to enable the forgiver *not* to confront the guilty party, or is issued in such a way as to avoid any assessment of the objective guilt involved. In Barth's words, the one who confesses Christ says, "He and not I will judge others"—but the fact should not be missed is that this *does* entail a belief that the Lord will judge.[33] Without some such belief forgiveness is almost nonsensical. Forgiveness without judgment simply decides that sin is *good*, or at least *understandable*. But mercy triumphs *over*

---

[31]*CD* IV/1, 668.
[32]See David Konstan, *Before Forgiveness: The Origins of a Moral Idea* (Cambridge: Cambridge University Press, 2010), 2, and Alice MacLachlan, *The Nature and Limits of Forgiveness* (PhD diss., Boston University, 2008), 16.
[33]*CD* IV/1, 233.

judgment, not without it.[34] In his saving work Jesus revealed true God and true humanity, both *naming* and *overruling* sin at once.[35] Compelled by Christ to freely forgive, the forbearing person looks for Christ's further reconciliation, entering into confrontation with a yoke that is easy, trusting the Prince of Peace who not only transcends every situation but also enters into it. In the precedence of forgiveness, persons are *freed for* confrontation as they entrust it to God and come under the judgment of grace themselves. Our concern in this section is to explore how this is so.

Geoffrey Scarre suggests that "to have been on the receiving end of some offensive behaviour is *not* . . . a sufficient ground of fitness to forgive," and adds that the "right to forgive must be earned by the display of moral qualities in the forgiver."[36] Unfortunately, he gets it only half right. Whether by achievement or accident, moral high ground does not supply the capacity or the right to forgive. When forgiveness is made subservient to a narrative of moral superiority it severely problematizes the attempt to find mutuality and to discern—let alone accomplish—justice or truth. A confrontation of sin that is *based* on moral high ground—no matter how legitimate—is bound to produce "superficial shamings" that are "always at bottom reciprocal," thus perpetuating the spiral of enmity.[37] In Barth's view, the "revolt against disorder" and "struggle for human righteousness" is lost when it is reduced to such an inevitable "conflict of mere self-interests."[38]

Apart from faith these suggestions sound scandalous. It appears as if there will be no conflict and therefore no justice, only a supposedly level playing field that actually remains slanted against victims. But faith in Christ means that the active sloth of conflict seeking is displaced by trust in the Spirit's power and presence. At the same time, the passive sloth of conflict avoidance is also challenged by the conviction that when "the question of truth is sacrificed to that of love and peace, we are not on the way to the one Church."[39] In Christian communion, peace is neither "the opposite of quarrelling" nor

---

[34]See Jas 2:13. On this point see Ray S. Anderson, *The Shape of Practical Theology: Empowering Ministry with Theological Praxis* (Downers Grove, IL: InterVarsity Press, 2001), 298.

[35]See *CD* IV/1, 401, 490, and *CD* IV/3.2, 700.

[36]Scarre, "Political Reconciliation," 174.

[37]*CD* IV/1, 385-86. On the dangers and the appropriateness of shame, see Aaron Lazare, *On Apology* (New York: Oxford University Press, 2004), 114-17.

[38]*ChrL*, 205-8.

[39]*CD* IV/1, 680; see also 675-77, 683.

the Trojan horse for "petty, self-opinionated bickering"; rather, it is always "the fruit of grace."[40] Jesus is the mediator; the minister of reconciliation. With Hebrews 12:7-8 Barth calls us to trust ourselves to his conflict with both the old self and the old world, reminding us that conflict is neither to be sought nor feared. In fact, on this side of redemption "if ye be without chastisement . . . then are ye bastards, and not sons."[41]

As has been discussed regarding self-judgment, so it is with confrontation. With Jeremiah the weeping prophet as his exemplar, Barth asks,

> How could the man who had to proclaim to the people the failure of their own self-help be himself a man who succeeded in helping *himself*? . . . I am already putting myself in the wrong with others, and doing them wrong, when—it makes no odds how gently or vigorously I do it—I confront them as the one who is right, wanting to break over them as the great crisis. For when I do this I divide myself and I break the fellowship between myself and others. I can only live at unity with myself, and we can only live in fellowship with one another, when I and we subject ourselves to the right which does not dwell in us and is not manifested by us . . . the right of His Word and commandment alone, the sentence and judgment of His Spirit.[42]

What this means is that faith in Christ's universally extended mercy frees us to courageously bring a situation before the Lord and the offender, seeking Christ's judgment in the hope for grace and reconciliation. If we are sure we are in the right, folk wisdom tells us we have nothing to fear. However, whether we are sure or unsure, Christian wisdom tells us that we have more to fear from trusting our own judgment than from trusting the Judge who was judged in our place.

Of course, to those accustomed to conflict-avoidant spirituality, even the most gracious confrontation may appear to be a self-assertive aggravation. Worse, the victim who confronts sin may be cast as the perpetrator of discord. Such appearances are unavoidable to some degree, and while they are not to be feared they may be taken into account as one considers how to approach a situation wisely. In some contexts resistance to confrontation may be understandable, and in others it may even be temporarily wise, but as a regular

---

[40]*ChrL*, 77, and *CD* IV/3.2, 881.
[41]*CD* IV/1, 537 (KJV).
[42]Ibid., 476, 451.

practice and ethos it is wholly unbecoming a church. In fact, in Barth's view, confrontation will be more rather than less likely within a Christian community: in the case of "one's fellow-man generally," he says, "much may be overlooked," but a "real Church" is a "theatre of conflict."[43] The Christian

> is in no position to make easy and cheap for men the hearing and receiving of what he has to attest. No self-evident friendliness, humanity and serenity with which he turns to them will deceive them. The glorious divine Yes . . . is necessarily enclosed in the No which they never like to hear because it not only gets on their nerves but touches them on the raw, radically challenging and overthrowing their existence. Not even in the name of love can he, to make it more acceptable, blunt either edge of the two-edged sword of the Word of God (Heb. 4:12f.). He cannot make the free grace of God a comfortable grace, nor transform the good Lord into a good man.[44]

However, what must be made clear about Barth's fully expressed view is that "a real Church . . . is only a theatre of conflict between the true Church and the false," and as such it is

> humbly content to be thrown back entirely upon faith. . . . A prudent guest at the Lord's table (Lk 14:10) will seat himself with the other guests whatever proud looks he may have to face . . . [and will] try to hear, and perhaps actually hear, the voice of the others. Where a Church does this, in its own place, and without leaving it, it is on the way to the one Church.[45]

Freed by the grace which they mutually confess, both the offended party and the offender are open to be "confronted by the one truth superior to both him and them."[46] This is not to call confrontation a *means* to fellowship, but to recognize its place in the up-building of the community as the Holy Spirit quickens its members to love and forgive.

How then does such confrontation proceed? It is hard to be more straightforward than Jesus' instructions in Matthew 18, which call for directness and, in the face of unsatisfactory results or resistance, a discreet expansion of the circle of mutual accountability and assistance. As seen in verse 15, the goal of such confrontation is not personal vindication but reconciliation. Often

---

[43]*CD* IV/2, 834, and *CD* IV/1, 708.
[44]*CD* IV/3.2, 627.
[45]*CD* IV/1, 708, 684.
[46]*CD* IV/3.1, 91; see also *CD* IV/3.2, 899.

overlooked is the fact that before he outlines his instructions and tells the
parable of the unforgiving servant in Matthew 18, Jesus upheaves social hier-
archies and gives a strong word about the mutual accountability for rooting
out sin. Where some might see a tension between the strong warnings on
one hand and the implications of relentless forgiveness on the other, Barth
quite clearly does not. In his view the most pronounced judgment is the
one that comes in Christ's triumphant mercy—what Gregory Jones calls
the "judgment of grace."[47] The church takes sin seriously precisely because
it is taken not with "ultimate" but *"penultimate* seriousness."[48] In the
freedom of a church's "being in 'the forgiveness of sins,'" Christ interrupts
the "mercilessly critical self-judgement" and "liberates" people for the "un-
compromisingly sober assessment" that comes as the Spirit guides into
truth between the prayerful rhythms of Word and sacrament.[49]

When a confrontation is tempted toward vengefulness or violence, Christ
is invoked not only to reveal the sin but also to divert slothful attempts to
manage the judgment that is Christ's alone. When there is sin and harm to
be addressed, there is a difference between confrontation in Christ and a
self-managed attempt to disturb the other's sin whether by sarcasm, accusation, guilt trip or passive-aggressive provocation.[50] Of course, efforts at
confrontation—especially in settings where conflict is frowned upon and
marginalized—will often be clumsy and questionable. (Sometimes confrontation is not even possible, due to absence or death.) But this is exactly why
such matters are best put in context by the priority of Christ's mercy.

If interpersonal forgiveness is conditional upon a sufficient display of confession and repentance it is hard to imagine how the confrontation of sin can
take place in the judgment *of grace.* Conversely, if intrapersonal forgiveness is
only concerned with personal therapy it is hard to imagine how there is to be a
judgment of grace at all. Forgiveness is connected to, manifested in and hopeful
of proper confrontation in Christ. To understand this further we must consider
forgiveness and confrontation in the context of interpersonal confession.

[47]See L. Gregory Jones, *Embodying Forgiveness: A Theological Analysis* (Grand Rapids: Eerdmans,
    1995), 135-37, 145-50, 156, and "The Judgment of Grace: Forgiveness in Christian Life," *Theol-
    ogy Matters* 3, no. 4 (July/August 1997): 7-16.
[48]*CD* IV/3.2, 717; see also *ChrL*, 26.
[49]*CD* IV/1, 94, and *CD* IV/2, 402-3. See also Jn 16:13.
[50]See *CD* IV/3.1, 475-76, *CD* IV/1, 772 and *CD* IV/2, 524, 545.

Truth Telling, Apology and Agreement: Forgiveness and Confession

In the New Testament, two words are normally translated in terms of confession: ὁμολογέω and ἐξομολογέω. In the case of the former (which is used more often, in terms of both confession of sin and confession of Christ), the literal meaning is "to say the same thing as another" or "to agree."[51] In the positive sense it is the yes of persons to the Yes of God; in the negative sense it is the yes of persons to the No of God.[52] Interestingly, there is a thick resonance between this and the pre-Christian ponderings of Aristotle on the notion, not of confession, but forgiveness. As David Konstan notes, in *Nicomachean Ethics* Aristotle's use of συγγνώμη (translated "forgiveness") "bears the sense of 'know with another,'" carrying a meaning that falls somewhere between commending and condemning, understanding and pardoning.[53] Harm is acknowledged, but the offense is understood in its larger, regrettable, context. This "knowing with" is thus an *agreement* about what transpired, expressed by the offended party from the side of lament and from the offending party from the side of empathy. As such, we consider this an inadequate account of forgiveness, but it does rather aptly illustrate the Christian process of interpersonal confession. When Christians confess their sins to one another they are seeking a *knowing with* or an *agreement about* the situation between forgiven and forgiver alike, on the basis of a judgment of grace in Christ.

Perhaps it is odd to speak of a forgiver making a confession, but in a very important sense this is what a forgiver seeks to do. An expression of forgiveness for sin is not offered on the basis of moral high ground but in agreement with the Yes and No of God in Christ. Without disavowing the responsibility to discern perpetrator from victim, a church must recall that neither a self-grounded confession nor a self-grounded pardon are particularly Christian.[54] In the grace of Christ there is freedom *from* self-justification and judgment, and freedom *for* a community wherein one can hope

---

[51]See O. Michel, "ὁμολογέω, ἐξομολογέω, ἀνθομολογέομαι, ὁμολογία, ὁμολογουμένως," in *Theological Dictionary of the New Testament*, ed. Gerhard Kittel and Gerhard Friedrich, trans. Geoffrey W. Bromiley (Grand Rapids: Eerdmans, 1967), 5:199-220.

[52]See *CD* IV/1, 572. It would be here that we encounter Barth's equivalent to what Miroslav Volf calls "remembering truthfully." See Miroslav Volf, *The End of Memory: Remembering Rightly in a Violent World* (Grand Rapids: Eerdmans, 2006), 51-65, especially 64-65, 75.

[53]See Konstan, *Before Forgiveness*, 23-29, 41.

[54]See *CD* IV/1, 575-76, 611-13, and *ChrL*, 58-59.

to be both helped and held to account. The church is meant to be a community in which such interpersonal confession and forgiveness of sin are most richly and hopefully embedded.

When he comes to Jesus' parable of the proud Pharisee and the penitent publican, Barth makes the standard remark about the only way forward being "the way of the real publican," but he also very tellingly adds the unique observation that "the most evil Pharisaism of all" is "the Pharisaism of the publican," which is the way of "self-chosen humility" often guised in the "clever psychology" of "weariness with the world."[55] Barth's remonstrations on this score evoke a natural follow-up question to Jesus' parable: What happens when "real publicans" turn to one another after prayer? As it regards the Lord's Table, Barth leads us to believe that they must "honestly and seriously try to hear and perhaps hear the voice of the Lord . . . and then try to hear, and perhaps actually hear, the voice of the others."[56] An agreement about the offense may not be immediately attainable or even foreseeably possible, but there is still more meaning in an account of forgiveness and reconciliation that has such a hope in view than in one that does not.

In regard to those circumstances in which a genuine meeting of offender and offended is possible, Beverly Flanagan names three possible outcomes: it may turn out (1) that the offender was both wrong and responsible, (2) that the offender was wrong and yet both parties held some responsibility or (3) that both the parties were both wrong and responsible.[57] Left out of Flanagan's analysis is the possibility of a reversal in which (4) the confronter of a wrongdoing is discovered to have been in the wrong, or (5) no wrong occurred apart from a misunderstanding. Regardless, the point lit up for us in Flanagan's observation is this: in a community where the confrontation is aimed at mutual confession of Christ—and is based in his forgiveness—there should be the freedom for such a discernment process to unfold. In circumstances where the confession of Christ is not shared, such agreement should still be encouraged and sought where possible, and may even be considered a work of the Holy Spirit who intercedes for our groaning and

---

[55]*CD* IV/1, 617-19; see also Lk 18:10-17, and *CD* IV/1, 404.

[56]*CD* IV/1, 684.

[57]See Beverly Flanagan, *Forgiving the Unforgivable: Overcoming the Bitter Legacy of Intimate Wounds* (New York: Wiley Publishing, 1992), 109-10.

guides into truth. Those unguided by Christian convictions ought to benefit from Christian engagement, and even before the gospel is articulated verbally there may be a considerable witness that takes place.

Of course, this is not to deny that there are manifold ways confrontation of wrongdoing can go badly, within the church or without. In fact, experience tells us that a congregation accustomed to confession of sin may find its own unique modes of abuse and misuse. Quoting Bonhoeffer, Jones observes, "On the one hand, the 'act of confession can easily turn into exhibitionism.' On the other hand, 'gossip is usually the worst evil in the congregation.'"[58] Given these (and many other) perils, in a competitive and reputation-obsessed environment we can understand why it is considered safer simply to keep one's sins and struggles to oneself, or to keep confession general and anonymous. Indeed, private forgiveness is often preferred to the forgiveness that seeks engagement and an agreed-upon confession. But here we have a reminder to invoke the mercy of Christ upon the entire process, and to look to be churches that perpetually do the same. We will explore this further by delineating connections and distinctions between confession and apology.

The apology phenomenon in Western culture has been broad and shallow. A general suspicion of apologies has arisen due to the fact that exposure to it often relates to the public-relations concerns of celebrities and politicians. Such public relations tend to be concerned neither with the *public* nor with *relations*, but with amplification and vindication of the self.[59] This is no anomalous cultural triviality. As Aaron Lazare puts it,

> Examples of failed apologies are everywhere. When an acquaintance says to you, "I apologize for whatever I may have done," he or she has failed to apologize adequately, because he or she has not acknowledged the offense and may not even believe an offense was committed. Another common example is the statement, "if you were hurt, I am sorry." Not only does this statement begin with a conditional acknowledgement of the offense . . . but it even suggests that your sensitivity may be the problem. . . . With failed apologies growing in prevalence . . . it is no wonder that many observers of the American scene have grown cynical about apologies, seeing them either as efforts to manipulate

---

[58]Jones, *Embodying Forgiveness*, 19, quoting Dietrich Bonhoeffer, *Spiritual Care*, trans. J. C. Rochelle (Philadelphia: Fortress, 1985), 39-40.
[59]See this point in Wannenwetsch, *Political Worship*, 321.

others or as shallow attempts by the offenders to free themselves from guilt. But I have another view of this phenomenon. I see the proliferation of pseudo-apologies as eloquent testimony of the power of "real" apologies. In fact, I believe pseudo-apologies are parasitical on that power.[60]

Pseudo-apologies like these are a prevalent means of avoiding not only true confession, but also repentance, reparation and commitment to a new future.[61]

Lazare offers a very perceptive analysis of the problem and a good deal of practical corrective wisdom, but his diagnosis is rather different from Barth's when it comes to naming the "power" of real apology. In Lazare's view, what is needed is the growth of virtues such as "honesty, generosity, humility, commitment, courage, and sacrifice"—in other words, to have true apologies we need people with the internal means available to transcend not only their own offenses, but also whatever societal and personal conditions aided them.[62] Certainly it may often be the case that our better convictions lead to a confession of wrong, but are we willing to make a rule out of this? Must an offender be morally superior to his or her own past self, and quite possibly to the victim, in order to make a real apology? We would not want to downplay the importance of the virtues Lazare recommends, but his account does leave something to be desired in contrast to a life of confession that invokes the power and mercy of Christ.

There are two factors that might be said to separate Christian confession from parasitic forgeries; namely, the priority of forgiveness upon the enterprise and the hope for seeing through initial exploratory attempts to true agreement in Christ. Given the many ways that an apology can fall short, we can see the benefit of combining the precedence of mercy with the freedom it brings to refine an apology's accuracy together over time. As Lazare observes, even inadequately motivated apologies may yet "have their place in the world of reconciliation":

These "strategic" apologies—motivated by the offender's attempt to change how others perceive them or keep their relationships intact or enhance their social stature—are valuable even if the offenders do not exhibit or experience shame, guilt, and empathy. . . . To believe that a "pragmatic" apology is

---

[60]Lazare, *On Apology*, 8-9, 22-23.
[61]Ibid., 9.
[62]Ibid., 10.

somehow less truthful or less effective than a more impassioned one is to value style over substance, as if we believe that the manner in which an apology is delivered is more important than the goals it seeks to achieve.[63]

Indeed, if we were to refuse to proceed until a confession was adequately motivated or articulated we might ensure that it never occurred at all, thereby stifling if not suffocating the ministry of reconciliation altogether. On other accounts we might reach a stalemate at this point, but with faith in the establishment of grace by Christ, forgiveness may precede the requital of confession and be expressed in some form even before its own fullest expression is possible.

At the same time, a naive acceptance of any and all apologies may settle for something other than truth and reconciliation precisely at the point when a reconciliation is being pretended. Forbearance will appear to do this at times. Because of the precedence of mercy, forgivers will often forbear shortfalls of confession and will often accept that which is but a pale reflection of a truthful apology—but this is no reason to make shallow apologies normative. The forgiveness given freely in Christ will not be immune to manipulative apologies, but properly conceived it will be less likely to presume to have found its fullness in them.

As sociologist Pumla Gobodo-Madikizela asserts, "A genuine apology focuses on the feelings of the other rather than on how the one who is apologizing is going to benefit in the end. It seeks to acknowledge full responsibility for the act, and does not use self-serving language to justify the behaviour of the person asking forgiveness."[64] Ideally, confessors of wrongdoing will give their forgivers the room to reiterate that the "actions can never be regarded as part of what it means to be human," even as they open the door to new relationship and "the possibility of transformation." "Managed carefully," she observes, "dialogue condemns—but not too hastily, lest it foreshorten the accountability process and, perversely, excuse the criminal by dismissing him into the category of the hopelessly, radically other."[65] With this Gobodo-Madikizela offers a very insightful sociological perspective, and its veracity is

---

[63]Ibid., 156-57.
[64]Pumla Gobodo-Madikizela, *A Human Being Died That Night: A South African Woman Confronts the Legacy of Apartheid* (New York: Mariner Books, 2004), 98-99.
[65]Ibid., 103 and 119.

illuminated (and put in different words) by the call to the Lord's Table and his Prayer: There, forgiver and forgiven seek a common confession in Christ and an agreement with his judgment of grace, one from the angle of contrition and the other from the angle of forgiveness.

Obviously this can break down in many ways, and putting it in Christian language does not give the apology process any special immunity from the contingencies involved. Indeed, Barth observes that it is a fear of moral and doctrinal deliberation that often paralyzes the Christian community, brings it to a retreat into generalities, fosters denial of the fundamental issues at stake and renders moot not only its witness but its self-awareness of the gospel![66] In confession, the crushing burden of earnest is replaced with the yoke of faith. Forgiveness is neither a foolproof plan nor a quick-fix to the grievous situation in which we find ourselves as sinful people in a world of enmity. In the church there is a unique call and freeing grounds for much forbearance and grace. In the church there is always a call to faith, to a freely shared forgiveness that daily invokes Christ and trusts the Holy Spirit for direction and empowerment for whatever else may come. As Lois Malcolm suggests, in the freedom of Christ we do not pretend to be able to sort things out instantaneously, but we do "find ourselves in the 'space' of God's reign of justice and mercy, a 'space' created and permeated by the Spirit, which makes our forgiveness of one another—as both victims and perpetrators—possible."[67]

For the Christian, forgiveness precedes holiness; grace goes before sanctity. Jacques Derrida poses a penetrating question when he asks, What is forgiveness if it is only applied when something is deemed forgivable? Interestingly, led by his reflections to consider forgiveness an impossibility, Derrida gestures toward it nonetheless. Given the alternatives, he even suggests that the only unforgivable sin might be to insist on the impossibility of forgiveness despite the fact that it somehow seems to have entered human possibility. This is resonant with Barth's conclusion, arrived at from faith in the risen Christ, which is to say that we cannot decide whether a sin is mortal or venial, or whether penitence is satisfactory or not, before we offer

---

[66]See *CD* IV/3.2, 814-15.
[67]Lois Malcolm, "Forgiveness as New Creation: Christ and the Moral Life Revisited," in *Christology and Ethics*, ed. LeRon Shults and Brent Waters (Grand Rapids: Eerdmans, 2010), 121.

the grace of forgiveness.[68] In forgiveness we are not looking for a way to declare something pardonable. In confrontation we are not considering whether to forgive. Forgiveness is freely given, and this does not preclude judgment, but opens it up to Jesus. Gone is the need for the confessor of sin to dilute personal responsibility on one hand or dismiss proper discernment on the other—all in the desperate attempt to garner exoneration. Gone is the need for the forgiver to withhold forgiveness out of fear that there will then be no truth, justice or healing. Christ is invoked to direct confrontation and confession. The offender is pursued by the offended within the freedom of forgiveness and not besides. Those outside the faith who are forgiven in this way may find themselves in touch with the gospel for the first time. Those who forgive each other in faith will find themselves at home in Christ's ministry of reconciliation.

In many cases of confronted sin and confession of wrong there will arise between those parties involved not only an awareness of other infractions in the relationship but also of their shared complicity in systems of thought and structures of enmity that provided the scaffolding for the sinful episode in the first place. A striking illustration of this is Pumla Gobodo-Madikizela's postapartheid encounter with one of its most infamous perpetrators, Eugene de Kock, also known as "Prime Evil," wherein she was able to see *both* the depth of the evil that he perpetrated *and* her smaller but nonetheless highly significant part in it—all without desecrating the memory of the victims or excusing de Kock's actions. She did not exonerate him but saw the powers implicated in his evil, noting "that the same society that had created de Kock, that had accepted his murderous protection of their privilege, had ostracized him and was now standing in judgment of him."[69] As we have already discussed, this is far better than calling him inhuman, or naming his a radical evil. It does not decrease his responsibility to say there is even more culpability to go around than was originally thought. Responsibility is not a zero-sum game with a total that is already clear.

Consider another illustration from South Africa, this time told by Antjie Krog in regard to an "Amnesty for Apathy" brought before the Truth and

---

[68]See Jacques Derrida, *On Cosmopolitanism and Forgiveness*, trans. Mark Dooley and Michael Hughes (London: Routledge, 2001), 32-34, along with *CD* IV/2, 492, and *CD* IV/3.2, 587.

[69]Gobodo-Madikizela, *A Human Being*, 34.

Reconciliation Commission on the brink of its 1997 amnesty application deadline. In what turned out to be both a rebuke and an adulation of the Commission, on that day a rather poignant application came forward from six youths *who claimed to have done nothing*. When the youths were pressed for an explanation, they explained they had "neglected to take part in the liberation struggle" and therefore stood "as a small group representative of millions of apathetic people who didn't do the right thing."[70] Though offered in jest, the application also stood as a vicarious confession on behalf of the complicit masses who might otherwise have granted themselves amnesty even from the need for amnesty. On the other hand, did it also call into question the whole process altogether? If everyone is complicit, how can anyone be held responsible for what occurred? Might a process of discernment lead to a confession that is really a statement of relative guilt by association?

To an important degree, a situation of confession must stick to the particularities of the offense at hand, even if it becomes the occasion for more widespread realizations. An apology that seeks to dilute its responsibility in measurements of grand complicity is likely an evasion, whereas a full confession that *also* laments the lordless powers and systems of enmity in which it was entangled might lead not only itself but its community to deeper repentance. Indeed, we should *expect* that when we confess (or even forgive) a particular sin we will also likely end up confessing a more or less active participation in the systems of enmity all around.[71] Even if we are relatively blameless in the causal structures of that system, we will not cling to our purity but will follow Christ into the mess with the prayer for kingdom come.

None of this requires that those involved in a particular confrontation are required to make apologies for everyone within the system of enmity in which they are intertwined. This would more rightly put us in the realm of lament, and while this has a place it should not be turned into a distraction from facing the particularities of sin and harm in question.[72] A particular exchange of confession and forgiveness will involve substantial healing in

[70]Antjie Krog, *Country of My Skull: Guilt, Sorrow, and the Limits of Forgiveness in the New South Africa* (Toronto: Times Books, 1998), 159.
[71]See *CD* IV/1, 396, 406, 771, *CD* IV/2, 397 and *CD* IV/3.1, 468.
[72]See *CD* IV/1, 771.

its own right, and ought to be celebrated and sought after in that regard—even and especially by those who are taken up in prayer to be zealous for an expansion of that healing.[73] Who knows if such loving attention to detail might open up avenues to peace otherwise unaffected by large-scale revolution? Every shared confession opens up language on which to build unity. For all that forbearance may mean as a first manifestation of the free gift of forgiveness, it is here in the humble process of engaging one another in the act of confession that forgiveness finds its most vocal and visible expression. Jacques Derrida was right to ask what forgiveness could possibly mean "without a shared language," since "two sides must agree on the nature of the fault" and "must know consciously who is guilty of which evil toward whom"—which means that offender and offended need some reason to "plunge . . . lucidly . . . into the night of the unintelligible" and take on the risks that such agreement requires.[74]

Some will suggest that there are occasions where the sin is just too horrible to be forgiven—let alone comprehended—by its victims, perpetrators and bystanders, but no matter how horrific our sin in this world, the horror is only illumined by the greatest horror of all: the death of the incarnate Son. We learn the gravity of our situation precisely in the lengths to which God goes to address it. And "when we consider what the debt is, we see that no other reaction to it is adequate but the divine forgiveness."[75] To withhold forgiveness is to exalt oneself as the Lord to whom all confessions must be given, rather than coming under the lordship of Christ in confrontation of sin by grace. Christ does not ask for a pretended peace, but frees forgivers for peaceable conflict in the fellowship of the Holy Spirit. To suggest that the Christian community is the *home* of true confession and forgiveness is not to say that it never happens in other contexts, but that Christ lights up these scenes of confession and forgiveness for their provisional goodness, so that the Spirit led should notice them and engage appropriately. Kindness breaks the cycle of violence, and while there is no guarantee of reciprocity in this fallen world, it is kindness that leads to repentance (Rom 2:4).

---

[73]This point about seeking substantial healing rather than giving up because we can't achieve the totality is one that is wonderfully made in Francis A Schaeffer, *True Spirituality* (Wheaton, IL: Tyndale House Publishers, 1971). See especially chapters ten through thirteen.
[74]Derrida, *On Cosmopolitanism*, 48-49.
[75]CD IV/1, 484.

PREREQUISITE FOR A GIFT? FORGIVENESS AND REPENTANCE

The dilemma whether repentance precedes forgiveness is as old as the acts themselves. In the Synoptic Gospels even Jesus appears to be of two minds on the issue: Matthew 18:22 has him telling Peter to forgive a brother's recurrent sin "seventy-seven times," and Luke 17:4 has him adding the condition that the brother says "I repent" each time. The early church's concern over deathbed confessions and the salvation of "the lapsed" indicates that they felt divine forgiveness was conditioned by penitence. Sociological arguments exist that suggest an order in this regard, but can be found persuasive in either direction.[76] On one hand, to insist that forgiveness precede repentance might diminish genuine engagement and promote a lack of respect for oneself and the other. On the other hand, to insist that repentance precede forgiveness might turn the decisive act of penitence into a more trivial and momentary display than it often needs to be, especially where enmity runs deep. The complexities are numerous, and sloppiness about forgiveness will likely aggravate them.

A further complexity is that repentance may frequently be directed to God without any expression toward others. Andrew Sung Park argues that Christian treatments of forgiveness can tend to favor offenders by privileging an experience of freedom from guilt over a shared freedom from sin and an amelioration of its effects. With attention to the Korean experience of han, Park raises our sensitivity to those situations where a perpetrator's "preoccupation with their own turning away from sin to God" may be trumpeted to the neglect of an attempt to "see the side of those they have wronged, genuinely caring about their pain and seeking forgiveness from them."[77] We should take particular note of Park's observation of a post-Christian context where cheap tolerance borrows so much from Christian rhetoric. A construal that puts all its emphasis on a crisis moment wherein a repentant act ushers in an expression of forgiveness may well be settling for a climactic experience of piety at the expense of rich involvement in Christ's ministry of reconciliation. The focus becomes the divine *exchange* rather than the freedom that Christ's forgiveness opens up. As a means of

---

[76]See both arguments put cursorily and illustrated for their complexity in Murphy, *Getting Even*, 36-37, 78-86. See also Konstan, *Before Forgiveness*, 8, and Anthony Bash, *Forgiveness and Christian Ethics* (Cambridge: Cambridge University Press, 2007), 63.

[77]Andrew Sung Park, *The Wounded Heart of God: The Asian Concept of Han and the Christian Doctrine of Sin* (Nashville: Abingdon Press, 1993), 90-92.

gaining exoneration, repentance becomes a self-serving shortcut. So it can be seen that withholding forgiveness until repentance is no more a guarantor against shortcuts than granting forgiveness as a precursor.[78] Observed phenomena on either side of the dilemma do not decide the matter for us. What, then, does Barth's theology suggest?

In the final baptism part-volume of Barth's *Doctrine of Reconciliation*, he referenced the divine-human relationship and said that repentance does not *condition* forgiveness, but is in fact "the first natural breath in the air of the forgiveness which has already come to pass and which is already present to men." John's baptism of repentance was one that could "only look forward to forgiveness" as a "free, uncontrived act of God," but with Jesus' baptism (and subsequent work) we now look *back* upon forgiveness the same way, even as we look ahead to its further actualization in time.[79] Repentance does not *cause* but *relies upon* forgiveness. It is one of the "moments of the new freedom" that comes in the "new page which is opened with the forgiveness of sins."[80] Worldly sorrow leads to death *because it never quite emerges from the darkness of guilt, shame, fear and condemnation*; godly sorrow leads to repentance because it *arises from the light and love of Christ*.[81]

In relation to God, our repentance relies on a confession of truth that is Jesus Christ. In this there arises the confrontation of our sin, and if we try to either avoid that confrontation or wallow in it we may be the beneficiaries of his longsuffering forbearance without really apprehending his gift of forgiveness. The forgiveness is already there. Where there is repentance it has sprung from apprehension of it. Where there is not, the forgiveness is not withheld so much as held at bay; it is given lip service but not realization. With that in mind, the question before us is this: How does this translate to our human fellowships?

Does interpersonal forgiveness precede or prompt repentance? On the interpersonal level things may certainly be more complicated, particularly since we are talking about a relationship between sinful creatures rather than their relationship with their Holy Creator. When it comes to the relation of

---

[78]See also Anderson, *Shape of Practical Theology*, 294-96.
[79]*CD* IV/4, 81-82 and 57.
[80]*CD* IV/1, 598. The others Barth names involve perseverance and humility.
[81]See *CD* IV/1, 361-62 and 2 Cor 7:10.

one aspect of the ministry of reconciliation to another, however, the burden
of proof should be on that construal that alters the relationships rather than
maintains them. If people participate in Christ's ministry of reconciliation by
faith in the prior gift of divine forgiveness, it would be odd to insist that interpersonal forgiveness depends upon repentance. But if a Christian is con-
victed of a sin, it would be doubly odd to wait to be forgiven before repenting.
In Matthew 5:23-24 it is the offender who is led by the imperatives of worship
to approach the offended for reconciliation. In Matthew 18:15 it is the offended who initiates the conversation. At this point it may come as no surprise that we will not try to define a phenomenological *chronology* but to
explore a practical-theological *relation*. In a Christian community there is no
rigid order. But as far as the two are related, it is the promise and presence of
forgiveness that makes way for repentance.

Perhaps the main concern for those who would *require* that forgiveness
wait until after repentance is that it otherwise becomes cheap grace and
closes off the opportunity for confrontation and correction. As discussed,
however, forgiveness can be free without entailing ignorance of the days that
have gone before. In fact, as we have argued, we cannot even begin to face
our sins for what they are until they are seen in light of Jesus' mercy.

A legitimate practical concern arises at this point, however, and that has
to do with the perpetuation of victimhood that seems to be implied when
the imperative is self-giving and forgiving love. But this is founded on a
misconception of the call to cruciform discipleship. As a living sacrifice the
Christian does not simply submit to fate but carries a cross at Jesus' command.
An abused person should not be led by an abstraction like "unconditional
forgiveness" to piously and quietly embrace the abuser. Self-giving love also
involves receiving the other, which in such a case does not require the perpetual reception of drunken blows but actually entails the freedom to seek
help where needed, not only for one's own sake but for the other's. Forgiving
an abuser in Christ will free one up to hope rather than lock one up in fate,
prompting the search for a respected third party who could offer assistance
toward gracious confrontation and corrective accountability.

Even if the abusive party is unrepentant, the result is not unforgiveness,
but an acknowledgment of nonreconciliation. The unrepentant offender
who resists forgiveness becomes responsible for freezing the reconciliation

process as it stands. The forgiver's response will be forbearance, but this does not necessitate denial of the circumstance in which this places them. Further confrontation may ensue, this time involving others and likely taking the form of an aim for healthy accountability, safe boundaries, preferably nonviolent resistance and, where appropriate, submission to the social justice system. But this will be informed by the sought-after mutuality in Christ that stems from the freedom of mercy confessed, rather than from a self-righteous posture of superiority or manipulation. Forgiving the abuser is not the perpetuation of victimhood but the free offer of further reconciliation.[82]

Miroslav Volf answered objections to free forgiveness rather poignantly when he observed that "forgiveness *after* justice is not much different from forgiveness *outside* justice," since both entail "treating the offender as if he had not committed the offense." The difference, he observes, is that after justice "one would *not* be going beyond one's duty in offering forgiveness," but would actually be wrong *not* to forgive![83] To withhold forgiveness until after an acceptable expression of confession and repentance would be to define forgiveness as little more than a declaration of satisfaction with the contrition and change displayed. Such a thing is important to reconciliation, but is not to be equated with forgiveness itself. It is better to say that the sharing of God's free forgiveness is a precursor and partner to the whole journey of reconciliation, which involves a series of related activities that depend on each other but that are not ours to arrange sequentially.

Barth's concern is to relay the historicity of grace without succumbing it to an interpersonally manageable system of exchange. Overly systematized, an order of reconciliation would lose its unique character within the churchly dynamic of *faith seeking mutual understanding together in the context of enmity*, powered by the Prince of Peace. Where such faith is not commonly held, all the more reason for the forgiver to freely open the way to reconciliation in Christ. Thus we are inclined to say that forgiveness both precedes and follows repentance, to speak of its beginnings in self-giving love and its flourishing in reciprocity of reconciliation.

---

[82]See also Anderson, *Shape of Practical Theology*, 293.

[83]Miroslav Volf, "Forgiveness, Reconciliation, and Justice: A Christian Contribution to a More Peaceful Social Environment," in Helmick and Petersen, *Forgiveness and Reconciliation*, 40-41.

Charles Moule gestures in this direction with his reflections on the "as we forgive" of the Lord's Prayer:

> However eager the forgiver may be to offer forgiveness, it cannot be received, and reconciliation cannot be achieved, without repentance. But repentance cannot earn the forgiveness or make the recipient worthy of it, for, by definition, forgiveness is always an act of unearned generosity.... That forgiveness is conditioned by repentance is true, because reconciliation is a personal relationship, and cannot be achieved without responsiveness on both sides of the relationship. But that forgiveness is earned by repentance or deeds of reparation is not true ... [and] to insist on appropriate response is not to rob the forgiveness of its character as an unmerited free gift.[84]

George Soares-Prabhu brings us even closer to our construal with his depiction of an interdependence of imperatives rather than a strictly causal sequence:

> Genuine forgiveness, genuinely accepted, leads to the repentance of the person forgiven—which in turn feeds back into and energises the original act of forgiveness. If this spiral of interhuman forgiveness breaks down something obviously has gone wrong. Either our forgiveness has not been genuine; or the person to whom the forgiveness is directed does not want to be forgiven.[85]

Barth puts forgiver and repenter, victim and perpetrator, together under the reconciling work of Christ, where repentance is clearly a correlate to true confession and forgiveness. In this he honors the complexity of interpersonal situations but does not allow sin or its correction to take a definitive role. Forgiveness is a *response*, but it is a response to the provision and command of Christ. The further work of Christ's reconciliation is sought in freedom. If repentance does garner a fuller expression of forgiveness, it is to be celebrated and will make for a unique milestone in the reconciliation of those concerned. But it is like a flowering of forgiveness and not the dam burst after it has been withheld.

The one who confesses sin in Christ knows the need is for more than a second chance or a do-over; the need is for his new creation. But what new

---

[84]C. F. D. Moule, "'... As We Forgive ...': A Note on the Distinction Between Deserts and Capacity in the Understanding of Forgiveness," in *Essays in New Testament Interpretation* (Cambridge: Cambridge University Press, 1982), 282, 285.

[85]George Soares-Prabhu, "'As We Forgive': Interhuman Forgiveness in the Teaching of Jesus," *Concilium* 184 (1986): 64.

creation is there apart from Jesus Christ? After witnessing the Rwandan genocide, Roméo Dallaire's guttural cry for a "transfusion of humanity" indicated not only the need for a miracle but also recognized that if something new is to come about in the ebb and flow of history it is going to involve a good deal of sacrifice and effort.[86] This brings us back to a consideration of the cruciform nature of an account wherein forgiveness is given freely. As Moule observes,

> Forgiveness and repentance are both costly. Just as the wronged party will be less than his full self as a person if he retaliates and is not willing to pay for his gift of forgiveness, so the offender will be less than his full self if he does not wish to compensate. Notoriously, real repentance "feels like death." Repentance cannot take place except by the penitent's stooping low and losing all *amour propre* and giving up all thoughts of deserving forgiveness. And the very repudiation of any attempt to pay turns out (by a strange paradox) to be itself infinitely costly.[87]

There is no doubt that Jesus puts the onus on his followers to love the enemy at cost to themselves, compelled by his love, by hope in his resurrection and by faith in his reconciliation against all odds. As discussed, an account of interpersonal forgiveness that allows for confrontation and accountability puts to rest some of the fears of a victim-perpetuating account of abstract and unconditional amnesty, but we do need to return to the question of how a forgiver confronts someone who is resiliently unrepentant. This will lead us into the next section on the place of discipline in the church's ministry of reconciliation.

In response to confrontation of sin, Barth explains that any "unwillingness to repent is the constant renewal of [one's] sin."[88] The implication of this is that if free interpersonal forgiveness meets a refusal to repent, it does not turn back on itself and withdraw its prior offer; instead it confronts a new strain of sin, now performed as a constant addition to the original. To return to our example briefly, then, we can see that it is one thing to confront an abuser for an *occasion* of physical abuse, and another thing to confront a *sustained upholding* (let alone recurrence) of that abusiveness in the face of

---

[86]Roméo Dallaire with Brent Beardsley, *Shake Hands with the Devil: The Failure of Humanity in Rwanda* (Toronto: Vintage Canada, 2003), 522.

[87]C. F. D. Moule, "The Theology of Forgiveness," in *Essays in New Testament Interpretation*, 253-54, 256.

[88]*CD* IV/1, 258.

urges to get help and accountability. The abused forgiver would be directed by Jesus' words to seek a community that can offer that accountability, and in the event of resistance that community must be prepared to discern and confront not only the sin but the added strain of impenitence or false repentance as well. Perhaps in the process it will be revealed that the offender is imprisoned by oppressive addictions and psychological trauma. Perhaps it will be revealed that greater complicities are at stake. In any case, if forgiveness is held back until demands are met, the confrontation and confession process is more likely to be hampered and confined to the logic of eros exchange rather than freed in hope for agape and healing. Where forgiveness is withheld, repentance will be harder to discern for sincerity. In that event, getting to the bottom of recurrent sin may likely be *more* difficult to address, not less. The alternative is to offer forgiveness to the unrepentant. In the face of unrepentance, that offer takes the form of further, hopefully loving, confrontation.[89]

As Gregory Jones argues in critique of Richard Swinburne, an "insistence on the causal priority of repentance preclude[s] . . . from adequately articulating the ways in which the priority of God's forgiveness actually creates new social contexts for repentance (and hence ongoing forgiveness of sins) to occur."[90] It is better to forgive and, in the freedom of that mercy, to have a new confrontation if it turns out that penitence has been false or repentance has faltered. Of course, the strength required to forbear until an adequate response is forthcoming is often precisely what victims are in no position to hold. Jesus' victim-favoring but truth-seeking exhortation to community discernment and accountability is where such a forgiver is told to look in the act of trusting healing and reconciliation, justice and reform, to God. Trusted to Christ's ministry of reconciliation in this way, an offender will in turn hopefully be freed by forgiveness rather than manipulated by it, and if there is a hope for them to walk through the door of grace it will be because the truth was spoken in love. We pursue the ministry of reconciliation from a place of shared grace, or we do not pursue it at all. This sharing

---

[89]For further practical analysis of the ways this can happen, see Elaine Enns and Ched Myers, *Ambassadors of Reconciliation*, vol. 2, *Diverse Christian Practices of Restorative Justice and Peacemaking* (Maryknoll, NY: Orbis Books, 2009), 1-46.
[90]Jones, *Embodying Forgiveness*, 84-87, 152-53.

of grace cannot be coerced but, at the same time, recognition of the unique qualities of a Christian community require that churches know what to do when they have brothers and sisters in their midst who by their actions refuse such engagement. This is a considerable challenge for an ecclesial account of forgiveness, and is the subject of the next section.

CORRECTION AND ACCOUNTABILITY: FORGIVENESS AND DISCIPLINE

Knowing full well that he had commanded forgiveness, Jesus nonetheless told his disciples that there might be occasions to leave a town and "shake off the dust that is on your feet as a testimony against them" (Mk 6:11). It is not unimportant that they were travelers to begin with—and the New Testament would lead us to expect that if there are to be acts of intentional separation they should only come after "making every effort to maintain the unity of the Spirit in the bond of peace" (Eph 4:3)—but this nonetheless raises the issue of recusing the unrepentant from fellowship.[91] Barth's perspective is this: "Temporary separations may be necessary in order that new and better future fellowship may be possible—but only for this reason."[92] To explain this we must recall that Christian confrontation and confession are to operate directly, openly and hopefully within a confessing community that daily shares not an entitlement to grace but faith in the mercy of Jesus Christ. Any separation of fellowship is due to a persistent refusal of *this confessing community*, and not simply due to the occurrence of sin or scandal. If the offender remains unrepentant after a discreet but direct process of mutual accountability and confession, then and only then is the mutual Christian fellowship sundered *as such*. The sin in question is still the relevant manifestation of the offender's nonrepentance— and may itself be the necessitating factor in calling for a time of separation for the sake of safety or unflustered discernment—but the community that considers a formal separation from fellowship will base that decision not on the level of the offense itself, but on the standstill that has been effected in the ministry of reconciliation.

In the event of a separation, an offender might declare that an injustice has been done—even going so far as to defame and accuse the congregation

---

[91]See Mt 10:14; Lk 9:5; Rom 14:19; Heb 12:14.
[92]*ChrL*, 83.

for making the sin itself the reason for the separation—but the community that has made every effort to seek a common confession will look to the Lord for confidence about what has transpired.[93] Myers and Enns note that in Jesus' instructions in Matthew 18 the "victim alone determines whether or not she has been truly 'heard,'" but if the conflict does come to involve the church leadership, then witnesses are deliberately sought to confirm "every word."[94] There is the possibility that a false accusation will have slipped by undetected, and precautions should be taken to avoid the acceptance of false testimony, but there is a certain Christian wisdom in having a system that errs on the side of the victim. Even then, if it decides that a separation is necessary, no matter what accusations are sent its way the church will do everything it can to avoid shaming the offender, and will entrust itself to God's judgment rather than run to vindicate itself at the expense of the other. At the same time, the church should be willing and able to explain itself discreetly, but not in the interest of "public relations" propaganda or according to the premises of competition. It takes no comfort in the separation of the individual, but only in the hope of Christ.[95]

The main heading for this section is *correction* rather than *discipline* because we should not think of church discipline only in terms of its worst-case scenarios. What easily goes unnoticed when we are discussing such things is the fact that "church discipline" normatively proceeds within a positive life of discipleship wherein there is mutual correction and accountability. If the confrontations that take place are met with penitent cooperation, then the mutual accountability and reform proceed with relatively little fanfare. If not, things may get tenuous and dramatic, but these flares of controversy should not be taken to entirely typify church discipline, let alone define it. For Barth, mutual correction in the living congregation is actually rather hopeful. In the best case, when a judgment of grace is received, the person "obeys it, not mechanically impelled from without, but in the freedom which is given" and known "only in . . . togetherness with them, as one of the fellowship of the saints."[96]

---

[93]Jones, *Embodying Forgiveness*, 20, 183, 194-95.
[94]Ched Myers and Elaine Enns, *Ambassadors of Reconciliation*, vol. 1, *New Testament Reflections on Restorative Justice and Peacemaking* (Maryknoll, NY: Orbis Books, 2009), 67.
[95]See *CD* IV/1, 675-77, 683.
[96]*CD* IV/2, 596; see 710.

Such mutuality does not entail a denial of either individual worth or responsibility. Seeing oneself as part of a body means a prayerful desire to contribute to it as a healthy member.

> He cannot take the chance that the brethren will make up for his failures. He cannot think that he is excused because apart from himself there are others who seem to be doing a good job, or more of a good job than a bad one. Nor, if his fellows seem to be doing more of a bad job than a good one, can he think that he is released from any responsibility for these others who are at fault. . . . The existence of the community . . . must always have a new reality and truth, and therefore must always be sought and discovered and practiced anew.[97]

Ideally, the freedom of Christ's grace involves forgiveness on the part of the offended, mutual discernment of wrong, submission to correction on the part of the offender and attention to reform by all those implicated in the deeper lines of enmity revealed.

When this ideal proves unreachable, however, it is highly telling that Jesus recommends a preference for *naming* the grievous division rather than veiling it in false peace, and cloaking it in pretended Christian fellowship. Recall the last resort described by Jesus in Matthew 18:17, wherein he instructs the church to treat the unrepentant offender "as you would a pagan or a tax collector" (NIV). Gregory Jones explains this well:

> Before we move too quickly . . . we need to remember how Jesus treats such "enemies" as Gentiles and tax collectors. He continues to reach out to them, to bring them (back) into the fold of God's covenant of grace. We should not coerce them into the fold, nor should we pretend that the conflict and division do not exist. But neither should we "demonize" them, as we so often want to do with enemies, or turn them into "scapegoats."[98]

Myers and Enns explain that when the resistant party is "redefined as an outsider" Jesus is not to be understood as recommending punishment or "shunning"; rather, he is naming a "change in the community's approach" wherein they take up a "strategy of engagement" according to the lead of Jesus' own treatment of such persons.[99] Love proceeds undaunted and mercy prevails,

---

[97]*ChrL*, 83.
[98]Jones, *Embodying Forgiveness*, 195.
[99]Myers and Enns, *Ambassadors of Reconciliation*, 1:68; see also Mt 11:19.

but pretended Christian communion is not an option. Formally naming a person's resistance to this communion is an act of trusting them to God and refusing to manipulate them against their will. Despite the scandal it confesses (and the risk of public scorn it opens up), such an act is more true to the nature of that communion than an attempt to cover up or to coerce.

In all of this the goal remains reconciliation with the offender, which continues to place invocation-based self-giving and forgiving love at the heart of the encounter. The decision regarding separation is not a condemnation, but a matter of truth in fellowship. Barth is explicit that in such an event the determination "is not that they lack Jesus Christ" but only that in this case "what they lack is obedience to His Holy Spirit."[100] This is no small matter, of course. It may be very difficult. Indeed, as Myers and Enns contend, in cases of criminal or abusive behavior there will be a call for careful cooperation with the justice system and a "nonviolent strategy of defending against a predatory person."[101] This brings us to the question of a church's level of participation with the politics and justice systems of the society in which it is located.

As we have seen, forgiveness does not refuse but redefines confrontation and reform, shifting everything to a new axis, even as it carries on in the history it is given. Barth is very interested to express the uniqueness of Christian community, but he is not interested in forcing a division of church and state wherein the church operates by grace in one realm and the logic of "coercion" in the other.[102] How hypocritical if the church were to disavow the state's methods and claim to be a uniquely operating community, all the while depending upon the state's forces of coercion to afford it its cloistered existence! For Barth, the church and the society are not in "absolute antithesis and mutual exclusion"; in fact "there is no reason in principle why there should not be reciprocity between them" or a desire to see the provisions of governmental authority conform to the measures of justice recommended in Amos and Isaiah and filled in by Jesus Christ.[103]

In fact, in post-Christendom's separation of church and state it is entirely possible that the accountability structures of the state may exceed those of

---

[100]*CD* IV/1, 93; see also 693, 698.
[101]Myers and Enns, *Ambassadors of Reconciliation*, 1:68.
[102]See Carl Reinhold Bråkenhielm, *Forgiveness*, trans. Thor Hall (Minneapolis: Fortress, 1989), 8.
[103]*CD* IV/2, 724.

local churches in provisional functionality or even in terms of situational wisdom.[104] While Barth rejects natural theology and its implications of a moral law incipient within humanity, he nonetheless asserts, "We can and must be prepared to encounter 'parables of the kingdom' in the full biblical sense . . . in the secular sphere."[105] The church seeks to engage with the worldly systems—"wise as serpents and innocent as doves" (Mt 10:16)—from within its own convictions. At the same time, the Christian conviction is that the church, because of its common life of Christ-confession, can function in such a way that is alien to any other citizenship. This does not mean retreat or revolution, but patient and self-giving social action, alongside careful attention to the particular integrity of the Christian communion.

Miroslav Volf contends that "forgiveness does not stand outside of justice" but in fact "presupposes" that there is work to be done, thus ushering in a "process of reconciliation . . . in which the search for justice is an integral and yet subordinate element."[106] So how does this proceed when there are similar efforts going on in society, but on the basis of premises other than those found within Christian faith? Criminal justice lawyer Walter Dickey argues that because Christian forgiveness is concerned with "community, interpersonal wholeness, and social and individual healing," a "restorative justice" system is where it is most at home, such that Christians will seek to promote such a thing in societies where this is not normative.[107] Gregory Jones suggests that Barth's view toward societal justice might be more eclectic than that, perhaps including "elements of retribution, deterrence, and rehabilitation theories" while also "challeng[ing] the adequacy of even thinking in terms of such theories." Jones proposes that a Christian

---

[104]See *CD* IV/3.2, 525, 565, and *CD* IV/2, 725.

[105]*CD* IV/3.1, 117.

[106]Volf, "Forgiveness, Reconciliation, and Justice," 45-47. See also Marilyn McCord Adams, "Forgiveness: A Christian Model," *Faith and Philosophy* 8 (July 1991): 299.

[107]Walter J. Dickey, "Forgiveness and Crime: The Possibilities of Restorative Justice," in *Exploring Forgiveness*, ed. Robert D. Enright and Joanna North (Madison: University of Wisconsin Press, 1998), 107. Timothy Gorringe suggests that for Barth the church takes a posture toward the criminal justice system that prompts it toward restorative justice, and where this is not present, moves to restoratively engage society in that direction. Timothy Gorringe, "Crime, Punishment, and Atonement: Karl Barth on the Death of Christ," in *Commanding Grace: Studies in Karl Barth's Ethics*, ed. Daniel L. Migliore (Grand Rapids: Eerdmans, 2010), 159-60. Katherine Sonderegger argues that Gorringe overlooks the priority of grace in Barth's *Dogmatics*, and sees more complex disparity between grace and law. Sonderegger, "For Us and for Our Salvation: A Response to Timothy Gorringe," in Migliore, *Commanding Grace*, 163-67, 172-73.

residing within a societal arrangement at odds with this vision (either by
leniency or oppression) "ought to work within established social and political contexts to enhance the prospects of reconciliation and, at the very
least, to minimize the deleterious effects of punishment's pain and
domination."[108] This seems correct—and if the church does engage from
within its own convictions it may be able to have a part in revealing flaws
in that system (or its background culture), in supporting and restoring
victims of harm and oppression, and also in aiding the discernment, discipline and rehabilitation of offenders.

So it is that a Christian community looks to be an ambassador of reconciliation, and is discerningly cooperative in provisional systems of justice
without being defined by them.[109] As Barth writes, "If it is to remain the true
Church, it cannot be essentially determined by any of these societies . . .
Christians will always be Christians first, and only then members of a specific culture or state or class or the like."[110] Illustrative here is Paul's exhortation to the members of the church in Corinth to not take each other to
court.[111] This is not to be stretched into an argument for a cloistered existence, but recommends itself as an indication of Paul's trust in the power
and presence of the reconciling Christ. It certainly does not preclude all
submission to the societal justice system. In fact, Paul's indication in another
context is that the church should be operating in the ministry of reconciliation while *also* aiming to submit to the provisional good of government.[112]
Should a church be found harboring a child abuser from legal justice because it thinks itself more capable of handling things? On the other hand,
should a church harbor a person who it deems innocent and in danger of
injustice or persecution? It would be wrong to refuse solidarity with the
world in concerns of justice, and at the same time it would be foolish to trust
entirely to the machinations of social progress, presuming total obeisance

---

[108]Jones, *Embodying Forgiveness*, 275-76. See also Matthew Rose, *Ethics with Barth: God, Metaphysics and Morals* (Surrey, UK: Ashgate, 2010), 166, and Oliver O'Donovan *The Desire of the Nations: Rediscovering the Roots of Political Theology* (New York: Cambridge University Press, 1999), 214.
[109]Such political involvement may resemble something like Olga Botcharova's "two-track diplo-macy." See Botcharova, "Implementation of Track Two Diplomacy: Developing a Model of Forgiveness," in Helmick and Petersen, *Forgiveness and Reconciliation*, 274.
[110] *CD* IV/1, 703.
[111]See 1 Cor 5:12–6:11.
[112]See Rom 13, *CD* IV/3.1, 157 and *CD* IV/3.2, 490.

without remainder.[113] The church is neither *aloof from* nor *defined by* its context. By engaging prayerfully it will hope to be a witness of the special visibility of the church, especially as it joins in the societal pursuit of justice and goes above and beyond, taking greater responsibility for compassionate restoration of offender and offended alike.[114]

Returning our attention to the inner life of the church, then, one issue that remains to be addressed is the situation wherein there *is* a repentant party who nonetheless persists in a recurrent sin. As previously indicated, we do well in such cases to confront not just the sin but the condition of "relapse" as well.[115] Compassion needs to be extended not only to victims but also to those caught in the grip of lordless powers. Barth warned against dealing with recurrent sin by legalistically "relapsing into the ways of thinking of later Judaism" that led to the sacrament of penance.[116] But this did not preclude recognition of the benefits of heightened accountability. As it proceeds, the Christian life remains substantially as it was: the repentant but recurrent offender calls for daily invocation and obedience, upheld in the richness of up-building community. New every morning, this community proceeds as self-aware but hopeful because it relies not on its own faithfulness but the Lord's (Lam 3:19-21). As William Telfer relays from Peter Lombard (and, in turn, Ambrose): "If absolution is followed by a repetition of the same sin, it does not prove that the penitence was vain. It brought hallowing for a time, which, though lost, is ready to revive at a subsequent conversion."[117] There will be recurrences of past temptation and sin—what Barth calls the "sorry remains" and relics of the old self, old wrongs and age-old enmity—but the way forward is neither a private battle nor a system of penance; rather, it is reciprocity in the ministry of reconciliation, mediated by Christ and alive in the church by his Spirit.[118]

What faith in God's mercy is not to become is a means of withdrawal, so that it might be said against fellow believers, "You were no help to me in my

---

[113]See *CD* IV/3.1, 91, 120-21.

[114]*CD* IV/3.2, 741.

[115]*CD* IV/3.1, 464.

[116]*CD* IV/2, 567-69.

[117]W. Telfer, *The Forgiveness of Sins: An Essay in the History of Christian Doctrine and Practice* (London: SCM Press, 1959), 102.

[118]*CD* IV/3.2, 571.

history which was interwoven with yours. . . . You only appeared to help, but
in reality harmed me. . . . You confirmed me in that from which you ought
to have kept me. And you kept me from that in which I needed confirmation." At the same time, as suggested by Barth's subsequent lines, neither
should Christians consider forgiveness a means of manipulative altruism, so
that it might be said, "In your great righteousness, or simply because you
were the stronger, you pushed me to the wall. You humiliated and wounded
me. You trampled over me contemptuously and perhaps even derisively,
pursuing your own ends."[119]

The people who confess and forgive sin between each other are those who
confess participation in a community that "will not avoid the care and effort
and labor and inward and outward conflict which it costs sincerely to build
only on the Son of God who gathers and protects and maintains it as His
community."[120] We do well to notice when the community has a breakdown
of hope and trust in this regard. The church cannot seek to spread the gospel
without seeking to be this community.

Unique in the world, then, this is a people rallied in faith to invoke the
freedom and continuity of Jesus' most basic guarantee: that "they will
always be awakened again."[121] From this point of view, the direst eventu-
ality is not the recurrence of sin but the "lost and false situation" of
stepping away from this faith, of denouncing this encounter with Christ.[122]
If unrepentant sin occurs among its members, the Christian community
continues to love, but does not pretend the mutual fellowship of shared
forgiveness and reconciliation is unbroken. In Christ it is always looking
to restoration not only of the offender but also of the offended person, as
well as the community that was wrapped up in what occurred. If this
sounds trying, that is because it is. But the hope for reform is the heartbeat
of the church that comes on the basis of Jesus' free forgiveness—and it is
in this light that discipline should be understood. So it is that we turn to
the final section of this chapter, which considers the relation of forgiveness
to healing and restoration.

[119]CD IV/2, 444.
[120]CD IV/1, 711.
[121]ChrL, 94-95; see also CD IV/4, 204.
[122]CD IV/3.1, 466.

REBUILDING TRUST AND SEEKING HEALING: FORGIVENESS AND RESTORATION

It would be naive to assume that reparation—let alone confession or forgiveness—can "make up for" all aspects of a harmful infraction. Aware that he could not right his wrongs, apartheid enforcer Eugene de Kock knew how trivial an apology would sound: "I wish I could do much more than [say] I'm sorry. I wish there was a way I could bring their bodies back alive. I wish I could say, 'Here are your husbands,' . . . but unfortunately . . . I have to live with it."[123] Pumla Gobodo-Madikizela wondered whether to believe him—after all, this could have been a sign of the man's further self-absorption—but she also considered de Kock's expression of paralysis a possible sign of genuine repentance. With statements like his we can understand the impetus to penance. For instance, a father who feels remorse for angrily shaking or frightening his child may be moved by his love for the child to resist the idea of God's free forgiveness and to wish instead for the catharsis and preventative measures of severe punishment for his offense. Disturbed by the ease with which public worship services will dole out the experience of amnesty, he may wish for a way to honor his child by not letting himself off so easy. Certainly the impulse to penance could be selfish—simply wishing to assuage his sense of regret by means of self-judgment and self-forgiveness—but it could also be motivated by concern and remorse. An offender's access to divine forgiveness may feel like an affront to the one who suffered as a result of the offense.

Then again, the same might be said about one's efforts at repair. Consider the objections of Vladimir Jankélévitch, who asked after the Holocaust, "Should We Pardon Them?"

> Reparations, alas! Reparations for little Jewish children whom German officers, to amuse themselves, chose as living targets for shooting practice. . . . In our turn, we say to the Germans, Keep your indemnities, crime doesn't pay. There are no damages that can compensate us for the execution of six million; there are no reparations for the irreparable. We don't want your money. Your marks horrify us, as does, even more so, your truly German intention of offering them to us. No, business isn't everything. No, vacationing isn't everything, nor is tourism, nor are lovely trips or festivals, if they are Austrian. But you can't

---

[123]Gobodo-Madikizela, *A Human Being*, 32.

understand that. We give up all of these very attractive benefits wholeheartedly. And as we cannot be friends with everyone, we choose to irritate the fans of Franco-German sister-city agreements rather than hurt the survivors of hell.[124]

Jankélévitch reminds us how relative forgiveness is to the entirety of reconciliation. The two are not one and the same. When restoration or repair is unavailable, what is the point of forgiveness and reconciliation?

In any event, there is no sense denying the grief. In fact, the lamentations and the imprecatory prayers of the psalmists lead us to put faith in Jesus' solidarity with sinners and suffering and to entrust ultimate justice to his hands. This is the only thing to do with one's desire for vengeance, but it is also the only thing to do with one's desire to do penance. Confession of Christ no longer bows to sin and death, but this is precisely why it involves lament over the grief that persists while the full experience of victory awaits. Confession is untruthful and forgiveness is triumphalistic if the result is a denial of the residuals of sin and enmity that still have to be confronted. No matter how fulfilling an experience of forgiveness may feel, or how unrealistic restoration may be, one is called to invoke the Holy Spirit of the living Lord Jesus Christ to lead the provisional work of healing, reconciliation and repair. The community's life of forgiveness and mutual accountability is not immune to the abuses and misuses of a self-assuring system of penance, but this is all the more reason to invoke the Lord and double back on one's situation within the penitent rhythms of the Lord's Supper, his prayer and his mercy ever new.

One way to ask Jankélévitch's question—which asked whether one should pardon what cannot be repaired—is to ask whether the alternative of *not* pardoning makes more sense. Perhaps on an anemic notion of forgiveness it is preferable to withhold the sentiment rather than use it to gloss over the past—but in the version we are describing, the free gift of forgiveness is not arbitrarily dispensed apart from any confrontation or pursuit of reconciliation. Neither does the forgiveness we are describing necessitate an immediately restored or previously unheard-of intimacy between perpetrator and victim.[125] Forgiving an estranged marriage partner will entail reform and

---

[124]Vladimir Jankélévitch, "Should We Pardon Them?" trans. Ann Hobart, *Critical Inquiry* 22, no. 3 (Spring 1996): 570-71, referring to André Neher, "Non a l'Allemagne," *L'Arche* (March 1965).
[125]See McCord Adams, "A Christian Model," 299.

rebuilding, but the historicity of grace prompts patient regard for the break in trust and intimacy that occurred. Forgiving an acquaintance or stranger—while it does entail an offer of fellowship that transcends the situation—does not necessitate a romanticized blossom of friendship to delight those greedy for a dramatic outcome. Forgiving someone who is absent or dead is impossible to do in person, and so the imperative of mercy has more to do with an internalized confession of faith. However, even then there should be openness to further ramifications of forgiveness that may not be interpersonal but familial, social or political—depending on the nature of what occurred.

In Jankélévitch's example, the question is whether a victimized social group forgives the perpetrator's social group within the circumstantial legacies and ongoing complicities of an obscene and widespread evil. There are more particulars at stake in that case than this project can suitably address, but the point is wholly relevant that in a Christian account of forgiveness there is a newly created situation in which the other is genuinely respected as an other God has intervened to restore. They are neither to be trampled with restorations or assuaged with empty apologies.

When an offer of grace goes unreciprocated, and restoration seems never to be realized, the path is not one of injury and reinjury but the patient pilgrimage of a new creation. To object to forgiveness due to the perceived impossibility of timely healing is to enthrone the offense and opt for another strategy wherein the impossibility not only remains but is exacerbated further. Christian forgiveness is not offered on the condition of the perceivable prospects for repentance and restoration. It is an act of faith. Most objections to forgiveness pertain to its caricature. Glib expressions of pardon and presumptuous claims of reparation are both bound to be a matter of self-help or self-serving philanthropy, and Jankélévitch is right to oppose them. But an obsession with severity of sorrow is hardly better than a flippantly granted amnesty—in either case the offense maintains its dictatorial hold on life. As Bernd Wannenwetsch has rightly observed, the path to rebuilt trust may be marked by suffering, but the path of mistrust is no less marked, and "the primacy of mistrust leads political life into devious paths which involve suffering that is unnecessary."[126] Forgiveness and

---

[126]Wannenwetsch, *Political Worship*, 316.

reconciliation are commendable and intelligible responses to sin if understood in the context of faith in Christ. But there is no sense denying that
the demands of such forgiveness and reconciliation may appear scandalous
and foolish apart from faith. It is often very clear that only in the faith and
hope of Christ does self-giving and forgiving commend itself.

It is very important that we understand that restoration of persons and
relationships does not suddenly take a form other than the life of invocation
and shared confession that brought the ministry of reconciliation this far.
Forgiveness and repentance do not open the door to a reform that operates
by other means. Healing and restoration cannot return to the sin of sloth
from whence the problem arose. This is illustrated well by a remarkable
excursus in Barth's second part-volume where he discusses the faithlessness
of the Hebrew spies on the cusp of the promised land, who, he says, manifested "extreme rebellion against Yahweh" by coming that far only to cower
in fear of the giants encountered.[127] (On this occasion, let the reader of
ethics understand, the character building of the desert wandering does not
seem to have helped.) When Moses prays for pardon on the basis of Yahweh's mercy, it is granted, but there are still consequences. The ten unfaithful
spies are condemned to the death that their unwillingness to enter the
promised land has chosen. This is an alarming incident worthy of commentary on a number of levels, but our focus here is on Barth's intent in
relaying the story. Particularly relevant is his observation that the sin of the
spies had been one of passive sloth (namely, inaction due to faithlessness),
and that, after mourning the loss of the spies and receiving God's pardon,
the seemingly repentant congregation immediately repeated this very sin. They
perceived that the spies were punished simply for not doing *that thing*, and
upon their reception of mercy simply presumed that they could reverse the
wrong now *by doing it.* Now the sin was an action of faithlessness. Apart
from God's renewed command to go forward, they were merely perpetuating the sloth of the spies—this time actively rather than passively.

It makes no difference whether they acted out of fear of punishment or
the fear of the giants. In Barth's view, their defiance continues even in what
appears to be repentance. They cling to a worldly sorrow that leads to death.

---

[127]See *CD* IV/2, 482-83, and Num 14.

Instead of living from Yahweh's grace they continue on in mere self-preservation. They are forgiven, but they have not repented of their sin. Before there can be restoration, further confrontation is required. This is informative of the relationship between forgiveness and restoration. The latter is not a means of securing the former. As we have seen, after forgiveness there may be further need of forbearance, more confessions to be made, recurrent calls for repentance and commitment to pursue correction. Healing is hardly ever a one-time event on its own, but is a life of mutual Christ seeking. Hauerwas evocatively calls the church to be "the people of the second-chance," but it must not let such rhetoric convince us that forgiveness is simply a do-over.[128] To be forgiven is not to be given a "clean slate" and set back on the same old path to try again; it is to be set on a path that carries on in the grace that remains grace—that is, in the life of daily invocation and obedience of the fellowship of the Holy Spirit.

In God's economy, he has clearly established that much of personal healing will take place within (but not *via*) the "mutual consolation" of a fellowship that seeks that healing in its totality together. In Barth's focus on the ministry he calls the "cure of souls," he insists that personal healing is always primarily something that *God* brings about, and we can apply this to interpersonal healing as well. In the ministry form Barth calls the "diaconate," he reckons that the community will be freed to face the "disorders" of the "prevailing social, economic and political conditions," aiming to contribute to them neither by silence nor by complicity but looking instead to participate in the healing of the "social roots" of those disorders. Because the healing for which forgiver and forgiven are freed is an event rather than a program, it cannot be canalled into another paradigm other than one of invocation and faithfulness to the living Christ. This does not mean that there is no place for those who are specifically "called and gifted" for what we now call pastoral counseling—but it does mean that the proper integration of social and psychological sciences will take place in service (rather than replacement) of the ministry of reconciliation to which the whole confessing community is called.[129]

---

[128]Stanley Hauerwas, *Dispatches from the Front: Theological Engagements with the Secular* (Durham, NC: Duke University Press, 1991), 88.
[129]See *CD* IV/3.2, 885-86 and 892-94.

This is a people who are gathered in faith that the cosmos has been reconciled to God in Christ. As "creation waits with eager longing for the revealing of the children of God" (Rom 8:19), so those children wait on God to quicken them to love and call them to serve his purposes in the world. They are made ready to engage in many different ways as that reconciliation is revealed in time on the way to full redemption. Healing and reform in the lives of victims and offenders are sought each day as given from the living Lord.

This is no reason to dismiss a victim's fear of being mistreated again, nor to overlook the call for accountability, correction and restorative measures. If someone steals something, repentance implies a desire to pay it back. If one is addicted to a pattern of sin, repentance implies a desire to seek help. If someone harms another person, repentance implies a new respect for their healing and rebuilt trust. Their forgiveness is not a license to carelessness any more than it is a license to slothful care. The establishment of boundaries and accountability structures may indeed be a way that the freedom of forgiveness is followed up in the ministry of reconciliation. But none of this is to succumb to the narratives of either victim's vengeance or perpetrator's penance. In the exercise of such things Christians will seek discretion out of freedom in Christ rather than "absolute fear of evil."[130] No matter what the extent of enmity, addiction or trauma, Christians are awakened to reality within a "lively hope" that leads them to the invocation of Christ and peaceable action in the church.

In all of this we should not leave the impression that restoration is a *means* by which *we* re-create communion; rather, it is what we do in the "occurrence of this communion" that is provided only by "the mighty work of Jesus." The church cannot pretend that it possesses a power or a "general rule for improved social relationships"; nor can it present itself as "the means to an end which can be dispensed with . . . when other and perhaps better means are perceived."[131] Forgiveness is of central vitality to the church's life and witness. Because of Jesus' cross and emptied tomb, and because of his ascension and sending of the Spirit, there is a fellowship made on earth wherein people look to "continually receive afresh" their freedom from sin

---

[130]*CD* IV/1, 408-9.
[131]*CD* IV/2, 642, 654, 549 and 621.

and allow themselves "to be set forward on the road ahead."[132] The occurrence of sin (however trivial or grave) will complicate the situation considerably, but sin does not change the fundamental fact that Christ was *always* the mediator of fellowship, the one on whom it depended.

Whether we are enemies or friends, acquaintances or family, for fellowship in a fallen world we are and always have been "unfit, but continually fitted."[133] The narrative of "futile vacillation or movement in a circle" is simply not believed in anymore, replaced as it is by the "constant prevailing of the promised forgiveness of sins" and the "constant differentiation" of future from past, right from wrong and life from death.[134] In aiming to be a community uniquely defined by this new belief, the church will still persist in addressing all people as "*christiani designate*"—which is to say that the gospel is assumed to be "valid and effective" for others as well.[135]

New every morning, with faith and hope in Christ, Christians forgive. They may not then excuse themselves from Christ's work of reconciliation, even when they have been wronged, and especially when they have been wrong. Whether one has been wronged or has been doing the wronging is not a cut-and-dry either/or as often as one might think. The best hope of discerning which is which is to find oneself in the rhythms of a Christ-confessing community.

Now that forgiveness has been so defined and embedded within a series of interrelated imperatives, it should be clear why Barth thought Christian love, while evident in the world, would be at home within such a common confession. To gather up the ethic of reconciliation that has been delineated here, we will now come to a conclusion by refocusing on the unique character of the church wherein an ethos befitting this account of forgiveness is pursued.

---

[132]*CD* IV/3.2, 531.
[133]*CD* IV/2, 623, see *ChrL*, 83.
[134]*CD* IV/1, 602.
[135]*CD* IV/3.2, 852-53.

6

New Every Morning

The Life of a Confessing Church

WE HAVE SEEN BARTH'S VIEW that to grasp a God-for-me-alone is to clasp at a wisp of the self-centered imagination, and that a forgiving community on earth is not incidental but integral to the movement of God with humanity in Christ. Despite the vitality of forgiveness to the life of this community, we have also seen Barth's reticence to delineate this ethos in a separable program. Indeed, he would likely agree with Jacques Derrida, whose *On Cosmopolitanism and Forgiveness* asserts, "One could never, in the ordinary sense of the words, found a politics or law on forgiveness."[1] This did not stop Barth from highlighting and describing the *extra-ordinariness* of the church's life, however, as if he wanted to fill it in as specifically as possible without usurping grace with law. Perhaps he would agree with Derrida that one cannot found a *law* on forgiveness, but we have seen evidence that he thought of the church as a politic wherein forgiveness finds its home. Having drawn out the interconnected imperatives that give definition and texture to this, in this final chapter we return to ecclesiology, motivated to root that multidimensional politic in core church practices and to indicate how this fits in the world. To do this we will take our cues from the final sections of Barth's *Church Dogmatics*.

Before his death Barth began what was to be his ethics of reconciliation, organizing it under the rubric of invocation, following the pattern of the

---

[1] Jacques Derrida, *On Cosmopolitanism and Forgiveness*, trans. Mark Dooley and Michael Hughes (London: Routledge, 2001), 39.

Lord's Prayer and framing it within a treatment of baptism on one side and the Lord's Supper on the other. Although the unfinished fragments only reach the third line of the Prayer, Barth did deem the section on baptism to be not only publishable but important, and declared it a good indication of what would have followed.[2] The remainder was published posthumously in *The Christian Life*. In the move from general to special ethics one encounters in these final portions, one sees Barth striving to supplement his depiction of the church event with a further delineation of "certain lines" and "certain directives" that merited tracing out.[3] James Buckley thinks Barth "shows" more than he "states" in this regard—but the showing is certainly there.[4] In what follows we will focus squarely on the life of the Christian community by extrapolating important points from two of Barth's most controversial—but still highly instructive—decisions. The first is his treatment of the sacraments as foundational to ethics, and the second is his treatment of ethics as fundamentally prayer.

THE LORD'S BAPTISM AND SUPPER: SHAPERS OF CHRISTIAN COMMUNITY (§74–§75)

When Barth returned in his ethics of reconciliation to the topic of sin, he did so with particular attentiveness to "the situation from which Christians are freed," describing it in terms of *ambivalence to the living God* and *service to lordless powers*.[5] In the course of time, ambivalence and the lordless powers continue to threaten church and world, giving reason to pray for forgiveness and deliverance as often as for daily bread. It is not our purpose in this chapter to retread ground already covered in the hamartiological

---

[2]*CD* IV/4, ix-x.

[3]*ChrL*, 7. Nicholas Healy used the terms *general ecclesiology* and *special ecclesiology* to differentiate Barth's work in certain ways as well. See Nicholas M. Healy, "Karl Barth's Ecclesiology Reconsidered," *Scottish Journal of Theology* 25, no. 3 (2004): 293-94, 297; see also *CD* IV/3.2, 790, and Nicholas M. Healy, "The Logic of Karl Barth's Ecclesiology: Analysis, Assessment and Proposed Modifications," *Modern Theology* 10 (1994): 253-70.

[4]See James J. Buckley, "A Field of Living Fire: Karl Barth on the Spirit and the Church," *Modern Theology* 10 (1994): 88-89, 91.

[5]*ChrL*, 115 and 213. Churches do not need to point fingers to understand ambivalence, Barth explains: not only are they frequently complicit in the evasive maneuvers of unbelievers, but they also manifest an "incomparably more sinister" form of the sin when they are ambivalent to the call of Christ they claim to have received. See ibid., 116, 118, 120-21 and 134-39. For more on the complicity of the church in the world's ambivalence, see *CD* IV/2, 444-45, *CD* IV/3.1, 468 and *CD* IV/3.2, 873-82.

sections of chapter two, but it is worth gathering up final insights into Barth's ecclesiology by considering the way baptism and the Lord's Supper set up a perpetual battleground against the besetting social systems of sin. To put it more positively, we want to see how Barth saw the politic of forgiveness and reconciliation taking shape *within* the contours of the sacraments.[6]

Barth's treatment of baptism under the rubric of *ethics* (rather than *sacraments*) in the fourth part-volume opened him to criticism on several levels: it drove too much of a separation between Spirit baptism and water baptism, it made more out of Jesus' baptism than did the apostles and it rejected infant baptism.[7] It is not necessary for us to vindicate Barth from these criticisms here, but it is worth noting that by risking charges of ethicized sacraments on one hand and mystified ethics on the other, Barth aimed to issue a challenge to all parties concerned.[8] In fact, he thought of his construal not as a

---

[6]To speak of the church as having a "shape" runs consciously against the grain of critiques that say Barth's ecclesiology lacked constancy and character. His intent was to counter *both* an institutionalized *and* a dehistoricized vision of the church by describing the church event in terms of its "special visibility." Ignoring the visibility of the church event would be tantamount to "ecclesiastical Docetism," while ignoring the unbridled nature of that event would be tantamount to ecclesiastical Ebionism. See *CD* IV/1, 653, 655. In Barth's distinction of *geistlich* (spiritual) from *geistig* (religious) we see that *if* there is to be any religiosity to the Christian life, it is only in service of its proper spirituality, and thus is open to the perpetual definition and redefinition of the Holy Spirit. This rules out any sense of latent religiosity in humankind that only needs kindling by christocentric or cruciform practices. What it does not rule out, however, is that there might be a defined corporate spirituality provided by Christ. Would baptism and eucharist be considered *geistig* or *geistlich*? Barth's point in his final fragments seems to be that they have the *potential* to be either, but are set aside by Christ as the promised sphere for the proper spirituality of his community. In prayerful observation of baptism and the Lord's Supper, we are attending to the corporate dimensions of proper Christian spirituality. See *ChrL*, 92. In Barth's view, baptism "aims at something which can indeed be called a sacramental happening," but this is "endangered, obscured and hampered" if we try to distill the event to "certain inner processes" that might just as well replace it. The way to make sense of this is to say that for Barth there remains a mystery to baptism, but it is on the divine side, not ours. *CD* IV/4, 105-9.

[7]For typical objections to Barth's exegesis, see John Yocum, *Ecclesial Mediation in Karl Barth* (Aldershot, UK: Ashgate, 2004), 165-66, and Thomas F. Torrance, *Theology in Reconciliation: Essays Towards Evangelical and Catholic Unity in East and West* (Grand Rapids: Eerdmans, 1975), 83, 88. Barth makes this move as early as *CD* IV/3.2, 517. He later admits taking "a certain exegetical liberty," but claims a "solid foundation" for it in (1) the New Testament's call for baptism *in the name of Jesus* (Lk 3:3; Acts 2:38, 10:48; 1 Cor 1:13, 15), (2) its willingness to relate subsequent baptisms to Jesus' own (Rom 6:3-4; 1 Cor 12:13; Gal 3:27) and (3) its placement of the baptismal command in the context of Christ's promise of ongoing presence (Mt 28:18-20). See *CD* IV/4, 30, 90-100, and *ChrL*, 20. For a full account of Barth's views, see W. Travis McMaken, *The Sign of the Gospel: Toward an Evangelical Doctrine of Infant Baptism After Karl Barth* (Minneapolis: Fortress, 2013).

[8]Criticisms of Barth's ethicization of the sacraments may not have fully grappled with the fact that Barth was in turn treating ethics as invocation. See *ChrL*, 37-39, 42-43, 88, and *CD* IV/4, 37,

novel break from an otherwise uniform tradition but an attempt to recast and appropriate already divergent views in a constructive manner.[9] For our purposes, the most relevant criticism is the one that says Barth's separation of water baptism from Spirit baptism leaned toward an uncharacteristic dualism, and his focus on the human activity involved meant a diminishment of the uniqueness of the sacraments as *acts of God*.[10]

One can see the tightrope Barth was trying to walk when, in a vexing combination of emphases, he called the sacraments "free and responsible . . . actions of human obedience for which Jesus Christ makes his people free and responsible."[11] However, if we probe past the false dilemma between divine and human action, we are well situated to incorporate the ecclesial and ethical imperatives that come in the "specific content of what is always a special event between God and man."[12] Barth's final placement

---

112. As it turned out, in the reception of Barth's ecclesiology and ethics a pair of criticisms arose that, when put together, questioned not only Barth but each other. The first criticism—which followed Barth from early on in his theological career and stuck with him to such an extent that it clouded readings of his later work—said that Barth's account of the church as event rendered his ecclesiology esoteric and ahistorical. The second—which emerged at the end of Barth's theological career but served to stall what might have been a more productive rendering of his ethics of reconciliation—said that his treatment of the sacraments in ethical terms put all its weight on human action in an improper bifurcation between it and the divine. As the dust has settled on the debate, however, it has become possible to see an answer to the first critique in the source of the other.

[9]See *CD* IV/4, 5.

[10]Such a dualism was explicitly not Barth's intent, but his rhetoric may have let him down. In his critique of Barth, Torrance insists that God can set up a sacrament without falling into its "control," remaining freely grounded even as "reciprocity between divine and human *agency*" is "established" by Jesus Christ and "maintained" by the Holy Spirit. See Torrance, *Theology in Reconciliation*, 95, 99-102. Barth would likely have agreed for the most part, and simply pointed out that the word *established* undermines an otherwise good point. See *CD* IV/4, 4, and *ChrL*, 16, 105-6. In the end, Barth's division is more rhetorical than material. He is mainly interested to get first things first in the asymmetry of divine and human action, to cast human agency not in terms of *division* but *derivation* from divine agency. For a critique that reaches a similar conclusion, see Yocum, *Ecclesial Mediation*, 175.

[11]*ChrL*, 46. See John Webster, *Barth's Ethics of Reconciliation* (Cambridge: Cambridge University Press, 1995), 8-9. What Barth says baptism *is not*, he says about it *as it stands apart from* or *in front of* the actualizing presence and prior work of Christ via the Holy Spirit. By grounding Christian life in the resurrection rather than the "miracle of the incarnation" (as Yocum puts it), Barth tries to see past a "disjunction of divine and human acts" to a different view of how they are related and work out in history. See Yocum, *Ecclesial Mediation*, 27, 30. Typically Barth thinks water baptism will follow Spirit baptism "at once." *CD* IV/4, 102; see also 42-43, *CD* IV/2, 556 and *ChrL*, 85, 91, 108. It is worth noting in this context that when the apostles discovered someone had been baptized with the Holy Spirit but not with water they immediately sought to rectify the disconnection rather than expound upon it. See Acts 8:16-17; 10:47-48; 11:16-17; 19:1-6.

[12]*ChrL*, 4-5.

of the sacraments under ethical categories may not satisfy every analysis, but it stands to reason that whether one views baptism as a symbolic ordinance or a mediatory sacrament it is best to include (at least proleptically, as in the case of infant baptism) the element of human participation.[13] Human agency must not be a *controlling* factor in this, but it is graciously included despite the fall. One's views about *when* baptism should occur are not incidental, but in any case the point (articulated by Franz Leenhardt and reiterated by Travis McMaken) remains that baptism is "the sign of what God *has done*" and "*wants to do* through Christ in the sinner."[14]

For Barth, no matter when it happens, properly speaking one's baptism begins a life defined by perpetual submission to the "lordship of God," setting the paradigm for the "sequence and fellowship" to follow. As the "first step of the Christian life," it contains also "the secret of its constantly renewed dynamic." In baptism *and in every moment afterward*—"Christian life begins with a change."[15] As McMaken puts it, "Baptism's concern is primarily with what one might call the formal beginning of that history, while the Supper's concern is with its continual renewal."[16] This has considerable import not only for the church's practice of the Lord's Supper but for the form of common life it perpetuates. Even though we lack his finished account of this, Barth suggested that attentive readers might "deduce from the [baptism] fragment how [he] would finally have presented the doctrine of the Lord's Supper."[17] Our goal in what follows is not to speculate in that regard, but to fill out his picture of the Christian community via the trajectories already laid.[18]

---

[13]See George Hunsinger, "Baptism and the Soteriology of Forgiveness," *Call to Worship* 35, no. 3 (2001): 23, and *CD* IV/3.2, 518.

[14]Franz J. Leenhardt, *Le Baptême Chrétien: Son Origine, sa Signification, Cahiers Théologiques de l'Actualité Protestante*, vol. 4 (Neuchâtel et Paris: Delachaux & Niestlé, 1945), 71, emphasis added. For this citation and its explication see Travis McMaken's compelling appropriation of Barth for an evangelical practice of infant baptism in McMaken, *Sign of the Gospel*, 274. While Barth's polemic against infant baptism may be overstated, it is worth bearing in mind that, at its best, believer's baptism underlines *first* the freedom of God in grace working in and through the church, *and then* the grace of God to make for human participation. As a sign of this, it *includes* the will of the individual *such as it is* at the point of baptism without hinging the power or the significance of the event upon the individual's choice. See *CD* IV/4, 101, 188-90; *CD* II/2, 178; *ChrL*, 27-28, 32, 41 and Webster, *Barth's Ethics*, 29, 50, 123, 185.

[15]*CD* IV/4, 61, 197-98, and 8-9.

[16]McMaken, *Sign of the Gospel*, 201.

[17]*CD* IV/4, x.

[18]Thoughts in this section were spurred in part by Paul Nimmo, "With and After Barth on the Eucharist" (paper, King's College, Aberdeen, May 9, 2011). In keeping with the baptism fragment,

Discerning the body: The politic of Barth's approach to the sacraments.
In the celebration of the sacraments there is a real event that has personal
and political proportions each time it occurs. Forgiveness is not the whole
of that event, but is vital to it. As in baptism, so it is in the meals of the
church: people are placed in communion under "the judgment of God" and
"referred only to his free remission of their sins."[19] The sacraments are in-
stantiations of the Lord's presence that give concrete shape to the community and its witness. In this section we pay attention to two of the ways
Barth's approach to baptism and the Lord's Supper provide an important
ecclesiological and missiological framework for the imperatives of forgiveness and reconciliation outlined in this book. The first has to do with
the sociopolitical ramifications of these sacred acts, and the second has to
do with the ethos they perpetuate and entail.

In his 1948 address to the World Council of Churches in Amsterdam,
subtitled "The Living Congregation of the Lord Jesus Christ," Barth spoke
of a "polity" that is continually awoken to combat against three besetting
"threats to the church"; namely, the sleepy-eyed tendency to neglect "dependence on its living Lord," the "squint-eyed" tendency to fall in love with the
"particular arrangement" of its own "forms of faith and worship" and the
blind-eyed tendency to give itself over to a "self-made world of [its] own
religious dreams."[20] In contrast to these, the "living congregation" has a
fellowship that is definitively *attentive* rather than *self-productive.*[21] In the
second part-volume of *Church Dogmatics*, Barth later described "the
crowning act of worship" as "the common eating and drinking of the disciples" wherein Christ commands and initiates "*the work of His real
presence.*"[22] Having emphasized this as a "nexus of human relationships,"
Barth concluded that baptism is taken "with positive seriousness" when it
includes an acceptance by both the candidate and the community of the
"specific point in this nexus" Christ means to give them.[23]

Barth would likely have interpreted 1 Cor 11 and the early church suppers through the lens of Jesus'
Last Supper before his death as well as the meals he shared with disciples after his resurrection.
[19]*CD* IV/4, 54.
[20]Karl Barth, *God Here and Now* (London & New York: Routledge, 2003), 68-71, 76.
[21]Ibid., 62, 64-66.
[22]*CD* IV/2, 658, emphasis added. See also *CD* IV/1, 665, and *CD* IV/3.1, 395.
[23]*CD* IV/2, 806-7; see *ChrL*, 82-83.

What merits commentary at this point is Scott Prather's suggestion that it would be a significant failure on Barth's part if he emphasized the "intra-ecclesial" points of this nexus without an account of its sociopolitical realities as well.[24] Indeed, how tragic if a church community exercises the ministry of reconciliation we have been outlining to such an extent that it experiences a *merely internal* harmony to the neglect of attention to its embeddedness in social enmity. Such a church could happily be reconciling itself to the premises and privileges of its participation in systemic injustice. Against this mistaken trajectory, Prather draws out Barth's point that the prayer for kingdom come is a prayer for the lordless powers to be exposed and overcome.[25] In Prather's view, if a church loses this "prophetic sensitivity," it faces the "dire consequences" of neglecting its "vocation of confession and witness," allowing its so-called *ever-new politic* to become an "ever-new naivety about the powers determining our sociopolitical and economic relations."[26] In short, a community that is new every morning ought to wake up not only to the mercy of God, but to the graciously renewed call to resist rather than ossify the lordless powers.

What needs to be elaborated in greater detail is the implication that Barth saw this call perpetuated in the sacraments themselves, wherein a relatively stable reconciling communion may be upheld even in the midst of great sociopolitical oppression or upheaval.[27] In these divinely mandated church

---

[24]It is to Prather's credit that he draws out the sociopolitical trajectory of Barth's posthumously published fragments to such good effect that one becomes convinced that Barth did not mean to neglect this altogether (however focused on the inner life of the church his published part-volumes might have been). For his part, Prather asserts that Barth's "intra-ecclesial description of God's reign is prioritized over socio-political awareness of its presence." Our hope is to join Prather in calling for attention to *both* the intraecclesial and the sociopolitical, but without losing sight of Barth's prioritization of a *proper ecclesial dynamic*, since it is that ecclesial politic that is so crucial to its sociopolitical witness. See Scott Thomas Prather, *Christ, Power and Mammon: Karl Barth and John Howard Yoder in Dialogue* (London: T&T Clark, 2013), 10.

[25]Prather expresses disappointment with Barth for backing away from the language of "revolt," but finds that the notion is nonetheless retained. Ibid., 45-46, 52; see also *ChrL*, 218-19.

[26]Prather, *Christ, Power and Mammon*, 171, 201 and 222. These points are developed in dialogue with essays by Kathryn Tanner, "Karl Barth on the Economy," and by Christopher Holmes, "Karl Barth on the Economy: In Dialogue with Kathryn Tanner," in *Commanding Grace: Studies in Karl Barth's Ethics*, ed. Daniel Migliore (Grand Rapids: Eerdmans, 2010), 176-215. See also Daniel M. Bell Jr., "Forgiveness and the End of Economy," *Studies in Christian Ethics* 20, no. 3 (2007): 325-44.

[27]This speaks to what Barth tentatively called Jesus' "passive conservatism" in relation to the political orders *and* revolutions of this world. In emphasizing this Barth wished not to foreground revolt to such an extent that the sociopolitical conditions remain a negatively defining factor for the church, even in its earnestness to overturn them. *CD* IV/2, 175-79.

events he envisioned participants who are made "mutually ready to accept each other as Christians" with all of the responsibilities and privileges entailed.[28] In this would be found both the resources for mission and a positive witness of what the church is praying for, proclaiming and pursuing. By foregrounding the intraecclesial even in mission, Barth is articulating the call for a church to be more than a cultural critic but a microcosm of that which it would recommend to the world in the name of the gospel.

As Barth saw it, in the Lord's Supper the Spirit gathers a community that is not drawn along preferential, socioeconomic or familial lines but is "freely and newly called and assembled out of Israel and all nations"— making it "an open Church" that "crosses its own frontiers into the territory of the people which walks in darkness."[29] In reiterating this we are inclined to point out that both of the sacraments set the church up to see its own frontiers crossed as well. Presupposed outsiders may theoretically disrupt the church's comfort zone at any time. Baptism and the Lord's Supper hold the promise of upsetting the social boundaries within which local communities might otherwise be based. Where this is neglected, the participants show "contempt for the church of God," eating and drinking (and receiving people in baptism, one might add) "without discerning the body" (1 Cor 11:22-29). The life initiated at baptism entails a change not only for the baptized but also the baptizers. In the openness of baptism to all persons, the preference-based social structures of baptizing churches have the potential to be greatly disrupted. The very entry point of Christian community is decidedly *not* the privilege of class or family, nor the preference-based congeniality of kindled friendship.

As warm as the experience of the Lord's Supper promises to be, for exactly that reason it is the Lord's Table where the threat of a merely friendship-based communion may be most palpable. To call this a threat is not to say that the desire for friendship is sinful in itself or inappropriate in the church, but is to say that it is a poor substitute for the gathered fellowship of the Holy Spirit that takes place in the throes of an as-yet unconsummated kingdom. Practically speaking, of course, friendships often serve as appropriate points of first contact between unbelievers and local churches, but this does not

---

[28]CD IV/1, 699.
[29]CD IV/4, 178 and 200.

mean that a church fellowship ought to base its ethos or its mission on such a thing.[30] This would soon be the sign of an insipid ecclesiology. Christian communion is not built or maintained on the guarantee of requited love or reciprocated good feelings, even if it hopes for such things to arise. The church is not an "organization for the common cultivation of the very private concerns of its individual members," wrote Barth; it is rather "a *people*" who are "related, responsible and united to one another" as siblings adopted by a common Father via the brotherhood of Jesus.[31] This common adoption ought to displace the tendency to centralize natural associations or, worse, to set any one community in the patronizing primary role of *adopter*. As Willie Jennings suggests, if we learn nothing else from honest reflection on the "colonialist wound," it should be that the church's identity as *grafted in* ought to bring about a "conceptual recalibration" wherein gospel receivers have as much "creative authority" as gospel proclaimers in the reconceived social imagination of the missionary event.[32] Jennings found this implicit in Barth's theological anthropology, and it is incumbent upon us to fill in the lines of his ecclesiology with this point as well.

Looking to the Lord's Supper, then, we may rightly appropriate some of Barth's claims about communion, which he describes as "an action in which on the basis of an existing union" the saints are "engaged in a common movement towards the same union."[33] Despite the traction gained by articulating forgiveness within a well-defined matrix of reconciliatory imperatives, it has not been our intention to portray the sacraments of the church as dispensable tools in the task of fellowship creation. The imperatives of Christian community are not a self-help regimen or a politic unto themselves. However, the alternative is not to shrug the shoulders and say that baptism and the Lord's Supper magically create human fellowship. In these Christ-commanded common practices we *do* have the establishment of an ethos within which koinonia is at work in an unjust and self-justifying

---

[30]See *CD* IV/2, 819.
[31]*ChrL*, 82-83, 95. Reconciliation is not based on natural common ground or a contrived egalitarianism. It is the event of new creation. See John H. Yoder, "The New Humanity as Pulpit and Paradigm," in *For the Nations: Essays Evangelical and Public* (Grand Rapids: Eerdmans, 1997), 41, 44-45. See *CD* IV/3.2, 858, 900.
[32]See Willie James Jennings, *The Christian Imagination: Theology and the Origins of Race* (New Haven, CT: Yale University Press, 2010), 60-61, 150-68 and 286-94.
[33]*CD* IV/2, 641.

world.[34] In this there is not a prescription for self-managed community, but the promise of a "common ordering" of the people of God in which they are "integrated and engaged in self-integration" by his Spirit.[35] Thus, as LeRon Shults and Steven Sandage suggest, "the main question in the practice of the Lord's Supper is not whom we should exclude from it" but the Supper's exposure of those already "exclusive practices that characterize our whole lives as we [otherwise] eat our fill in a hungry world."[36] As Barth would have it, the table is not to be fenced off but *focused on Christ*, so that the Supper is the place of thankful invocation wherein the community finds itself uniquely equipped for truth-speaking attentiveness to the gospel-driven social significance of the meal.[37]

The Christian community has not been employed in the mission of God because of any particular usefulness it possesses; it is caught up in that mission to be "forgiven for all its uselessness."[38] In this forgiveness there is not an excuse for inaction but the freedom for action. The contours of the Christian life are to be lived in and not ignored. As Barth put it, "The community is given the task of listening to its self-explanation and then of using the human means at its disposal, not to proceed independently, but to follow it."[39] This is made abundantly clear in the sacraments, wherein the Holy Spirit gathers people to forgive and to love one another amidst the differences of diversity, the hurts of enmity and the temptations of success.[40] Baptism and the Lord's Supper "are not empty signs"; rather, "they are full of meaning and power. They are thus the simplest, and yet in their very simplicity the most eloquent, elements in the witness which the community

---

[34]See Joseph L. Mangina, "The Stranger as Sacrament: Karl Barth and the Ethics of Ecclesial Practice," *International Journal of Systematic Theology* 1, no. 3 (1999): 332, translating Ulrich Kühn, *Sakramente*, Handbuck Systematischer Theologie Bd. II (Gutersloh: Gutersloher Verlagshaus Mohn, 1985), 182.

[35]*CD* IV/2, 642, 707-8.

[36]F. LeRon Shults and Steven J. Sandage, *The Face of Forgiveness: Searching for Wholeness and Salvation* (Grand Rapids: Baker Academic, 2003), 220.

[37]*CD* IV/2, 626. See this gospel-attentive action in Barth's account of baptism in *CD* IV/4, 152, 165, 193.

[38]*CD* IV/1, 647, and *CD* IV/2, 637; see also *CD* IV/2 623, 638, and *CD* IV/3.2, 800-801. The church may appear the most fragile institution on earth, but it nonetheless stands on an "impregnably firm foundation." In the church we are not "thrown back on our own resources." *ChrL*, 150, 167; see also 95.

[39]*CD* IV/3.2, 846.

[40]*ChrL*, 84; see 1 Jn 4:20.

owes to the world, namely, the witness of peace on earth."[41] Thus it is that the church's internal ethos is part and parcel of its sociopolitical activism.

As has been discussed in previous chapters, this can hardly be the stuff of false peace. Indeed, at one point in the working out of his ethics of reconciliation, Barth gestures at the human inclination to strike a peace accord "between light and darkness" and insists that *"for the sake of peace with God and true peace on earth, that peace cannot stand."*[42] The church is to resist both forced homogeneity and hegemonic pseudocommunity in order to be formed in the ebb and flow of baptism and communion as a diverse fellowship of pilgrims. So potent is the temptation to rebuild the Tower of Babel at this point, however, that before we proceed we do well to contrast the pathology of pseudocommunity with the ecclesiology of Christ confession.

For the sake of peace, that false peace cannot stand. Having used Jeremiah to frame his *Doctrine of Reconciliation*, again in *The Christian Life* Barth looked to the weeping prophet to set the tone, this time for an evocative depiction of our fallen disorientation. Despite God's commitments—"I will be their God, and they shall be my people" and "I will forgive their iniquity, and remember their sin no more" (Jer 31:33-34)—the people have lamentably been content to say "'Peace, peace,' when there is no peace" and "have treated the wound of [God's] people carelessly" (Jer 6:14; 8:11).[43] With this reference Barth brings attention to the *social* component of evil, highlighting the *pseudocommunity* that is entailed in the "scurrying hither and thither" of pride, sloth and falsehood.[44] In our account of the common life shaped by baptism and the Lord's Supper, it behooves us to briefly contrast the pathology of false peace with the health of a community that lives from faith in the Prince of Peace. In this it will be seen once more how essential to the sacrament-shaped life are the interlocked imperatives of interpersonal forgiveness and reconciliation.

---

[41]*CD* IV/3.2, 901.

[42]*ChrL*, 193-94, emphasis added.

[43]See *CD* IV/1, 22, 33, 42, and *ChrL*, 193-94.

[44]*CD* IV/3.1, 470-71. Gregory Jones calls this "an aura of 'community'" and a "pale, synthetic substitute." Jones, *Embodying Forgiveness. A Theological Analysis* (Grand Rapids: Eerdmans, 1995), 44. Miroslav Volf calls it a "delicate bubble of false peace." Volf, *The End of Memory: Remembering Rightly in a Violent World* (Grand Rapids: Eerdmans, 2006), 74. LeRon Shults and Steven Sandage refer to a "cheap forgiveness" that "maintain[s] the artificial façades." Shults and Sandage, *Face of Forgiveness*, 170.

In the ethics fragments Barth used the term *lordless powers* to refer not
to positive forces that provide a viable alternative to Christ's lordship, but to
creaturely manifestations of the implosive power of imagined lordlessness.
The issue at stake is not godlessness per se, for there is no such thing. These
powers have no power of their own. Nonetheless, Barth writes, they are
"palpable for all their impalpability in every morning and evening newspaper
in every corner of the globe," and from their threat the church is not immune.[45] With specific reference to the "isms" and slogans of marketplace,
politics and ideology, as well as the obsessions of technology, fashion and
sport, Barth perceptively depicts the many ways that human energies bend
toward lordlessness rather than the living Lord. In this he is not calling for
a community of legalists or Luddites, but highlighting the unification de-
vices that can "rob [the Lord] of his freedom under the pretext and appearance of granting every kind of freedom."[46] Were we to focus on the
critical implications of this we might descend quickly into the kind of cultural analysis that paints the church as little more than a film negative of its
times. We would also be veering from our present focus, which is the health
of a Lord-full church in the middle of the world.

How might one describe the church that is resistant to lordless powers in
positive terms? Most interestingly, when this theme appeared earlier in §64.4,
"The Direction of the Son," Barth spoke of the influence of "alien forces" in the
promotion of false peace. There he explained that the privations of sin tear us
apart in any one of three ways, offering either (1) "a supposed peace with God"
that contradicts "peace with men," (2) "a supposed peace with men" that is
"not grounded in peace with God" or (3) "a supposed peace with God and our
fellows" that "does not carry with it peace with ourselves."[47] In each of these

---

[45]*ChrL*, 218-19; see also 134-37, 143-44, 149-55, 214-15 and 222.
[46]Ibid., 224-29.
[47]*CD* IV/2, 315; see also *ChrL*, 279-80. Within this third type is the inverse "peace and harmony
with himself" in which the "undisturbed sinner" conjures an illusory self-contentedness apart
from the peace of God. *CD* IV/2, 524. These "dimensions" are anticipated earlier in the ethics
section *The Doctrine of Creation*. See *CD* III/4, 43-44. Indeed, Barth arranged the final part of
volume three according to the dimensions of "Freedom Before God" (47-115), "Freedom in Fellowship" (116-323), "Freedom for Life" (324-564) and "Freedom in Limitation" (565-685). The
final two of these sections could arguably entail what Barth later called the third dimension of
"peace with ourselves," but it could also be argued that "Freedom in Limitation" anticipates a
fourth dimension unnamed by but appropriate to Barth: namely, our interdependent relation with
creation and its other creatures, which is implied when we confess our "limitation" or finitude.

cases, Barth said, there exists the powerful charm of a peace that will "be very pleasant in some respects" but is "worthless" and not to be trusted because it forgoes or short-circuits that which "is effected *in all three dimensions at once*" by "the peacemaking power of the resurrection of Jesus Christ."[48] The peaceable church, then, is attentive to the lead of a living Lord who effects his accomplishment in all three dimensions at once: the reconciliation of God with us, of us with each other, and of each of us with our individual selves. Each dimension of this vision of peace begs for further description, but our particular focus is on the dimension of interpersonal reconciliation and the lines of Barth's missional ecclesiology.

In keeping with the prior depictions of active and passive sloth, in §77 Barth describes two types of false peacekeeping that plague Christian communities that have strayed from their proper form of life: the tendencies either to be presumptuous rather than penitent or to despair instead of hope. One way of illustrating these twin temptations is through Barth's dialectic of ecclesial visibility and invisibility. On one hand, the presumptuous church becomes so invested in the *visibility* of its unity that in the face of its own imperfections it begins to produce "energetic and skilful propaganda" in order to maintain its sense of purity and cohesiveness.[49] On the other hand, the despairing church becomes so troubled by the *invisibility* of its unity that in the face of its obstacles and enemies it will expend more and more of its efforts on staying afloat, keeping face, maintaining borders or pointing fingers.

If "successful," the presumptuous church may pacify more than make peace, uttering a vacuous "prayer for peace" that ends up "committing no one."[50] If decidedly "un-successful," the despairing church may rally around what it presumes to be the only genuine spirituality possible: private piety and collective concern.[51] So it goes that the modes of false peacekeeping Barth describes are but two sides of the same coin, the corporate manifestations of either active or passive sloth.

As these forms of sloth feed off each other, the vicious cycle of false peace goes on, and those who feel the brokenness most acutely may be left little

---

[48]*CD* IV/2, 315, emphasis added.
[49]*ChrL*, 136-38.
[50]*CD* IV/3.2, 814.
[51]See *CD* IV/3.1, 453.

room within the prevailing rhetoric for an exploration of their concerns. Any confrontation of the modus operandi is likely to be framed as rebellion. Simply diagnosing these tensions and presuming to strike a middle way is no solution, however. In the disorientation of sin we will inevitably be "contentious where it is unnecessary and harmful" or else retreat into secluded ambivalence when it would have been right to "confidently attack."[52] In Barth's depiction of the back and forth between conflict avoidance and consent management, he shows how the "balm in Gilead" (Jer 8:22) loses out to a placebo and the ministry of reconciliation gives way to a smoothing over of discord.[53] The pull to run away from such churches may be strong (and in some cases legitimate), but Barth warns that this, too, may amount to "running away from God," entailing a denial of the reach of the Spirit and the "remission of sins."[54]

In his ethics of reconciliation Barth sought to explain how we "can no longer dream either the bad dream of a church that is merely unholy or the all too beautiful dream of one that is merely holy."[55] It is to those who would deny their strife in order to worship that Jesus says to "first be reconciled . . . and then come and offer your gift" (Mt 5:24).[56] As Barth put it, "Peace is not just the opposite of quarrelling, strife, and warfare." This was not to depict peacemakers as a quarrel-seeking "centrifugal people disintegrating in all kinds of peculiarities," but to depict them as a "concentrated people" whose

---

[52]Or they will speak "faith and the Gospel when what is needed is a little sound commonsense," or reason when what is needed is trust. CD IV/2, 413.

[53]See CD IV/1, 676, and CD IV/3.1, 442. This pathology of false peace has not escaped the notice of psychological and sociological analysis. Robert Schreiter observes seven dysfunctional ways we approach diversity in community: faced with potential conflict we "demonize," "romanticize," "colonize," "generalize," "trivialize," "homogenize" or "vaporize" the other rather than deal with them peaceably from a place of solidarity and hope. Robert J. Schreiter, Reconciliation: Mission and Ministry in a Changing Social Order (Maryknoll, NY: Orbis Books, 1992), 51-53. See also Ofelia Ortega, "Conversion as a Way of Life in Cultures of Violence," in Forgiveness and Reconciliation: Religion, Public Policy, and Conflict Transformation, ed. Raymond G. Helmick and Rodney L. Petersen (Philadelphia: Templeton Foundation Press, 2001), 374. With Barth we might gather these under two basic trajectories: either "the might of right" justifies "the right of might," or people "serve peace yet pursue cold war," bringing a "provisional peace" that veils a "corresponding provisional hell." ChrL, 221-24.

[54]ChrL, 191, 189.

[55]Ibid., 193-94, emphasis added.

[56]See also Jer 6:14; 8:11; Is 58; Amos 5; Mt 18; Eph 4–5. Barth makes surprisingly little of these passages, but this may prove nothing more than that he thinks his case strong enough without proof texts.

unique mutuality gives witness to the One in whose name they are gathered.[57] Theirs is a "mutual respect and forbearance in love" that refuses "safe restriction to the sphere of a general, abstract and neutral Christianity."[58] Opposing amorphous peace and espousing a "very definite freedom," Barth resisted "rounding off of the picture of Jesus into a kind of ideal-picture of human existence," since it would "necessarily degenerate into a free sketch" of utopia that has turned from its living Lord.[59]

Ironically, one of the things that *conceals* the church from the skeptical world is its refusal of false unity, its willingness to remain open to all kinds of mess. Such is its special visibility. Communion in Christ is as such describable, but ascertainable only to awakened faith. As members of a *believed union* that is *seeking manifestation in time*, believers are repeatedly gathered around the Lord's Table to expose themselves to the healing work of God afresh.[60] This focus on the ever-new quality of the church's fellowship may seem to leave us with no way to speak about church growth. It is certainly the case that it calls into question any focus on church-growth strategies, but does not denounce visible growth entirely. Growth and healing are neither a possessed state nor a hope forever deferred. For Barth the church lives in a "commonly given freedom" of obedience that it "*grows in rendering*" unto God.[61] We misunderstand this growth if we construe it in terms of a character building or habit forming that displaces utter dependence on the Spirit, but we also misunderstand Barth if we think that he has *no* account of growth at all. The church may grow in prayerful obedience, but as such it is never an *achievement* and always an *event*. Whatever health and growth is experienced carries forward "with constant reference to the promise of the Lord."[62]

It is the Spirit of Pentecost (and not some other commonality) that unifies in diversity and reconciles in enmity—overcoming disputes and disparities by reminding people that "they must always reassemble and be brought into harmony" in Christ.[63] Each celebration of the Lord's Supper

---

[57] *ChrL*, 77 and 84.
[58] *CD* IV/3.2, 815.
[59] *CD* IV/2, 361, 363, and *CD* IV/1, 167.
[60] *CD* IV/1, 668 and 684.
[61] Ibid., 151, emphasis added.
[62] Ibid., 684-85.
[63] *CD* IV/3.2, 800-801; see also 900.

looks to be both a grateful celebration and a prayerful instantiation of the darkness's dispelling in this regard. So it is that the eccentric fellowship of God's children does not bow to the presuppositions of a "friendfoe relationship," but "includes human and Christian brotherhood with all the problems entailed."[64] Rather than reveling in the hegemonic unity of a conflict well avoided, then, we gather at the table of thanksgiving for the gracious provision of fellowship and peace. This peace may be difficult to pin down, but it is not completely invisible. Christians cannot rail against false peace and then, when put to the question, retreat into mystery thanking God that, somehow, "with all their false notes the Father hears his pure voice."[65] In Barth's view we need more than an "indefinite talk about a life of forgiveness" that lends itself to "a kind of nondescript Christianity."[66] Whether he intended to describe this in more detail or not, Barth certainly did not leave his ecclesiology indefinite. It has been the thrust of this book to draw out and build upon Barth's description of the earthly historical presence of Christ as it carries forward amid, but ultimately undefined by, the currents of conflict and enmity.

Rather than see the ministry of reconciliation as a series of bandages applied to what remains a definitive pathology, it has been important to underline the sacrament-shaped dynamics of faith and fellowship that surround and uphold the practices of interpersonal Christian forgiveness. Just as the less common medical rubric of *apithology* points to "the presence of health" rather than "merely the absence of sickness," so it may be argued that the ministry of reconciliation is not just a response to sin, but a foreshadowing of new creation.[67] Apart from the interruptions of sin and death we may look forward to real encounters of growing relationship with diverse others under the common reign of Christ. In a fully consummated kingdom it will be our experience that nothing is ultimately irreconcilable. In the meantime, the prayer for "the peace of God, which surpasses all understanding"

---

[64]*ChrL*, 210, 83; see 85-86.

[65]Ibid., 108.

[66]*CD* IV/2, 504, and *CD* IV/1, 678. "It is not the restoration of a parallelism and equipoise in which God and the world, God and man, will now continue to live together happily. This is—slightly caricatured—the this-worldly, immanentist and middle-class understanding of the being in Jesus Christ given by God." *CD* IV/1, 110; see *CD* IV/2, 368-69.

[67]Will Varey, "Apithology: An Emergent Continuum," *Aspects of Apithology* 1, no. 1 (2008): 3-4; www.aspects.apithology.org/Aspects.Vol.1.No.1.pdf.

(Phil 4:7) propels a life that is not afraid or reactionary but hopefully peaceable in the face of strife.[68]

So it is that we dispense with our illusions of either triumphalism or gloom and take an important step toward a truer vision of the church. Freed from lordless powers for those of a risen Lord, believers are called to follow the Prince of Peace in enemy-occupied territory, without the enemy setting the terms of engagement. This flavors the corresponding interdependence in important ways, beginning with the fact that believers do not "break solidarity with other Christians" to "make separate peace with God."[69] In Matthew 18 it is in the context of working out their problems that Jesus promises to be with the two or three who are gathered in his name.[70] This is not a promise to only be visible at the "sitcom ending" when everything has been "smoothed over," but to be there with a church that is with Christ on the way. Having seen how the sacraments shape Christian life, we turn our attention now to the ways that Barth looked to the Lord's Prayer to fill it in.

BETWEEN SUPPERS: LIVING BY THE LORD'S PRAYER (§76–§78)

In the introduction to his unfinished ethics of reconciliation, Barth indicated that the Lord's Prayer would be the centerpiece because it speaks to the question of "the continual renewal of the Christian life" wherein Christ's command will "newly acquire and maintain its actuality."[71] Jesus is the only one who can rightfully pray "*my* Father," but in his sending by "the Father of mercies" he has put "*our* Father" on the lips of those with whom he "accepts solidarity" in the events of his incarnation.[72] With this come the words of forgiveness, invoked from the Father and shared by his children in Jesus' name each day. That this forgiveness has already been provided does not negate the fact that it is also to be asked for on an ongoing basis along with the prayer for his kingdom to come.[73] In the same way that the prayer for daily bread does not define the kingdom by its hunger, so the

---

[68]*CD* IV/3.2, 593-94. See also *CD* IV/1, 711, 724.

[69]*ChrL*, 190, 192. "Where there is no 'Glory to God in the highest' even the sincerest longing and loudest shouting for peace on earth will never lead to anything but new divisions." *CD* IV/2, 421.

[70]*CD* IV/1, 680.

[71]*ChrL*, 45-46. Barth considered calling this life the "path from baptism to the Lord's Supper." Ibid., 288.

[72]Ibid., 68, quoting 2 Cor 1:3 (NASB), see also 83, 88 and 149.

[73]*CD* IV/1, 412.

prayer for shared forgiveness does not define it by its sins. Jesus leads believers to pray not just *against* evil but *for* the kingdom of heaven to come on earth. Put on the lips of his disciples, Jesus' prayer is an invitation to action. As Barth saw it, the prayer makes clear that "obedient human action in this vertical direction" also "implies . . . the horizontal of a corresponding human, and therefore provisional, attitude and mode of conduct."[74] The prayer evokes action that does not lose the character of a prayer. To gather up the ethic and ethos of forgiveness that has been thus far described, we thus conclude with a consideration of the place of invocation and lamentation in the life of a Christ-confessing church.

The art of correct asking: The invocations of the confessing church. On the cusp of his "special ethics" Barth set the tone for his foregrounding of invocation when he wrote, "The community works, but it also prays. More precisely, it prays as it works. And in praying, it works. Prayer . . . is a movement in which Christians jointly and persistently engage."[75] As discussed in chapter one, by selecting the rubric of invocation for his ethics Barth indicated that it would be neither the growth of skills nor the possession of virtues that would make an ethic Christian. What makes this ethic special is that we relinquish control, not by rendering ourselves adrift, inactive or fickle, but by fixating on the reconciling work of the Lord Jesus Christ, invoking the Spirit's guidance and empowerment in the community, and obeying accordingly. As Christians we stand under the "free commanding of God," and God will "always be new to us people each morning."[76] In this, *free* does not mean *fickle*, and *new* does not necessarily mean *novel*. To call it "ever-new" and "free" is to indicate the character of Christian life as day-to-day service in the timely grace of God.

Barth exhibits such a confidence in the perpetual guidance and empowerment of Christ that it has to be taken seriously if his ethic of forgiveness is to be understood. If ethics means daily asking God what we should *do*, Barth does not think it means starting from zero each time. In fact, asking God what to do is an "authentic and therefore a fruitful question" precisely

---

[74]*ChrL*, 212-13. This prayer is not truly prayed "without its determining their whole action as a direct response" to the Father to whom it is prayed. Ibid., 57.

[75]*CD* IV/3.2, 882.

[76]*ChrL*, 5 and 236. The task of special ethics is "to point to that event between God and man, to its uncontrollable content." Ibid., 4-5; see also 79.

because it "cannot be asked in a vacuum." In this so-called *command ethic* we expect not "an uncontoured plenitude of accidental or arbitrary individual acts" but a perceptible "encounter with the living God."[77] Barth does not deny the contingencies of historicity. Nor does Barth deny any constancy to the Christian life—instead he simply insists that Christ will be the one to provide it. To be a Christian is to trust Jesus precisely in the concrete corners of the everyday, where we live attentively to the Holy Spirit, in the context of his church, according to his Word.[78] In this account of Christian ethics it is the sheer centrality of prayerful deliberation that is most alarming. Is there a community that can sustain such vitality of invocation and action? It does not seem that even Barth thinks so. But divine forgiveness is the impetus and perpetual renewal of that community-dynamic nonetheless.

If invocation seems a shaky way forward, Barth thinks an ethic based on human will or virtue is even shakier. Perhaps what we are imagining is the "sham question" of the one "who knows very well" what the answer is and is only asking in order to avoid it.[79] God's particular guidance may be unpredictable and uncomfortable, but Christians trust that it will be intelligible and recognizable as the self-revelation of Jesus Christ. With Barth, what we are looking for in the church's common life is not a "controlling sociological mechanism" nor the "application of a general, natural, historical, social rule" but a "completely new and special event" wherein even the "sheer readiness to learn" cannot be treated in terms of a "schooled erudition."[80] The church's life has its constancy in invocation, and invocation is not a monologue. Ethics, Barth explains, "cannot itself give direction." What it can do is "give instruction in the art of correct asking about God's will and open hearing of God's command."[81]

It does sound like Barth is trying to have it both ways. Is there any difference if one calls ethics an *art* rather than a *skill*? This remains an important

---

[77]Ibid., 31 and 5.

[78]Ibid., 13-18. John Yocum is right to challenge Barth's polemic against continuities in church life, but it is misleading to describe Barth's alternative as an event with an "invisible occurrence, impossible to locate in space or time, or to describe psychologically or socially in any depth." Yocum, *Ecclesial Mediation*, 183. See Webster, *Barth's Ethics*, 123, 219-20, and Karl Barth, *The Teaching of the Church Regarding Baptism*, trans. Ernest A. Payner (London: SCM Press, 1948), 19.

[79]*ChrL*, 31-32; see also Lk 3:10; 12:17; Acts 2:36; Rom 12:1-3.

[80]*CD* IV/4, 133, and *ChrL*, 80; see also 267-68.

[81]*ChrL*, 34; see also 103-4.

question, but for our purposes the key is that ethics instructs in the *art of correct asking*. It seeks to be true, and it is true by seeking Christ. That this can be learned does not mean it ends in self-sufficiency. In such an ethic one learns ever to be seeking and confessing Christ. To say that such a life loses constancy and content may say more of one's view of Christ than of the ethic itself. In Barth's view one does not walk this path of invocation and obedience *alone*. The Christ invoked is the one received in the provision of Scripture. Scripture is heard with the church in which it comes, and in the world in which the Spirit works. This is not an isolationist ethic—not because of a prevailing fear of error or a prior commitment to social reasoning, but because the particularity of God's guidance to individuals is given in "togetherness with them, as one of the fellowship of the saints."[82]

This brings us back to what Webster calls "the reciprocal active life of humanity," which Barth says proceeds "solely by the free mercy of God."[83] This should make clear not only how vital is forgiveness to such a fellowship, but also how important is invocation to the practice of interpersonal forgiveness and reconciliation. Whether one is the forgiven or the forgiver, in either case one is confessing Christ as Lord over the sin-stained situation. In an important sense, sin is being confessed as sin by both parties in Jesus' name, just as the forgiveness of Christ is being confessed and his presence invoked for correction and restoration. When Barth says no "art or craft" or "organised improvement of the human lot" is being handed over by Jesus as a program to peace, it does not mean we should be overcautious about detailing the actual imperatives involved in this confession.[84] Is there an *art of correct asking* in this regard? In this book we have stopped short of prescribing a program of reconciliation, but have sought to give a thick description of the rhythms of reconciliation that are struck up in the freedom of divine forgiveness. Is this to say that there is a particular church order that ought to be encouraged in order to keep these rhythms alive?

Ordered by grace: Accountability in the reign of Christ. Given all that has been argued, it behooves us to consider whether there might be a church order more to be recommended than any other. For his part, Barth was

---

[82]*CD* IV/2, 596.
[83]Webster, *Barth's Ethics*, 46, and *ChrL*, 263-64.
[84]*CD* IV/2, 216-17.

frustrated by expectations that he dogmatically recommend a single church polity, suggesting that an obsession with order may result in "communities of interest" that can only be considered churchly "movements" if we do not "inquire too closely what it really is that unites them."[85]

However the church arranges itself, he said elsewhere, the "word 'Church' must point to this sovereignty of Jesus" or else it "points where there is no Church."[86] Barth was not the first to signify church order under the rubric of the *regnum Christi*, but he did insist most adamantly that this is not about *timeless rules* but an *ever-present reign*.[87] As we have shown, however, Barth was not interested in distilling the church to a formless existence. When Barth broached the issue of church order in the second part-volume, he questioned the notion that the "great campaign against chaos and therefore against disorder" could "fail to have its own order," suggesting that it does have "specific form" and "distinctness."[88]

In §67.4 Barth highlighted four normative presuppositions for "The Order of the Community": the community (1) exists as it serves Jesus Christ, and in that light, one another; (2) is centered in the event of its public worship; (3) orders itself in terms of a "living law"; and (4) offers the world an "exemplary law" in the form of a "living order of fellowship."[89] It has been the work of this book to inquire further into this living order for its exemplary Christianness, and this has led us to what might be called Barth's ecclesiological manifesto: "The promise of the Lord that where two or three are gathered together in His name He is there in the midst *will be true of this Church in spite of the doubtful nature of its separate existence*."[90] In other words, the church's existence is inseparable from its gathering in Jesus' name for shared forgiveness.

---

[85]*CD* IV/1, 706. Kimlyn Bender notes Barth's criticism of the Oxford Group on this score. See Bender, "The Church in Karl Barth and Evangelicalism," in *Karl Barth and American Evangelicalism*, ed. Bruce L. McCormack and Clifford B. Anderson (Grand Rapids: Eerdmans, 2011), 188-89. See Karl Barth, "Church or Group Movement?" *The London Quarterly and Holborn Review* (January 1937): 1-10.

[86]Barth, *God Here and Now*, 61, 63.

[87]Yoder uses Martin Bucer's rubric of "the rule of Christ" to steer toward reconciliation procedures. See Yoder, *For the Nations*, 30, and *Body Politics: Five Practices of the Christian Community Before the Watching World* (Scottdale, PA: Herald Press, 1992), 7. See also *CD* IV/2, 678-79, and *CD* IV/3.2, 898-99.

[88]*CD* IV/2, 676-77, 710 and 715.

[89]See ibid., 690, 695, 710 and 719. See also 640, 678, 691-93.

[90]*CD* IV/1, 680, emphasis added. See Mt 18:20, and *CD* IV/3.2, 899.

The point to be pressed home here is that this is an account of church "order" that could carry on within a number of organizational structures. Barth thinks there is "no such thing as universal Church law," but looks instead for what Erik Wolf called "confessing law."[91] Despite the fact that the people of the church are "well aware how imperfectly" they might pursue cooperation with their brothers and sisters, in Barth's view it is not this imperfection but "always perfectionism which makes Church law sterile." As baptized partakers in the Lord's Supper they "know themselves as people who stand in absolute need of . . . the forgiveness of their sins," who share communion "in spite of all the wrong committed."[92] For Barth this is not the doorway to merely tolerant, undisciplined community, but to mutual accountability in the free grace of God.

True to form, when Barth addresses the issue of church discipline he does not give us a methodology, but directs us to the life of *"mutua consolatio."*[93] If this sounds more in line with a free church ecclesiology, it goes with the grain of Barth's own leaning, but by his own insistence it does not preclude other forms of church polity.[94] Fully aware that there were missteps on either side of the Reformation (such as the system of indulgences or the failings of Bucer's *Christlichen Gemeinschaften*), Barth maintains the importance of churchly accountability and warns against the ways that this mutual care can break down.[95] In evangelical experience it has often been the case that this

---

[91]*CD* IV/2, 690, 682; see also 710-14.

[92]Ibid., 718-19, 701 and 704; see also 710.

[93]*CD* IV/3.2, 886. See *CD* IV/2, 694, 706; *CD* IV/3.2, 801 and *CD* IV/4, 210.

[94]Barth does lean toward a free church model, but this could pertain to almost any church order, if the authorities and structures thrived on rather than closed off mutual accountability and reform. See *CD* IV/2, 689, and Barth, *God Here and Now*, 76, 78. Bender thus observes that for all the critiques it brings to bear on evangelicalism, Barth's ecclesiology may be particularly suited to it, and indeed may supply Protestantism the theological impetus to finally blossom in this area. One of the reasons for this is that Barth's ecclesiology "gives rise to a new form of politics in the world" wherein locality and universality are well related. See Bender, "Church in Karl Barth," 197-200. For an apt warning against subsuming church order under the premises of democracy, however, see Bernd Wannenwetsch, *Political Worship: Ethics for Christian Citizens*, trans. Margaret Kohl (Oxford: Oxford University Press, 2004), 298.

[95]On Bucer's difficulties see Gottfried Hammann, "The Creation of the 'Christlichen Gemein- schaften,'" in *Martin Bucer: Reforming Church and Community*, ed. D. F. Wright (Cambridge: Cambridge University Press, 1994), 129-43, and David Lawrence, *Martin Bucer: Unsung Hero of the Reformation* (Nashville: Westview Publishing Co., 2007), 138. Besides Bucer, Barth notes Zwingli, Calvin, Spener, Wesley, "Georg Calixt, J. Duraeus, Jean Frédéric Osterwald and Leib- niz," and "Zinzendorf and his community." *CD* IV/3.1, 26, 36.

mutual accountability in the priesthood of believers has been the seedbed for all manner of shortcuts—including public shamings, indiscretions of intimacy, unspoken codes of honor, legalism, rampant gossip, slanderous politics and manipulative cults of leadership. If authority structures do not eliminate these problems, neither does the removal of them. Furthermore, in an uninstitutionalized church's efforts to combat these dysfunctions, Barth observes a prevalent temptation to defer once again to professionals—this time not of the priestly but the psychological variety. From this it is clear that Barth means to reserve a place for the counseling arts as long as they partake in the event character of the gospel-driven fellowship and *serve* rather than *replace* the unique mutuality of invocation and accountability that this entails.[96] The "true leader" is the one who ranges with all the others "most seriously and unreservedly" as a helper, and it is this investment in the "reciprocal responsibility" of the community that is the focus of pastoral energy and authority in the church.[97]

If church accountability is so mutual, and authority so defined, how does the church approach those difficult situations which seem to call for a person's separation from the community? The posture and procedure for such a thing was discussed in chapter five, but it is worth reiterating that the primary interest is not for the *appearance* of a church's purity but the "mutual trust" of its "glad and confident participation" in the fellowship of Christ.[98] The church is not to be caught up with "the form or quality of their character, culture, morality, or human appearance and achievement," but with the question whether there is a perpetual reorientation to God, others and self— even if this highlights rather than distracts from the struggles they face.[99]

Disturbed sinners: Hopeful lamentation in the confessing church. As has already been discussed, it is at the point of describing ethics as invocation

---

[96]*CD* IV/3.2, 885-86. "It certainly cannot be questioned that such emergencies and also such callings and endowments do in fact exist," but therapy cannot "take over" or "try to solve" what remains a "witness of the kingdom which only the community can set up." Psychological arts do not compete with but find their place within the larger sphere of the ecclesial "cure of souls." Ibid., 886-87. Gregory Jones observes "that much of the fascination with counseling in our culture is the direct result of failures to embody such Christian community, people marked by forgiving love for one another." Jones, *Embodying Forgiveness*, 178.
[97]*CD* IV/2, 709, 723.
[98]Ibid., 701.
[99]See *CD* IV/3.2, 877-78 and 895-96.

and the church as an event that Barth's account of shared forgiveness becomes susceptible to accusations of naiveté or blissful ignorance. With this
in mind we conclude by reckoning with the character of hope and the place
of lamentation in a confessing church.[100] The first thing to be reiterated is
that, for Barth, confession is misunderstood unless there is both the positive
confession of Christ and the negative confession of sin. In fact, it is the
former that undergirds and enables the latter. Confession is not simply the
name we give to the cry of those in misery; it is their "discovery of the true
situation" in Christ.[101] Confession is not about *coming to terms* with our
sin-stained situation, it is about "falling-out" with ourselves (and the lordless
powers), under the direction of the Spirit in communion under the Word
of God.[102] Confession is not a symbolic gesture used to rise above guilt and
take hold of a latent goodness, nor is it a "futile vacillation" between the old
self and the new. Confession invokes Christ's "constant differentiation" of
old from new in a "constant prevailing of the promised forgiveness of sins"
that is "sought and apprehended afresh every moment out of the deepest
need."[103] This *is* the Christian life. In Barth's view, as it is in baptism so it is
in everyday life: the Spirit forges a moving frontier between the old and the
new creation, freeing us for a "specific renunciation" and a "specific pledge"
along the lines of grace in Christ.[104]

Christian life and community is not a matter of affirming that *all is forgiven* but of confessing *the God who forgives*.[105] When John Milbank rightly

---

[100]"Confessing church" is a name attached to the group of German churches who resisted Nazi
influence, as represented by the Barmen Declaration cowritten by Barth. As a phrase it makes
sparse appearance in the *Church Dogmatics*, and has more political ramifications than we are
utilizing here. See *CD* IV/3.1, 21-22.

[101]*CD* IV/1, 579; see also *ChrL*, 24, 26-27.

[102]*CD* IV/2, 566, 570, 574; see also 548-52. Barth thinks English lacks a word that gets across the
significance of the German word *Auseinandersetzung*, but "coming to terms" may well be the
best English rendering, since it can refer to both acquiescence and genuine grappling with gritty
realities. In any case, Barth is clear: "What might sound a most intolerant statement must not
be suppressed in this connection. . . . Christians who refuse to sit with their Master at the table
of publicans and sinners, are *not* Christians at all." In fact, "the Christian ethos in big and little
things alike . . . depends at every time and in every situation on whether or not Christians come
before God as *beginners*." *ChrL*, 80.

[103]*CD* IV/1, 602; see also *CD* IV/2, 723.

[104]See *CD* IV/4, 153-54, 158-59. As we have seen, this frontier is traveled on every day not because
of a deficiency in Christ's accomplishment but because of the nature of its provision in time.
Ibid., 145.

[105]See *CD* IV/1, 577.

notes that the "economy of forgiveness could not be reduced to a workable calculus of self-interest," as an alternative he offers the rather abstract logic of "infinite giving," thereby losing some of the particularity of Christian confession.[106] For Barth, there is a similar problem when the renunciations and pledges of a confessing community are frequently generalized and rarely specific. On one hand, to dwell only on the level of negative renunciation is to stay on the underside of forgiveness, always coping with "worldly grief." On the other hand, to dwell only on the level of one's positive pledge is to pretend to reside topside of forgiveness, resisting "godly grief" and upholding an ahistorical self-righteousness (2 Cor 7:10). In either case one is at risk of turning the Christian life into a catharsis of self-managed forgiveness, wallowing in a deluded freedom that amounts to devotion to an unknown god. What separates false forgiveness from true is that the former is an "indefinite" amnesty and the latter a Christ-won liberation from death to life.[107]

With Barth we have seen emphasis on the point that, because Christ stands alone as both Judge and Justifier, the confessing church renounces not only sin but also its habits of self-justification and judgment. Once a "disturbed sinner" takes solace in such patterns of self-judgment and vindication, he or she begins to act more like an "undisturbed sinner" precisely by managing inner peace within a cycle of self-scouring guilt and self-earned release.[108] Barth explicitly warns against "systematizing the event of the confrontation" with Jesus Christ in this way: "To lose one's life is not of itself to find it."[109] In Christian baptism, Barth says, "further efforts at self-justification and self-cleansing" are renounced right along with sin.[110] The most succinct expression of this (and of the whole thesis of this book!) might be found in Barth's poignant quip, "The habit of self-forgiveness spoils [one's] taste for a life by free grace."[111]

Self-justification is not merely a personal temptation of which to beware; it can infect an entire church's worship and way of being. Barth makes us keenly aware how easy it is for Protestants to perpetuate the pattern of penance.

---

[106]John Milbank, *Being Reconciled: Ontology and Pardon* (London: Routledge, 2003), 46-47.
[107]See *CD* IV/1, 360, 364, 497-98 and *CD* IV/2, 504-5.
[108]*CD* IV/2, 524; see also 475, 492-93, and *CD* IV/4, 145.
[109]*CD* IV/3.1, 448, and *CD* IV/2, 283-84; see also *CD* IV/2, 288-89, 294-95, and *CD* IV/1, 628.
[110]*CD* IV/4, 159.
[111]*CD* IV/2, 461; see also *CD* IV/1, 372, and *CD* IV/3.1, 448.

"The priestly art as such," he says, "can turn into the very opposite of all that is intended by it. The priest as such can always be a deluded and deluding pope."[112] In *The Christian Life* Barth observes how, once freed from the institutionalized forms of penance, Christians nonetheless untheologically multiplied the temptation to enact it by psychological, political, aesthetic and moral means.[113] Such comments might elicit reflection on the ways that musical repetition, inspirational preaching and programmatic catering to the "felt needs" of "seekers" might be symptomatic of a grace that is cheapened not by passive but active sloth. The practice of penitence management may be alive and well in the context of Western individualism and consumerism, and it may be all too easy for a therapeutic and commodified version of forgiveness to be pressed into service in this regard. As Barth saw it, if a church fits into this mold too neatly, it becomes the harbinger of a "succulent lie" and works to "appropriate and domesticate" the message of Christ.[114] At its worst, its proclamation of the good news forsakes true witness for "energetic and skilful propaganda."[115]

In the confessing church wherein forgiveness finds its home, Christ's real presence is invoked to take the pulse of the community and move it to greater faithfulness. There is always the chance that people will turn penitence into penance by putting the impetus on self-preparation, or by conjuring up what psychologist's call "'witness stand' remorse" in order to evade the truthful grace of Christ, but this is also the place where such things are most likely to be seen for what they are.[116] As believers come to confess the preeminence of Christ's mercy in a community of faith, "the manoeuvres of lying man are constantly disrupted and thwarted as by an invisible hand."[117] Here the church is called not to be a gathering of sycophants, contrarians, guilt-trippers or fear-mongers, but a people freed to listen to God and one another as the Spirit guides into truth.

This brings us to an important question about the place of lamentation in Christ-confessing communities. How likely is this ethos of mutual confession

---

[112]*CD* IV/1, 429.
[113]*ChrL*, 151-53.
[114]*CD* IV/3.1, 438, 442.
[115]*ChrL*, 136.
[116]For an observation of this phenomenon see Pumla Gobodo-Madikizela, *A Human Being Died That Night: A South African Woman Confronts the Legacy of Apartheid* (New York: Mariner Books, 2004), 125.
[117]*CD* IV/3.1, 475.

if a fellowship of worshipers has little time for prayers that find their humble beginnings in inarticulate groaning? To put a sharper point on it, one might ask, How many occasions for interpersonal repentance and reconciliation have been short-circuited by too much presumption and not enough invocation on the part of the offended party, the offender, or both? Jesus begins his reconciliatory instructions in Matthew 18 with an all-important *if*, but it is too often presumed that the whole answer to that *if* will be perfectly clear from the outset. The scenario Jesus utilizes is one where the sin is clear—but what if it is not? As Gregory Jones observes, "Not all situations of brokenness call for specific words of forgiveness or requests for forgiveness," but may require endurance and lament instead.[118] If it is expected that people will come together with privately formed, fully articulated renunciations before they can take a common pledge together in Christ, far too much weight will be placed on personal introspection and not nearly enough room left for the interpersonal discourse required. Thus a confessing community such as we have been describing is going to need to make room in its common life and worship for prayers of lamentation—more room, in fact, than Barth's own account seems to have recommended.

Daniel Migliore is not the only commentator who has detected an "insufficient attention to the prayer of lament" in Barth's work. Indeed, despite his expressed opposition to such a thing, at times Barth's own rhetoric leaves us with a rather stoic, flat-lined sense of triumph.[119] On occasion he spoke pejoratively about "constant questioning, worrying, complaining, accusing and protesting against God and the world," suggesting that "the presence of the Spirit gives us no grounds for sighing," so "how can we help being merry even here and to-day?"[120] On the other hand, however, Barth also contrasted the admirable waiting and pleading of Job with the presumptuous eagerness of his friends to console. He explained that "the fact that God lives is what

---

[118]Jones, *Embodying Forgiveness*, 230.

[119]Daniel L. Migliore, "Freedom to Pray: Karl Barth's Theology of Prayer," in Karl Barth, *Prayer*, 2nd ed. (Louisville: Westminster John Knox Press, 2002), 112. See also Robert McAfee Brown, "Introductory Essay," in Karl Barth and Johannes Hamel, *How to Serve God in a Marxist Land* (New York: Association Press, 1959), 36; Alan Torrance, "Christian Experience and Divine Revelation in the Theologies of Friedrich Schleiermacher and Karl Barth," in *Christian Experience in Theology and Life*, ed. I. Howard Marshall (Edinburgh: Rutherford House Books, 1988), 111; and G. C. Berkouwer, *The Triumph of Grace in the Theology of Karl Barth* (London: Paternoster, 1956), 247-48, 279.

[120]CD IV/3.1, 243, 359-60; see also CD IV/3.2, 642, and ChrL, 59, 167.

makes it impossible for Job . . . to yield to his friends and to cease his cycle of questioning, petition, protest and resignation."[121] In other words, the hastiness of Job's friends to cheer him up ensured that there was "never any real contact" between them and Job, betraying the fact that they did not really believe God to be as self-involved in history as Job believed God to be.[122]

To some degree, then, if we look past the scarcity of explicit exhortation to lament in Barth's *Doctrine of Reconciliation* we do see resonances with the ecclesial ethos we are describing. In one place, Barth commends the imprecatory psalms on account of the observation that their authors betray no express intention "of avenging themselves on their oppressors," but invoke God to be "Defender and Avenger" instead. As an act of confession, then, they let their cries "ring out passionately and even wildly" in a manner "offensive to the abstract moral taste of the modern age" but nonetheless vital to the life of faith in the face of evil.[123] Such crying out can of course be little more than a rehearsal of rage, entitlement or despair, deflecting appropriate relational confrontation into a merely private catharsis. But this is exactly why lamentation needs to be enfolded in Christian community and rendered a part of its life of *invocation and confession*.[124]

When the prevailing enmity benefits from the repression of struggling voices, a church with no space for lament may stifle discernment and accountability, playing right into the lordless powers' hands. So Barth's warnings against false peace and the development of his special ecclesiology lead us toward agreement with Wannenwetsch, who says that "*as long as people can worship together, they can dispute freely with each other.*" Including lamentation and confession in the worship of the church "makes it possible for them to be led out of the vicious cycle of mere reaction" and into a community of real engagement.[125] In our view this not only fills in what was left implicit in Barth's ecclesial vision but also vividly explains why the Lord's Prayer for kingdom come carries on in a corporate supplication for daily nourishment, shared forgiveness and deliverance from evil.

---

[121]*CD* IV/3.1, 423-24; see also 366, and *CD* IV/2, 484.

[122]Ibid., 403, 425, 456, 458.

[123]Ibid., 209-10.

[124]See John Swinton, *Raging with Compassion: Pastoral Responses to the Problem of Evil* (Grand Rapids: Eerdmans, 2007), 138, 171-76.

[125]Wannenwetsch, *Political Worship*, 304 and 307.

When Emmanuel Levinas looked at the horrors of evil in our world he said, "No one, not even God, can substitute himself for the victim."[126] Notwithstanding the illegitimate limits this places on God, the statement does express a respect for life and for the victim that Christians ought to affirm. However, it also radicalizes evil to such an extent that it ultimately neutralizes talk of either mercy or justice. That Jesus Christ rose from the dead and reigns over creation as the reconciling God is our only hope for both justice and peace. To say this is not to discount Levinas's point about the trivialization of suffering, but is to take up the truth of his lament in faith, making it an invocation of none other than the dead and resurrected God-man, Jesus Christ.

We do well to remember that public attempts to come to grips with trauma often involve a clamoring for words that Christians should not be too quick, pastorally speaking, to pounce on for the sake of a well-argued theodicy. If Christians listen long enough to such incipient laments they are likely to hear the Spirit interceding amid the groans before they need to say a word. Consider the account of Nazi death camps in Elie Wiesel's *Night*, wherein the climactic expression of evil's profundity finds words in the imagined death of God, "hanging here on the gallows."[127] One does not need to be told that the child's death is horrific and deplorable, of course, but the reference to a divine hanging opens up space for empathetic resonance that actually puts that loss of life in its most tragic perspective possible: in the light of the value put on it by God himself at the cross. Or consider the account of Rwandan genocide given by Roméo Dallaire, wherein he describes his helplessness and undesired complicity in some of the worst evils imaginable and, searching for a conclusion devoid of religious jargon, declares that "we are in desperate need of a transfusion of humanity."[128] The best Christian response to these unaddressed lamentations, as to Levinas' objection, may be to groan in solidarity and nonetheless to ask this: What if God *can* substitute for the victim? What if God can instigate not only resurrection but a just and true reconciliation?

---

[126]Emmanuel Levinas, *Difficult Freedom: Essays on Judaism*, trans. Sean Hand (Baltimore: Johns Hopkins University Press, 1997), 20, cited in Nick Smith, *I Was Wrong: The Meanings of Apologies* (Cambridge: Cambridge University Press, 2008), 139.

[127]Elie Wiesel, *Night*, trans. Stella Rodway (New York: Bantam Books, 1982), 62.

[128]Roméo Dallaire with Brent Beardsley, *Shake Hands with the Devil: The Failure of Humanity in Rwanda* (Toronto: Vintage Canada, 2003), 522.

Without a risen Lord, such faith is futile. With a risen Lord there is reason for hope. In the hoping there is reason for lamentation, invocation and confession, and in the community gathered in faith there is room and reason for forgiveness and for the patient work of reconciliation.

Conclusion

THE CENTRAL CONVICTION underlining *The Doctrine of Reconciliation* is that the world is reconciled to God, by God, in Christ; thus from now on the followers of Jesus look at no one from a merely worldly point of view. This reconciling mission of God does not *depend* on those followers, but it also does not take place without them. So it is that the prayer for God's will to be done on earth as it is in heaven informs every aspect of Christian life and community. The remainder of Jesus' prayer provides the impetus to ask what on earth it means for us to ask *our Father in heaven* to *forgive as we forgive*, and to do so from within a theology attuned to the task. We found this in Barth, whose ecclesiology definitively declares, "It is the Church which . . . knows and confesses that it needs the forgiveness of sins."[1]

Our close reading of Karl Barth's *The Doctrine of Reconciliation* has sought to analyze and appropriate his theology of forgiveness at the height of its intersection with ecclesiology and ethics. In chapter one, we took the pulse of Barth's work on those two fronts and emerged largely sympathetic with Barth's project, albeit attentive to the cautions to be heeded. If Barth's practical account of Christian life is to be appropriated we must still specify the proper constancy and character of that community that seeks to be made ever new in Christ, while resisting the urge to overinvest ourselves in means and methods.

With this in view, in chapter two we began a section-by-section analysis of *The Doctrine of Reconciliation* that sought to gather up the points most

---

[1] CD IV/1, 658. The biblical references alluded to include Mt 6:9-15; Lk 11:1-52; Cor 5:11-21.

relevant to our project. This began with the insistence that a proper Christian account of forgiveness must find its central impetus in the positive mission of God in Christ rather than in reaction to the parasitic realities of sin and enmity. In the face of our selfishness, our self-help religion and our falsification of the created order, God's already gracious self-giving love has overflowed in the forgiving love of Christ that is freely shared with the world and is, as such, to be freely shared among its recipients. What we saw when we examined Barth's soteriology on this score was that he considered the ongoing ministry of reconciliation to be as much a work of Christ as its accomplishment once and for all. Because Jesus rose from the grave as Lord, justification is temporally and historically situated, and is as missional as it is personal. In the forgiveness of God there is not only freedom *from* sin but freedom *for* life and love. To separate these is to relinquish crucial aspects of what forgiveness entails.

With evocative points such as these, in chapter three we were able to trace out Barth's ecclesiology and see the importance of situating interpersonal forgiveness within the telos of Christ's reconciling work, particularly in the context of the church's fellowship and witness on the way to full redemption. There we saw that interpersonal reciprocity and mutuality are integral to Christian life and community, contained within the telos not only of sanctification but also justification. Here, too, we saw that the gift of forgiveness entails a vocation to share it freely, buoyed by the embeddedness of one's salvation within God's reconciling of the entire world to God's self in Christ, thereby canceling any grounds for self-righteous triumphalism or sequestered selfish piety.

With that we came to our fourth and fifth chapters, wherein we sought to work out a Christian definition of forgiveness by seeking to vitally embed it with other aspects of the church's ministry of reconciliation. There we followed through on Barth's insistence that forgiveness is a gift of God that we are either in process of sharing or relinquishing. To receive it personally is to receive it in the context of God's mercy to all. To harbor it privately is to indulge in a fabrication of the self-centered and depraved imagination. In order to differentiate freely shared forgiveness from cheap grace, however, it was incumbent upon us to follow through on Barth's thick description of justification (interwoven as it is with sanctification and vocation) with an equally nuanced account of the interpersonal realities therein entailed. Thus we sought to tease out the relation of forgiveness to other reconciliatory activities—including forbearance, gracious confrontation, reciprocal confession, repentance, correction and restoration—all the while aiming not to overprescribe a sequential order of reconciliation, thus turning gospel into law. Detailing these relations no doubt left a complex picture of interpersonal life, but not one that is more or less complex than the situations within which we find ourselves trying to be faithful. Forgiveness remains the simple imperative that opens up a host of opportunities for hopeful engagement with brothers, sisters, neighbors and enemies in the victorious love of Christ. That this is simple and profound, hopeful and difficult should be considered a statement about the perspicuity and relevance of the gospel.

The point expressed was this: while forgiveness is given freely, and is no guarantor of a timely experience of full reconciliation between persons, it loses its uniquely Christian meaning if it is pulled apart from that greater hope and offered in ambiguity. Often the opportunity to articulate it fully is not there, but that does not mean it should be understood according to its lowest common denominator. In fact, in churches where forgiveness serves as an escape from further reconciliation it needs to be corrected and brought into line with its deeper reality in Christ. Self-managed forgiveness does not stem from the true peace of Christ but the false peace that recycles human enmity.

Thus we returned to the delineations of Barth's mature ecclesiology in chapter six, in order to give an account of the common life of the Christ-confessing church. There we reflected on the whole of the Barth's *Doctrine of Reconciliation* from the perspective of its unfinished special ethics. With the baptism part-volume and *The Christian Life* in hand we ascertained the way Barth saw the sacraments and the Lord's Prayer providing the dynamic of mutual confession that comprises the ministry and mission of the church. There we saw the importance of following the Prince of Peace rather than succumbing to a contrived unity. Given the lordless powers and sinful ambivalences exposed by Christ, we were able to distinguish the forgiving love of this community from the strategies of self-forgiveness and false peace which so often prevail in a fallen world. Thus we drew from Barth's vision of the confessing community an even clearer depiction of the people who come together to invoke Christ to prevail upon their situations of experienced enmity. They are an ever-renewed fellowship speaking truth in love, buoyed by the peace that passes understanding and is offered to them all the same. There they find themselves freed to forgive.

Darrell Guder summed it up for us when he wrote that "for Barth, the good news of God's love-made-history in Jesus is the *gift* that becomes the *task* of the church."[2] Joseph Mangina pointed us further when he detected a "politics of forgiveness" in Barth's theology that could be said to proceed along certain lines even as it waited on the lead of the living Lord.[3] In this book we have tried to explore that task and that politic in greater detail. The outcome is a constructive practical theology of forgiveness that I believe is faithful to Barth and in line with the trajectory of his posthumously published fragments.

If divine forgiveness is a gift freely given, it is extended between persons in the hope of a fuller redemption. Such forgiveness is not *conditional* but properly *conditioned* by faith in Christ. It is related to interpersonal acts of reconciliation that are not only enabled by it, but in turn inform its possibilities. It is within the message, ministry and mission of God's reconciliation of the world to himself in Christ that the place and meaning of forgiveness is found. When Jesus healed the paralytic in Mark 2, it may have been to address the people's doubts about this divinity, but his challenge to the scribes may have something further to say to our hearts today as well. They asked, "Who can forgive sins but God alone?" and by showing them his "authority on earth to forgive sins" Jesus was not denying this divine prerogative (Mk 2:7, 10). But he also left us little doubt that his was a mercy to be shared.

---

[2]Darrell L. Guder, "Encountering Barth as a Missional Theologian," *Inspire* 8, no. 1 (Summer/Fall 2003): 15, emphasis added.
[3]Joseph L. Mangina, "The Stranger as Sacrament: Karl Barth and the Ethics of Ecclesial Practice," *International Journal of Systematic Theology* 1, no. 3 (1999): 332-33, 339.

Bibliography

Primary Sources

Barth, Karl. *Anselm: Fides Quaerens Intellectum.* Translated by J. Robinson. London: SCM Press, 1958.

———. *The Christian Life: Church Dogmatics,* IV/4: *Lecture Fragments.* Translated by Geoffrey W. Bromiley. Edinburgh: T&T Clark, 1981.

———. *Das christliche Leben: Die kirchliche Dogmatik,* IV/4: *Fragmente aus dem Nachlass, Vorlesungen 1959–1961.* Zürich: Theologischer Verlag Zürich, 1976.

———. *The Church and the Churches.* Grand Rapids: Eerdmans, 2005.

———. *The Church Dogmatics.* Translated by Geoffrey W. Bromiley and Thomas F. Torrance. Edinburgh: T&T Clark, 1956–1977.

———. "Church or Group Movement?" *The London Quarterly and Hoborn Review* (January 1937): 1-10.

———. "The Church—the Living Congregation of the Living Lord Jesus Christ." In *God Here and Now,* translated by Paul M. van Buren. New York: Routledge, 2003.

———. *Credo: A Presentation of the Chief Problems of Dogmatics with Reference to the Apostles' Creed.* Translated by J. Strathearn McNab. London: Hodder & Stoughton, 1936.

———. *Deliverance to the Captives.* London: Bloomsbury Street, 1961.

———. *The Epistle to the Romans.* Translated by Edwyn C. Hoskyns. London: Oxford Press, 1933.

———. *Ethics.* Translated by Geoffrey W. Bromiley. Edinburgh: T&T Clark, 1981.

———. *Ethik I 1928.* Zürich: Theologischer Verlag Zürich, 1973.

———. *Ethik II 1928/1929.* Zürich: Theologischer Verlag Zürich, 1978.

———. *Evangelical Theology: An Introduction.* Translated by Grover Foley. Grand Rapids: Eerdmans, 1963.

———. "An Exegetical Study of Matthew 28:16-20." In *The Theology of the Christian Mission*, edited by Gerald Harry Anderson. New York: McGraw-Hill, 1961.

———. *God Here and Now.* New York: Routledge, 2003.

———. *God in Action: Theological Addresses.* Translated by Elmer George Homrighausen and Karl Julius Ernst. New York: Round Table Press, 1936.

———. *The Gottingen Dogmatics: Instruction in the Christian Religion.* Edited by H. Reiffen. Translated by G.W. Bromiley. Grand Rapids: Eerdmans, 1991.

———. *The Holy Spirit and the Christian Life: The Theological Basis of Ethics.* Translated by R. Birch Hoyle. Louisville: Westminster John Knox, 1993.

———. *The Humanity of God.* Translated by John Newton Thomas and Thomas Wieser. Richmond, VA: John Knox Press, 1960.

———. *Die Kirchliche Dogmatik.* Zürich: Evangelischer Verlag, 1932–1970.

———. *Letters 1961–1968.* Edited by Jürgen Fangmeier and Hinrich Stoevesandt. Grand Rapids: Eerdmans, 1981

———. "An Outing to the Bruderholz." In *Fragments Grave and Gay.* London: SCM Press, 1971.

———. *Prayer.* Edited by Don E. Saliers. Translated by Sara F. Terrien. 2nd ed. Louisville: Westminster John Knox, 2002.

———. *Protestant Theology in the Nineteenth Century: Its Background and History.* Translated by Brian Cozens and John Bowden. Grand Rapids: Eerdmans, 2002.

———. *The Teaching of the Church Regarding Baptism.* Translated by Ernest A. Payner. London: SCM Press, 1948.

———. "Die Theologie und die Mission in der Gegenwart." *Zwischen den Zeiten* 10 (1932): 189-215.

———. *The Theology of John Calvin.* Translated by Geoffrey W. Bromiley. Grand Rapids: Eerdmans, 1995.

———. *The Theology of Schleiermacher: Lectures at Gottingen, Winter Semester of 1923/24.* Edited by Dietrich Ritschl. Translated by Geoffrey W. Bromiley. Edinburgh: T&T Clark, 1982.

Secondary Sources

Aagaard, Johannes. "Some Main Trends in Modern Protestant Missiology." *Studia Theologica* 19 (1965): 251-52.

Adams, Marilyn McCord. "Forgiveness: A Christian Model." *Faith and Philosophy* 8 (1991): 277-304.

Allender, Dan B., and Tremper Longman III. *Bold Love.* Colorado Springs, CO: NavPress, 1992.

Anderson, Ray S. *The Shape of Practical Theology: Empowering Ministry with Theological Praxis.* Downers Grove, IL: InterVarsity Press, 2001.

Anselm. *Cur Deus Homo.* Edited by Richard D. McCormack. Translated by Sidney Norton Deane. Fort Worth, TX: RDMc Publishing, 2005.

Apel, Karl-Otto. *Diskurs und Verantwortung: Das Problem des Übergangs zur postkonventionellen Moral.* Frankfurt: Suhrkamp, 1992.

Arendt, Hannah. *The Human Condition.* Chicago: University of Chicago Press, 1998.

Arnold, Johann Christoph. *Why Forgive?* Rifton, NY: Plough Publishing House, 2009.

Augsburger, David. *Caring Enough to Confront: Learning to Speak the Truth in Love.* Basingstoke, UK: Herald Press, 1980.

———. *Caring Enough to Forgive: True Forgiveness; Caring Enough Not to Forgive: False Forgiveness.* Scottdale, PA: Herald Press, 1981.

Augustine. *The City of God.* Translated by Marcus Dodds. New York: Random House, 1950.

———. *Confessions.* Translated by Henry Chadwick. Oxford: Oxford University Press, 1991.

Banner, Michael. "A Doctrine of Human Being." In *The Doctrine of God and Theological Ethics,* edited by Alan J. Torrance and Michael Banner. London: T&T Clark, 2006.

Barnes, Elizabeth. "Theological Method and Ecclesiology in Barth." PhD diss., Duke Divinity, 1984.

Barnes, Philip L. "Talking Politics, Talking Forgiveness." *Scottish Journal of Theology* 64, no. 1 (2011): 64-79.

Bash, Anthony. "Forgiveness: A Re-appraisal." *Studies in Christian Ethics* 24, no. 2 (May 2011): 133-46.

———. *Forgiveness and Christian Ethics.* Cambridge: Cambridge University Press, 2007.

Baumeister, R. F., J. J. Exline, and K. L. Sommer. "The Victim Role, Grudge Theory, and Two Dimensions of Forgiveness." In *Dimensions of Forgiveness: Psychological Research and Theological Speculations,* edited by E. L. Worthington Jr. Philadelphia: Templeton Foundation Press, 1998.

Bell, Daniel M. "Forgiveness and the End of Economy." *Studies in Christian Ethics* 20, no. 3 (2007): 325-44.

————. *Liberation Theology After the End of History: The Refusal to Cease Suffering.* New York: Routledge, 2001.

Bellah, Robert N., ed. *Habits of the Heart: Individualism and Commitment in American Life.* Los Angeles: University of California Press, 1996.

Bender, Kimlyn. "The Church in Karl Barth and Evangelicalism." In *Karl Barth and American Evangelicalism,* edited by Bruce L. McCormack and Clifford B. Anderson. Grand Rapids: Eerdmans, 2011.

————. *Karl Barth's Christological Ecclesiology.* Aldershot, UK: Ashgate, 2005.

Bercot, David W., ed., *A Dictionary of Early Christian Beliefs: A Reference Guide to More Than 700 Topics Discussed by the Early Church Fathers.* Peabody, MA: Hendrickson Publishers, 1998.

Berkouwer, G.C. *The Triumph of Grace in the Theology of Karl Barth.* London: Paternoster, 1956.

Beste, Jennifer Erin. *God and the Victim: Traumatic Intrusions on Grace and Freedom.* Oxford: Oxford University Press, 2007.

Biggar, Nigel. *The Hastening That Waits: Karl Barth's Ethics.* Oxford: Clarendon Press, 1993.

————. "Hearing God's Command and Thinking About What's Right: With and Beyond Barth." In *Reckoning with Barth. Essays in Commemoration of the Centenary of Karl Barth's Birth,* edited by Nigel Biggar. Oxford: Oxford University Press, 1988.

————. "Melting the Icepacks of Enmity: Forgiveness and Reconciliation in Northern Ireland." *Studies in Christian Ethics* 24, no. 2 (May 2011): 199-209.

Billman, K. D., and Daniel L. Migliore. *Rachel's Cry.* Cleveland: United Church Press, 1999.

Blain, Edward E. "Karl Barth and His Critics: A Study in Ecclesiology." PhD diss., Drew University, 2001.

Blondel, Jean L., "Prayer and Struggle: Karl Barth's *The Christian Life.*" *St. Luke's Journal of Theology* 23 (1980): 105-15.

Blondel, Maurice. *The Letter on Apologetics and History and Dogma.* Translated by Alexander Dru and Illtyd Trethowan. London: Harvill Press, 1964.

Bonhoeffer, Dietrich. *Discipleship.* Edited by Geffrey B. Kelly and John D. Godsey. Translated by Barbara Green and Reinhard Krauss. Dietrich Bonhoeffer Works, vol. 4. Minneapolis: Fortress, 2001.

————. *Ethics.* Edited by Clifford J. Green. Translated by Richard Krauss, Charles C. West and Douglas W. Stott. Dietrich Bonhoeffer Works, vol. 6. Minneapolis: Fortress, 2005.

———. *Life Together and Prayer Book of the Bible*. Edited by Geffrey B. Kelly. Translated by Daniel W. Bloesch and James H. Burtness. Dietrich Bonhoeffer Works, vol. 5. Minneapolis: Fortress, 1996.

———. "On Psalm 119." In *Meditating on the Word*, translated and edited by David McI. Gracie. Cambridge: Cowley Publications, 1986.

———. *Sanctorum Communio: A Theological Study of the Sociology of the Church.* Edited by Clifford J. Green. Translated by Reinhard Krauss and Nancy Lukens. Dietrich Bonhoeffer Works, vol. 1. Minneapolis: Fortress, 1998.

———. *Spiritual Care*. Translated by J.C. Rochelle. Philadelphia: Fortress, 1985.

Bosch, David J. *Transforming Mission: Paradigm Shifts in Theology of Mission.* Maryknoll, NY: Orbis Books, 1991.

Botcharova, Olga. "Implementations of Track Two Diplomacy: Developing a Model of Forgiveness." In *Forgiveness and Reconciliation: Religion, Public Policy, and Conflict Transformation*, edited by Raymond G. Helmick and Rodney L. Petersen. Philadelphia: Templeton Foundation Press, 2001.

Bowlin, John. "Contemporary Protestant Thomism." In *Aquinas as Authority*, edited by P. van Geest. Louvain: Peeters, 2001.

Bradshaw, Anita. "Church as Reconciling Community: An Assessment of Conflict Resolution Methods in Light of Theology." PhD diss., Luther Seminary, 2006.

Bråkenhielm, Carl Reinhold. *Forgiveness*. Translated by Thor Hall. Minneapolis: Fortress, 1989.

Brinkmann, Klaus. "Hegel on Forgiveness." In *Hegel's Phenomenology of Spirit*, edited by Alfred Denker and Michael Vater. New York: Humanity Books, 2003.

Brock, Brian. *Singing the Ethos of God: On the Place of Christian Ethics in Scripture*. Grand Rapids: Eerdmans, 2007.

Brown, James. *Subject and Object in Modern Theology*. London: SCM Press, 1955.

Brown, Robert McAfee. "Introductory Essay." In *How to Serve God in a Marxist Land*, by Karl Barth and Johannes Hamel. New York: Association Press, 1959.

Brudholm, Thomas. *Resentment's Virtue: Jean Améry and the Refusal to Forgive*. Philadelphia: Temple University Press, 2008.

Brudholm, Thomas, and Arne Grøn. "Picturing Forgiveness After Atrocity." *Studies in Christian Ethics* 24, no. 2 (May 2011): 158-70.

Brunner, Emil, and Karl Barth. *Natural Theology: Comprising "Nature and Grace" by Professor Dr. Emil Brunner and the Reply "No!" by Dr. Karl Barth.* Translated and edited by P. Fraenkel. Eugene, OR: Wipf and Stock Publishers, 2002.

Büchsel, Friedrich. "δέω (λύω)." In *Theological Dictionary of the New Testament,* edited by Gerhard Kittel. Vol. 2, *Δ–H.* Grand Rapids: Eerdmans, 1964.

Buckley, James J. "A Field of Living Fire: Karl Barth on the Spirit and the Church." *Modern Theology* 10 (1994): 81-102.

Busch, Eberhard. *Karl Barth: His Life from Letters and Autobiographical Texts.* Philadelphia: Fortress, 1976.

Busch, Eberhard, Darrell L. Guder, Geoffrey W. Bromiley and Judith J. Guder. *The Great Passion: An Introduction to Karl Barth's Theology.* Translated by Geoffrey W. Bromiley. Grand Rapids: Eerdmans, 2004.

Butler, Joseph. "Sermon VIII. Upon Resentment." In *Fifteen Sermons Preached at the Rolls Chapel.* Cambridge: Hilliard and Brown, 1827.

———. "Sermon IX. Upon Forgiveness of Injuries." In *Fifteen Sermons Preached at the Rolls Chapel.* Cambridge: Hilliard and Brown, 1827.

Cahill, Thomas. *Desire of the Everlasting Hills: The World Before and After Jesus.* New York: Doubleday, 1999.

Calvin, John. *Institutes of the Christian Religion.* Translated by Ford Lewis Battles. Edited by John T. McNeill. Philadelphia: Westminster, 1977.

Camps, A., L. A. Hoedemaker, and M. R. Spindler, eds. *Missiology: An Ecumenical Introduction.* Grand Rapids: Eerdmans, 1995.

Carson, D. A. "Matthew." *The Expositor's Bible Commentary 8.* Grand Rapids: Zondervan, 1984.

Case-Winters, Anna. *God's Power: Traditional Understandings and Contemporary Challenges.* Louisville: Westminster John Knox, 1990.

Chapman, Audrey R. "Truth Commissions as Instruments of Forgiveness and Reconciliation." In *Forgiveness and Reconciliation: Religion, Public Policy, and Conflict Transformation,* edited by Raymond G. Helmick and Rodney L. Petersen. Philadelphia: Templeton Foundation Press, 2001.

Chesterton, G. K. *Orthodoxy.* London: Hodder & Stoughton, 1996.

Childs, Brevard. *Biblical Theology of the Old and New Testaments: Theological Reflections on the Christian Bible.* Minneapolis: Fortress, 1993.

Cioffi, Todd V. "Karl Barth and the Varieties of Democracy." In *Commanding Grace: Studies in Karl Barth's Ethics,* edited by Daniel L. Migliore. Grand Rapids: Eerdmans, 2010.

———. "Stanley Hauerwas and Karl Barth: Matters of Christology, Church, and State." In *Karl Barth and American Evangelicalism,* edited by Bruce L. McCormack and Clifford B. Anderson. Grand Rapids: Eerdmans, 2011.

Clough, David. *Ethics in Crisis: Interpreting Barth's Ethics.* Aldershot, UK: Ashgate, 2005.

Cochrane, Arthur C. "Baptism as the Basis of the Christian Life: A Review Article." *Journal of Ecumenical Studies* 5 (1968): 745-57.

Collins, Paul M., Gerard Mannion, Garth Powell and Kenneth Wilson. *Christian Community Now: Ecclesiological Investigations.* London: T&T Clark, 2008.

Collins, Raymond F. "Binding and Loosing." In *Anchor Bible Dictionary*, edited by David Noel Freedman. Vol. 1. New York: Doubleday, 1992.

Congar, Yves M. J. *Christ, Our Lady and the Church: A Study in Eirenic Theology.* Translated by Henry St. John, OP. Westminster, MD: Newman Press, 1957.

Constantineanu, Corneliu. *The Social Significance of Reconciliation in Paul's Theology: Narrative Readings in Romans.* London: T&T Clark, 2010.

Crisp, Oliver D. "'I Do Teach It, but I Also Do Not Teach It': The Universalism of Karl Barth (1886–1968)." In *"All Shall Be Well": Explorations in Universalism and Christian Theology, from Origen to Moltmann*, edited by Gregory MacDonald. Eugene, OR: Cascade, 2011.

———. "On Barth's Denial of Universalism." *Themelios* 29, no. 1 (2003): 18-29.

Cunningham, Joseph William. "John Wesley's Moral Pneumatology: The Fruits of the Spirit as Theological Virtues." *Studies in Christian Ethics* 24, no. 3 (August 2011): 275-93.

Da Silva, Anthony. "Through Nonviolence to Truth: Gandhi's Vision of Reconciliation." In *Forgiveness and Reconciliation: Religion, Public Policy, and Conflict Transformation*, edited by Raymond G. Helmick and Rodney L. Petersen. Philadelphia: Templeton Foundation Press, 2001.

Dalfert, Ingolf. "Karl Barth's Eschatological Realism." In *Karl Barth: Centenary Essays*, edited by S.W. Sykes. Cambridge: Cambridge University Press, 1989.

Dallaire, Roméo, with Brent Beardsley. *Shake Hands with the Devil: The Failure of Humanity in Rwanda.* Toronto: Vintage Canada, 2003.

Daly, Erin, and Jeremy Sarkin. *Reconciliation in Divided Societies: Finding Common Ground.* Philadelphia: University of Pennsylvania Press, 2007.

Davaney, Sheila Greeve. *Divine Power: A Study of Karl Barth and Charles Hartshorne.* Philadelphia: Fortress, 1986.

Dawson, John. "Hatred's End: A Christian Proposal to Peacemaking in a New Century." In *Forgiveness and Reconciliation: Religion, Public Policy, and Conflict Transformation*, edited by Raymond G. Helmick and Rodney L. Petersen. Philadelphia: Templeton Foundation Press, 2001.

Dawson, R. Dale. *The Resurrection in Karl Barth.* Hampshire, UK: Ashgate, 2007.

De Gruchy, John W. *Reconciliation: Restoring Justice*. London: Student Christian Movement Press, 2002.

Derrida, Jacques. *On Cosmopolitanism and Forgiveness*. Translated by Mark Dooley and Michael Hughes. London: Routledge, 2001.

Dickey, Walter J. "Forgiveness and Crime: The Possibilities of Restorative Justice." In *Exploring Forgiveness*, edited by Robert D. Enright and Joanna North. Madison: University of Wisconsin Press, 1998.

Dietterich, Inagrace. "Missional Community: Cultivating Communities of the Holy Spirit." In *Missional Church: A Vision for the Sending of the Church in North America*, edited by Darrell L. Guder. Grand Rapids: Eerdmans, 1998.

Dorff, Elliot N. "Individual and Communal Forgiveness." In *Autonomy and Judaism*, edited by Daniel H. Frank. Albany: State University of New York Press, 1992.

Dulles, Avery. *Models of the Church*. New York: Doubleday, 1974.

Duncan, J., and M. Derrett. "Binding and Loosing (Matt 16:19; 18:18; John 29:23)." *Journal of Biblical Literature* 102, no. 1 (1983): 112-17.

Duquoc, Christian. "The Forgiveness of God." *Concilium* 184 (1986): 35-44.

Ellul, Jacques. *The Politics of God and the Politics of Man*. Translated and edited by Geoffrey W. Bromiley. Grand Rapids: Eerdmans, 1972.

Enns, Elaine, and Ched Myers. *Ambassadors of Reconciliation*. Vol. 2, *Diverse Christian Practices of Restorative Justice and Peacemaking*. Maryknoll, NY: Orbis Books, 2009.

Enns, P. "Biblical Interpretation: Jewish." In *Dictionary of New Testament Background*, edited by Craig A. Evans and Stanley E. Porter. Downers Grove, IL: InterVarsity Press, 2000.

Enright, Robert D. "Comprehensive Bibliography on Interpersonal Forgiveness." In *Exploring Forgiveness*, edited by Robert D. Enright and Joanna North. Madison: University of Wisconsin Press, 1998.

Enright, Robert D., Suzanne Freedman, and Julio Rique. "The Psychology of Interpersonal Forgiveness." In *Exploring Forgiveness*, edited by Robert D. Enright and Joanna North. Madison: University of Wisconsin Press, 1998.

Farrow, Douglas. *Ascension and Ecclesia*. New York: T&T Clark, 1999.

Ferguson, Everett, ed. *Encyclopedia of Early Christianity*. New York: Garland, 1990.

Feuerbach, Ludwig. *The Essence of Faith According to Luther*. Translated by M. Cherno. New York: Harper, 1967.

Fiddes, Paul. "Mission and Liberty: A Baptist Connection." In *Tracks and Traces: Baptist Identity in Church and Theology*. Carlisle, UK: Paternoster, 2003.

Findler, Richard S. "Reconciliation Versus Reversal: Hegel and Nietzsche on Overcoming Sin or Ontological Guilt." In *Hegel's Phenomenology of Spirit*, edited by Alfred Denker and Michael Vater. New York: Humanity Books, 2003.

Flanagan, Beverly. *Forgiving the Unforgivable: Overcoming the Bitter Legacy of Intimate Wounds*. New York: Wiley Publishing, 1992.

Flett, John G. "*Missio Dei*: A Trinitarian Envisioning of a Non-Trinitarian Theme." *Missiology: An International Review* 37, no. 1 (Jan. 2009): 5-18.

———. *The Witness of God: The Trinity, Missio Dei, Karl Barth, and the Nature of Christian Community*. Grand Rapids: Eerdmans, 2010.

Forsyth, P.T. *The Church and the Sacraments*. London: Independent Press, 1947.

Foster, Richard J. *Celebration of Discipline: The Path to Spiritual Growth*. San Francisco: Harper & Row, 1978.

France, R.T. *The Gospel of Matthew*. New International Commentary on the New Testament. Grand Rapids: Eerdmans, 2007.

Gadamer, Hans-Georg. *Truth and Method*. New York: Seabury, 1975.

Gibson, David. *Reading the Decree: Exegesis, Election and Christology in Calvin and Barth*. London: T&T Clark, 2009.

Gibson, David, and Daniel Strange, eds. *Engaging with Barth: Contemporary Evangelical Critiques*. Nottingham, UK: Apollos, 2008.

Girard, René. *The Scapegoat*. Translated by Yvonne Freccero. Baltimore, MD: John Hopkins University Press, 1986.

———. *Things Hidden Since the Foundation of the World*. Stanford, CA: Stanford University Press, 1987.

Gobodo-Madikizela, Pumla. *A Human Being Died That Night: A South African Woman Confronts the Legacy of Apartheid*. New York: Mariner Books, 2004.

Gonzalez, Justo L. *A History of Christian Thought: From the Beginnings to the Council of Chalcedon*. 2nd ed. Nashville: Abingdon Press, 1987.

Gorringe, Timothy. "Crime, Punishment, and Atonement: Karl Barth on the Death of Christ." In *Commanding Grace: Studies in Karl Barth's Ethics*, edited by Daniel L. Migliore. Grand Rapids: Eerdmans, 2010.

———. *God's Just Vengeance: Crime, Violence and the Rhetoric of Salvation*. Cambridge: Cambridge University Press, 1996.

Graham, Billy. *How to Be Born Again*. Nashville: Thomas Nelson, 1989.

———. *The Key to Personal Peace*. Nashville: Thomas Nelson, 2003.

Green, Clifford. "Freedom for Humanity: Karl Barth and the Politics of the New World Order." In *For the Sake of the World: Karl Barth and the Future of Ecclesial Theology*, edited by George Hunsinger. Grand Rapids: Eerdmans, 2004.

Green, Michael, and R. Paul Stevens. *New Testament Spirituality: True Discipleship and Spiritual Maturity*. Guildford, UK: Eagle, 1994.

Greene, Graham. *The Power and the Glory*. New York: Penguin Books, 2003.

Greggs, Tom. *Barth, Origen, and Universal Salvation: Restoring Particularity*. Oxford: Oxford University Press, 2009.

———. "'Jesus Is Victor': Passing the Impasse of Barth on Universalism." *Scottish Journal of Theology* 60, no. 2 (2007): 196-212.

———, ed. *New Perspectives on Evangelical Theology: Engaging with God, Scripture and the World*. New York: Routledge, 2010.

Grenz, Stanley J. *Theology for the Community of God*. Nashville: Broadman and Holman, 1994.

Grenz, Stanley J., and John Franke. *Beyond Foundationalism: Shaping Theology in a Postmodern Context*. Louisville: Westminster John Knox, 2001.

Grey, Mary, and Richard Zipfel. *From Barriers to Community: The Challenge of the Gospel for a Divided Society*. London: HarperCollins, 1991.

Griswold, Charles. *Forgiveness: A Philosophical Exploration*. Cambridge: Cambridge University Press, 2007.

Großhans, Hans-Peter. *Die Kirche—irdische Raum der Wahrheit des Evangeliums*. Leipzig: Evangelische Verlagsanstalt, 2003.

Guder, Darrell L. "Encountering Barth as a Missional Theologian." *Inspire* 8, no. 1 (Summer/Fall 2003): 2.

———. "*Missio Dei*: Integrating Theological Formation for Apostolic Vocation." *Missiology: An International Review* 37, no. 1 (January 2009): 63-74.

———, ed. *Missional Church: A Vision for the Sending of the Church in North America*. Grand Rapids: Eerdmans, 1998.

Guido of Monte Rochen. *Handbook for Curates: A Late Medieval Manual on Pastoral Ministry*. Translated by Anne T. Thayer. Washington, DC: The Catholic University of America Press, 2011.

Gunton, Colin E. "No Other Foundation: One Englishman's Reading of *Church Dogmatics*." In *Reckoning with Barth*, edited by Nigel Biggar. Oxford: Oxford University Press, 1988.

———. *On Being the Church. Essays on the Christian Community*. Edinburgh: T&T Clark, 1989.

———, ed. *The Theology of Reconciliation*. New York: T&T Clark, 2003.

Guretzki, David. "Life in the Mess: A Theology of Forgiveness and Reconciliation." Lecture series, Briercrest Seminary, Caronport, SK, October 2007.

――――. "Should We Forgive Those Who Show No Repentance?" *Faith Today*, September/October 2007: 36.

Gustafson, James M. *Can Ethics Be Christian?* Chicago: University of Chicago Press, 1975.

――――. *Christ and the Moral Life*. Chicago: University of Chicago Press, 1968.

――――. *Christian Ethics and the Community*. Philadelphia: Pilgrim Press, 1971.

――――. *Ethics from a Theocentric Perspective*. Vol. 2. Chicago: University of Chicago Press, 1984.

――――. *Protestant and Roman Catholic Ethics*. Chicago: University of Chicago Press, 1978.

Haber, Joram Graf. *Forgiveness: A Philosophical Study*. Baltimore, MD: Rowman & Littlefield Publishers, 1991.

Haddorff, David. *Christian Ethics as Witness: Barth's Ethics for a World at Risk*. Eugene, OR: Cascade Books, 2010.

Hagner, Donald A. *Matthew 14–28*. Word Biblical Commentary. Dallas: Word, 1993.

Hamber, Brandon, and Richard Wilson. "Symbolic Closure Through Memory, Reparation and Revenge in Post-Conflict Societies." *Journal of Human Rights* 1, no. 1 (2002): 35-53.

Hammann, Gottfried. "The Creation of the 'Christlichen Gemeinschaften.'" In *Martin Bucer: Reforming Church and Community*, edited by D. F. Wright. Cambridge: Cambridge University Press, 1994.

Harakas, Stanley S. "Forgiveness and Reconciliation: An Orthodox Perspective." In *Forgiveness and Reconciliation: Religion, Public Policy, and Conflict Transformation*, edited by Raymond G. Helmick and Rodney L. Petersen. Philadelphia: Templeton Foundation Press, 2001.

Hart, David Bentley. "A Gift Exceeding Every Debt: An Eastern Orthodox Appreciation of Anselm's *Cur Deus Homo*." *Pro Ecclesia* 7, no. 3 (1993): 333-49.

Hart, Trevor. *Regarding Karl Barth: Essays Toward a Reading of His Theology*. Carlisle, UK: Paternoster, 1999.

Hart, Trevor A., and Daniel P. Thimell, eds. *Christ in our Place: The Humanity of God in Christ for the Reconciliation of the World: Essays Presented to Professor James Torrance*. Allison Park, PA: Pickwick Publications, 1989.

Hauerwas, Stanley. *Character and the Christian Life: A Study in Theological Ethics*. San Antonio, TX: Trinity University Press, 1975.

――――. "On Honor: By Way of a Comparison of Karl Barth and Trollope." In *Dispatches from the Front: Theological Engagements with the Secular*. Durham, NC: Duke University Press, 1991.

———. *The Peaceable Kingdom: A Primer in Christian Ethics*. Notre Dame: University of Notre Dame Press, 1983.

———. "Why Time Cannot and Should Not Heal the Wounds of History but Time Has Been and Can Be Redeemed." *Scottish Journal of Theology* 53 (2000): 33-49.

———. *With the Grain of the Universe: The Church's Witness and Natural Theology; Being the Gifford Lectures Delivered at the University of St. Andrews in 2001*. Grand Rapids: Brazos Press, 2001.

Hauerwas, Stanley, and William H. Willimon. *Resident Aliens: A Provocative Assessment of Culture and Ministry for People Who Know That Something Is Wrong*. Nashville: Abingdon Press, 1989.

Healy, Nicholas M. "Karl Barth's Ecclesiology Reconsidered." *Scottish Journal of Theology* 25, no. 3 (2004): 287-99.

———. "The Logic of Karl Barth's Ecclesiology: Analysis, Assessment and Proposed Modifications." *Modern Theology* 10 (1994): 253-70.

Hegel, G. W. F. "The Consummate Religion." In *Lectures on the Philosophy of Religion: One-Volume Edition; The Lectures of 1827*, edited by P. C. Hodgson. Berkeley: University of California Press, 1988.

———. *The Phenomenology of Spirit*. Translated by A.V. Miller. Oxford: Oxford University Press, 1977.

Heller, Karin. "*Missio Dei*: Envisioning an Apostolic Practical Theology." *Missiology: An International Review* 37, no. 1 (January 2009): 47-61.

Helmick, Raymond G., and Rodney L. Petersen, eds. *Forgiveness and Reconciliation: Religion, Public Policy, and Conflict Transformation*. Philadelphia: Templeton Foundation Press, 2001.

Henderson, Michael. *No Enemy to Conquer: Forgiveness in an Unforgiving World*. Waco, TX: Baylor University Press, 2009.

Hodge, Charles. *The Way of Life*. Edinburgh: Banner of Truth, 1991.

Hoekendijk, J. C. *Kirche und Volk in der deutschen Missionswissenschaft*. Munich: Chr. Kaiser Verlag, 1967.

Holloway, Richard. *On Forgiveness: How Can We Forgive the Unforgivable?* Edinburgh: Canongate, 2002.

Holmes, Stephen R. "Trinitarian Missiology: Towards a Theology of God as Missionary." *International Journal of Systematic Theology* 8, no. 1 (2006): 72-90.

Holmgren, Margaret. "Forgiveness and the Intrinsic Value of Persons." *American Philosophical Quarterly* 30 (1993): 341-52.

Hood, Robert E. *Contemporary Political Orders and Christ: Karl Barth's Christology and Political Praxis.* Pittsburgh, PA: Pickwick Press, 1985.

Horne, Jon. "A Reservation About Miroslav Volf's Theory of Non-remembrance." *Theology* 114, no. 5 (September/October 2011): 323-30.

Horton, Michael Scott. *Putting Amazing Back into Grace: Embracing the Heart of the Gospel.* Grand Rapids: Baker, 2002.

Huebner, Chris K. "Can a Gift Be Commanded? Theological Ethics Without Theory by Way of Barth, Milbank, and Yoder." *Scottish Journal of Theology* 53, no. 4 (2000): 472-89.

Hume, David. *An Enquiry Concerning Human Understanding.* In *Principle Writings on Religion*, edited by J. C. A. Gaskin. Oxford: Oxford University Press, 1993.

Hunsinger, George. "Baptism and the Soteriology of Forgiveness." *International Journal of Systematic Theology* 2, no. 3 (November 2000): 247-69.

———. *Disruptive Grace: Studies in the Theology of Karl Barth.* Grand Rapids: Eerdmans, 2000.

———. *How to Read Karl Barth: The Shape of His Theology.* New York: Oxford University Press, 1991.

———. "Proposals for a Missional Hermeneutic: Mapping a Conversation." *Missiology: An International Review* 39, no. 3 (July 2011): 309-21.

———. "A Response to William Werpehowski." *Theology Today* 43 (1986): 354-60.

———. "To Hauerwas: On Learning Faithfulness in a Fallen World." In *Barth, Barmen, and the Confessing Church Today*, edited by James Y. Holloway. Lewiston, NY: Edwin Mellen Press, 1992.

———. ed. *For the Sake of the World: Karl Barth and the Future of Ecclesial Theology.* Grand Rapids: Eerdmans, 2004.

Hütter, Reinhard. *Evangelische Ethik als kirchliches Zeugnis. Interpretation zu Schlüsselfragen theologischer Ethik in der Gegenwart.* Neukirchen-Vluyn: Neukirchener Verlag, 1993.

———. "Karl Barth's 'Dialectical Catholicity': Sic et Non." *Modern Theology* 16, no. 2 (2000): 137-57.

———. *Suffering Divine Things: Theology as Church Practice.* Translated by Doug Stott. Grand Rapids: Eerdmans, 2000.

Ilibagiza, Immaculée, with Steve Irwin. *Left to Tell: Discovering God Amidst the Rwandan Holocaust.* Carlsbad, CA: Hay House, 2006.

Irenaeus. *Against Heresies.* In *The Ante-Nicene Fathers*, edited by Alexander

Roberts and James Donaldson. Vol. 1, *The Apostolic Fathers—Justin Martyr—Irenaeus*, Grand Rapids: Eerdmans, 1975.

Jaeger, Marietta. "The Power and Reality of Forgiveness: Forgiving the Murderer of One's Child." In *Exploring Forgiveness*, edited by Robert D. Enright and Joanna North. Madison: University of Wisconsin Press, 1998.

Jankélévitch, Vladimir. "Should We Pardon Them?" Translated by Ann Hobart. *Critical Inquiry* 22, no. 3 (Spring 1996): 552-72.

Jennings, Willie James. *The Christian Imagination: Theology and the Origins of Race*. New Haven, CT: Yale University Press, 2010.

Jenson, Matt, and David E. Wilhite. *The Church: A Guide for the Perplexed*. London: T&T Clark, 2010.

Jenson, Robert W. "You Wonder Where the Spirit Went." In *The Holy Spirit: Classic and Contemporary Readings*, edited by Eugene F. Rogers Jr. West Sussex, UK: Blackwell, 2009.

Johnson, Keith L. "The Being and Act of the Church: Barth and the Future of Evangelical Ecclesiology." In *Karl Barth and American Evangelicalism*, edited by Bruce L. McCormack and Clifford B. Anderson. Grand Rapids: Eerdmans, 2011.

Jones, L. Gregory. *Embodying Forgiveness: A Theological Analysis*. Grand Rapids: Eerdmans, 1995.

———. "The Judgment of Grace: Forgiveness in Christian Life." *Theology Matters* 3, no. 4 (July/August 1997): 7-16.

———. *Transformed Judgment: Toward a Trinitarian Account of the Moral Life*. Notre Dame: University of Notre Dame Press, 1990.

Jüngel, Eberhard. *Barth-Studien*. Gütersloh: Mohn, 1982.

———. "Invocation of God as the Ethical Ground of Christian Action: Introductory Remarks on the Posthumous Fragments of Karl Barth's Ethics of the Doctrine of Reconciliation." In *Theological Essays*, translated by John Webster. Edinburgh: T&T Clark, 1989.

———. *Karl Barth: A Theological Legacy*. Translated by Garrett E. Paul. Philadelphia: Westminster, 1986.

———. "Mission und Evangelisation." In *Ganz warden: Theologische Erörterungen V*. Tübingen: Mohr Siebeck, 2003.

Kant, Immanuel. *Conflict of the Faculties*. In *Religion and Rational Theology*, translated and edited by A. Wood and G. di Giovanni. Cambridge: Cambridge University Press, 1996.

Käsemann, Ernst. *Jesus Means Freedom: A Polemical Survey of the New Testament*. London: SCM Press, 1969.

———. *Perspectives on Paul.* Philadelphia: Fortress, 1971.

Keener, Craig S. *A Commentary on the Gospel of Matthew.* Grand Rapids: Eerdmans, 1999.

Kelsay, J. "Prayer and Ethics: Reflections on Calvin and Barth." *Harvard Theological Review* 82, no. 2 (1989): 169-84.

Keown, Gerald, Pamela J. Scalise and Thomas G. Smothers. *Jeremiah 26–52.* Word Biblical Commentary, vol. 27, edited by David A. Hubbar, Glenn W. Barker and John D. W. Watts, Nashville: Thomas Nelson, 1998.

Kerr, Nathan R. "Das Ereignis der Sendung: The Word of God, Apocalyptic Transfiguration, and the 'Special Visibility' of the Church." Paper presented at the conference of The Karl Barth Society of North America, Princeton Theological Seminary, Princeton, NJ, June, 2010.

Kierkegaard, Søren. "Becoming Sober." In *For Self-Examination: Judge for Yourself!*, edited and translated by Howard V. Hong and Edna H. Hong. Princeton, NJ: Princeton University Press, 1990.

———. "The Difference Between a Genius and an Apostle." In *The Book on Adler*, edited and translated by Howard V. Hong and Edna H. Hong. Princeton, NJ: Princeton University Press, 1998.

———. *Works of Love: Some Christian Reflections in the Form of Discourses.* Translated by Howard and Edna Hong. New York: Harper & Brothers, 1962.

Klooster, Fred H. *The Significance of Barth's Theology: An Appraisal, with Special Reference to Election and Reconciliation.* Grand Rapids: Baker Book House, 1961.

Komonchak, J. "Ecclesiology and Social Theory: A Methodological Inquiry." *Thomist* 45 (1981): 262-83.

Konstan, David. *Before Forgiveness: The Origins of a Moral Idea.* Cambridge: Cambridge University Press, 2010.

Kotsko, Adam. *The Politics of Redemption: The Social Logic of Salvation.* London: T&T Clark, 2010.

Kroetke, Wolf. *Sin and Nothingness in the Theology of Karl Barth.* Translated by P. Ziegler. Princeton, NJ: Princeton Theological Seminary, 2005.

Krog, Antjie. *Country of My Skull: Guilt, Sorrow, and the Limits of Forgiveness in the New South Africa.* Toronto: Times Books, 1998.

Kühn, Ulrich. *Sakramente. Handbuck Systematischer Theologie Bd. II.* Gutersloh: Gutersloher Verlagshaus Mohn, 1985.

Kung, H. *Justification: The Doctrine of Karl Barth and a Catholic Reflection.* London: Burns & Oates, 1964.

Lamb, Sharon, and Jeffrie G. Murphy, eds. *Before Forgiving: Cautionary Views of Forgiveness in Psychotherapy*. Oxford: Oxford University Press, 2002.

Lawrence, David. *Martin Bucer: Unsung Hero of the Reformation*. Nashville: Westview Publishing, 2007.

Lazare, Aaron. *On Apology*. New York: Oxford University Press, 2004.

Le Bruyns, Clint C. "Human Dignity and Moral Renewal." *Scriptura* 95, no. 2 (2007): 202-12.

Leenhardt, Franz J. *Le Baptême Chrétien: Son Origine, sa Signification*. Vol. 4, in *Cahiers Théologiques de l'Actualité Protestante*. Neuchâtel et Paris: Delachaux & Niestlé, 1945.

Lehman, Paul L. *Ethics in a Christian Context*. London: SCM Press, 1963.

———. *Forgiveness: Decisive Issue in Protestant Thought*. New York: Harper & Brothers, 1940.

Levinas, Emmanuel. *Difficult Freedom: Essays on Judaism*. Translated by Sean Hand. Baltimore, MD: Johns Hopkins University Press, 1997.

Lewis, C. S. *God in the Dock: Essays in Theology*. Edited by W. Hooper. London: Fount, 1979.

———. "On Forgiveness." In *The Weight of Glory and Other Addresses*. New York: Collier Books, 1980.

Lindbeck, George A. *The Nature of Doctrine: Religion and Theology in a Post-liberal Age*. 2nd ed. Louisville: Westminster John Knox, 2009.

Lovin, Robin. *Christian Faith and Public Choices: The Social Ethics of Barth, Brunner, and Bonhoeffer*. Philadelphia: Fortress, 1984.

Lowe, Walter. *Theology and Difference: The Wound of Reason*. Bloomington: Indiana University Press, 1993.

Lowrie, Walter. *Our Concern with the Theology of Crisis*. Boston: Meador, 1932.

Lutzer, Erwin W. *How You Can Be Sure That You Will Spend Eternity With God*. Chicago: Moody, 1996.

MacIntyre, Alasdair. "What Has Christianity to Say to the Moral Philosopher?" In *The Doctrine of God and Theological Ethics*, edited by Alan J. Torrance and Michael Banner. London: T&T Clark, 2006.

Macken, John. *The Autonomy Theme in the* Church Dogmatics: *Karl Barth and His Critics*. Cambridge: Cambridge University Press, 1990.

Mackintosh, H. R. *The Christian Experience of Forgiveness*. 2nd ed. London: Nisbet, 1934.

MacLachlan, Alice. *The Nature and Limits of Forgiveness*. PhD diss. Boston University, 2008.

Maclean, Iain S. "No Future Without Forgiveness, by Desmond Tutu." *Missiology* 31 (Oct. 2003): 505-7.

Malcolm, Lois. "Forgiveness as New Creation: Christ and the Moral Life Revisited." In *Christology and Ethics*, edited by F. LeRon Shults and Brent Waters. Grand Rapids: Eerdmans, 2010.

Mangina, Joseph L. "Bearing the Marks of Jesus: The Church in the Economy of Salvation in Barth and Hauerwas." *Scottish Journal of Theology* 52, no. 3 (1999): 269-305.

———. *Karl Barth on the Christian Life: The Practical Knowledge of God*. New York: Peter Lang Publishing, 2001.

———. *Karl Barth: Theologian of Christian Witness*. Aldershot, UK: Ashgate, 2004.

———. "The Stranger as Sacrament: Karl Barth and the Ethics of Ecclesial Practice." *International Journal of Systematic Theology* 1, no. 3 (1999): 322-39.

Mannion, Gerard, ed. *Comparative Ecclesiology: Critical Investigations*. London: T&T Clark, 2008.

Mannion, Gerard, and Lewis S. Mudge, eds. *The Routledge Companion to the Christian Church*. New York: Routledge, 2008.

Martin, Ralph. *Reconciliation: A Study of Paul's Theology*. Grand Rapids: Zondervan, 1989.

Matheny, P. D. *Dogmatics and Ethics: The Theological Realism and Ethics of Karl Barth's* Church Dogmatics. Frankfurt: P. Lang, 1990.

Mattison, William C. III, "Can Christians Possess the Acquired Cardinal Virtues?" *Theological Studies* 72, no. 3 (September 2011): 558-85.

Mbabazi, Isaac K. *The Significance of Interpersonal Forgiveness in the Gospel of Matthew*. Eugene, OR: Pickwick, 2013.

McCormack, Bruce L., ed. *Engaging the Doctrine of God: Contemporary Protestant Perspectives*. Grand Rapids: Baker Books, 2008.

———. *Karl Barth's Critically Realistic Dialectical Theology: Its Genesis and Development 1909–1936*. Oxford: Clarendon Press, 1997.

———. *Orthodox and Modern: Studies in the Theology of Karl Barth*. Grand Rapids: Baker Academic, 2008.

McDonald, H. D. *Forgiveness and Atonement*. Grand Rapids: Baker Book House, 1984.

McKenny, Gerald. *Analogy of Grace: Karl Barth's Moral Theology*. Oxford: Oxford University Press, 2010.

McMaken, W. Travis. *The Sign of the Gospel: Toward an Evangelical Doctrine of Infant Baptism After Karl Barth*. Minneapolis: Fortress, 2013.

McMaken, W. Travis, and David W. Congdon, eds. *Karl Barth in Conversation.* Eugene, OR: Pickwick Publications, 2014.

Michel, O. "ὁμολογέω, ἐξομολογέω, ἀνθομολογέομαι, ὁμολογία, ὁμολογουμένως." In *Theological Dictionary of the New Testament,* edited by Gerhard Kittel and Gerhard Friedrich. Translated by Geoffrey W. Bromiley. Vol. 5, *Ξ–Πα.* Grand Rapids: Eerdmans, 1967.

Migliore, Daniel L., ed. *Commanding Grace: Studies in Karl Barth's Ethics.* Grand Rapids: Eerdmans, 2010.

———. "Freedom to Pray: Karl Barth's Theology of Prayer." In Karl Barth, *Prayer,* 2nd ed. Louisville: Westminster John Knox, 2002.

———. "Participatio Christi: The Central Theme of Barth's Doctrine of Sanctification." *Zeitschrift für dialektische Theologie* 18 (2002): 286-307.

Mikkelson, Hans Vium. *Reconciled Humanity: Karl Barth in Dialogue.* Grand Rapids: Eerdmans, 2010.

Milbank, John. *Being Reconciled: Ontology and Pardon.* London: Routledge, 2003.

———. "The Midwinter Sacrifice." In *The Blackwell Companion to Post-Modern Theology,* edited by Graham Ward. Oxford: Blackwell, 2002.

———. *Theology and Social Theory: Beyond Secular Reason.* Cambridge, MA: Basil Blackwell, 1990.

Molnar, Paul. *Karl Barth and the Theology of the Lord's Supper: A Systematic Investigation.* New York: Peter Lang, 1996.

Moule, C. F. D. "'. . . As We Forgive . . .': A Note on the Distinction Between Deserts and Capacity in the Understanding of Forgiveness." In *Essays in New Testament Interpretation.* Cambridge: Cambridge University Press, 1982.

———. *Forgiveness and Reconciliation, and Other New Testament Themes.* London: SPCK, 1998.

Mueller, Joan. *Is Forgiveness Possible? A Scriptural-Pastoral Dialogue.* Collegeville, MN: Liturgical Press, 1997.

Mulholland, M. Robert, Jr. *Invitation to a Journey: A Road Map for Spiritual Formation.* Downers Grove, IL: InterVarsity Press, 1993.

Müller-Fahrenholz, Geiko. *The Art of Forgiveness: Theological Reflections on Healing and Reconciliation.* Geneva: World Council of Churches, 1997.

Muller, R. A. *After Calvin: Studies in the Development of a Theological Tradition.* Oxford: Oxford University Press, 2003.

Murphy, Jeffrie G. "Forgiveness and Resentment." *Midwest Studies in Philosophy* 7 (1982): 503-16.

———. *Getting Even: Forgiveness and Its Limits.* Oxford: Oxford University Press, 2003.

Murphy, Jeffrie G., and Jean Hampton. *Forgiveness and Mercy*. Cambridge: Cambridge University Press, 1988.

Myers, Ched, and Elaine Enns. *Ambassadors of Reconciliation*. Vol. 1, *New Testament Reflections on Restorative Justice and Peacemaking*. Maryknoll, NY: Orbis Books, 2009.

Neusner, Jacob. *Introduction to Rabbinic Literature*. New York: Doubleday, 1994.

———. "Rabbinic Literature: Mishnah and Tosefta." In *Dictionary of New Testament Background*, edited by Craig A. Evans and Stanley E. Porter. Downers Grove, IL: InterVarsity Press, 2000.

Neven, Gerrit W. "Just a Little: The Christian Life in the Context of Reconciliation." *Zeitschrift für dialektische Theologie* 18 (2002): 353-63.

Newbigin, Lesslie. *Truth to Tell: The Gospel as Public Truth*. Grand Rapids: Eerdmans, 1991.

———. *A Word in Season: Perspectives on Christian World Missions*. Grand Rapids: Eerdmans, 1994.

Niebuhr, H. Richard. *The Responsible Self*. New York: Harper & Row, 1963.

Niebuhr, Reinhold. "We Are Men and Not God." *Christian Century* 65, no. 43 (October 1958): 1138.

Nietzsche, Friedrich. *Beyond Good and Evil*. Translated by Walter Kaufman. New York: Vintage Books, 1966.

———. *The Gay Science*. Translated by J. Nauckhoff. Cambridge: Cambridge University Press, 2001.

———. *On the Genealogy of Morals*. Translated by Carol Diethe. Cambridge: Cambridge University Press, 1994.

Nimmo, Paul T. "Barth and the Christian as Ethical Agent: An Ontological Study of the Shape of Christian Ethics." In *Commanding Grace: Studies in Karl Barth's Ethics*, edited by Daniel L. Migliore. Grand Rapids: Eerdmans, 2010.

———. *Being in Action: The Theological Shape of Barth's Ethical Vision*. London: T&T Clark, 2007.

———. "With and After Barth on the Eucharist." Paper presented to the Systematic Theology Seminar of King's College, Aberdeen, UK, May 2011.

Nouwen, Henri J. M. *In the Name of Jesus: Reflections on Christian Leadership*. New York: Crossroad, 1989.

Nygren, Anders. *Agape and Eros*. Translated by Philip S. Watson. New York: Harper & Row, 1957.

Oakes, Kenneth. *Reading Karl Barth: A Companion to Karl Barth's* Epistle to the Romans. Eugene, OR: Cascade Books, 2011.

Oden, Thomas C. *Pastoral Theology: Essentials of Ministry.* San Francisco: Harper & Row, 1983.

O'Donovan, Oliver. *The Desire of the Nations: Rediscovering the Roots of Political Theology.* Cambridge: Cambridge University Press, 1996.

———. "Karl Barth and Ramsey's 'Uses of Power.'" In "The Ethics of Paul Ramsey," special issue, *The Journal of Religious Ethics* 19, no. 2. (Fall 1991): 1-30.

———. *The Problem of Self-Love in St. Augustine.* New Haven, CT: Yale University Press, 1980.

———. *Resurrection and Moral Order: An Outline for Evangelical Ethics.* Leicester, UK: Inter-Varsity Press, 1986.

O'Grady, Colm. *The Church in Catholic Theology: Dialogue with Karl Barth.* Washington, DC: Corpus, 1969.

———. *The Church in the Theology of Karl Barth.* London: Geoffrey Chapman, 1968.

Ortberg, John. *The Life You've Always Wanted: Spiritual Disciplines for Ordinary People.* Grand Rapids: Zondervan, 2002.

Ortega, Ofelia. "Conversion as a Way of Life in Cultures of Violence." In *Forgiveness and Reconciliation: Religion, Public Policy, and Conflict Transformation,* edited by Raymond G. Helmick and Rodney L. Petersen. Philadelphia: Templeton Foundation Press, 2001.

Ott, Craig, Stephen J. Strauss and Timothy C. Tennent. *Encountering Theology of Mission: Biblical Foundations, Historical Developments, and Contemporary Issues.* Grand Rapids: Baker Academic, 2010.

Outka, Gene, and Paul Ramsey, eds. *Norm and Context in Christian Ethics.* London: SCM Press, 1968.

Overbeck, Franz. *On the Christianity of Our Theology.* Translated by J.E. Wilson. San Jose, CA: Pickwick Publications, 2002.

Owen, John. *The Forgiveness of Sins.* Grand Rapids: Baker, 1977.

Pannenberg, Wolfhart. *Grundlagen der Ethik.* Gottingen: Vandenhoeck & Ruprecht, 2003.

———. *Systematic Theology.* Vol 2. Translated by Geoffrey W. Bromiley. Edinburgh: T&T Clark, 1991.

Park, Andrew Sung. *The Wounded Heart of God: The Asian Concept of Han and the Christian Doctrine of Sin.* Nashville: Abingdon Press, 1993.

Paton, Margaret. "Can God Forgive?" *Modern Theology* 4, no. 3 (1988): 225-33.

Petersen, Rodney L. "A Theology of Forgiveness: Terminology, Rhetoric, and the Dialectic of Interfaith Relationships." In *Forgiveness and Reconciliation: Religion,*

Public Policy, and Conflict Transformation, edited by Raymond G. Helmick and Rodney L. Petersen. Philadelphia: Templeton Foundation Press, 2001.

Peterson, Eugene H. *Working the Angles: The Shape of Pastoral Integrity*. Grand Rapids: Eerdmans, 1987.

Pinnock, Clark H. *Flame of Love: A Theology of the Holy Spirit*. Grand Rapids: Eerdmans, 1996.

Plantinga, Cornelius, Jr. *Not the Way It's Supposed to Be: A Breviary of Sin*. Grand Rapids: Eerdmans, 1994.

Post, Stephen G. *A Theory of Agape: On the Meaning of Christian Love*. Cranbury, NJ: Associated University Presses, 1990.

Prather, Scott Thomas. *Christ, Power and Mammon: Karl Barth and John Howard Yoder in Dialogue*. London: T&T Clark, 2013.

Price, Daniel J. *Karl Barth's Anthropology in Light of Modern Thought*. Grand Rapids: Eerdmans, 2002.

Puka, Bill. "Forgoing Forgiveness." In *Before Forgiving: Cautionary Views of Forgiveness in Psychotherapy*, edited by Sharon Lamb and Jeffrie G. Murphy. Oxford: Oxford University Press, 2002.

Purves, Andrew. *Reconstructing Pastoral Theology: A Christological Foundation*. Louisville: Westminster John Knox, 2004.

Quasten, Johannes. *Patrology*. Vol 4. Translated by Placid Solari. Edited by Angelo Di Berardino. Westminster, MD: Christian Classics, Inc., 1986.

Rae, Murray. "To Render Praise: Humanity in God's World." In *The Doctrine of God and Theological Ethics*, edited by Alan J. Torrance and Michael Banner. London: T&T Clark, 2006.

Rae, S. H. "Law, Gospel and Freedom in the Theological Ethics of Karl Barth." *Scottish Journal of Theology* 25 (1972): 412-22.

Ramsey, Arthur Michael. *The Gospel and the Catholic Church*. London: Longmans, 1956.

Ramsey, Paul. *Basic Christian Ethics*. Chicago: University of Chicago Press, 1950.

Redlich, E. Basil. *The Forgiveness of Sins*. Edinburgh: T&T Clark, 1937.

Ricoeur, Paul. *Figuring the Sacred: Religion Narrative and Imagination*. Minneapolis: Augsburg Fortress, 1995.

Rieneker, Fritz. *A Linguistic Key to the Greek New Testament*. Vol. 1, *Matthew Through Acts*. Edited by Cleon L. Rogers Jr. Grand Rapids: Zondervan, 1976.

Ritschl, Albrecht. *The Christian Doctrine of Justification and Reconciliation*. Translated by H. R. Mackintosh and A. B. Macaulay. Edinburgh: T&T Clark, 1902.

Rose, Matthew. *Ethics with Barth: God, Metaphysics and Morals.* Surrey, UK: Ashgate, 2010.

Scarre, Geoffrey. "Political Reconciliation, Forgiveness and Grace." *Studies in Christian Ethics* 24, no. 2 (May 2011): 171-82.

Schacter, Daniel. *How the Mind Forgets and Remembers.* London: Souvenir Press, 2001.

Schaeffer, Francis A. *True Spirituality.* Wheaton: Tyndale, 1971.

Schimmel, Solomon. *Wounds Not Healed by Time: The Power of Repentance and Forgiveness.* Oxford: Oxford University Press, 2002.

Schleiermacher, Friedrich. *On Religion: Speeches to Its Cultured Despisers.* Translated by Richard Crouter. Cambridge: Cambridge University Press, 1988.

Scholz, Heinrich. *Eros und Caritas. Die platonische Liebe und die Liebe im Sinne des Christentums.* Halle: Max Niemeyer Verlag, 1929.

Schreiter, Robert J. *Reconciliation: Mission and Ministry in a Changing Social Order.* Maryknoll: Orbis Books, 1992.

Scott, Waldron. *Karl Barth's Theology of Mission.* Downers Grove, IL: InterVarsity Press, 1978.

Seamands, Stephen. *Ministry in the Image of God: The Trinitarian Shape of Christian Service.* Downers Grove, IL: InterVarsity Press, 2005.

Sharpe, R. A. *Forgiveness: How Forgiveness Endangers Morality.* Exeter, UK: Imprint Academic, 2007.

Shriver, Donald W., Jr. *An Ethic for Enemies: Forgiveness in Politics.* New York: Oxford University Press, 1995.

Shults, F. LeRon, and Brent Waters, eds. *Christology and Ethics.* Grand Rapids: Eerdmans, 2010.

Shults, F. LeRon, and Steven J. Sandage. *The Face of Forgiveness: Searching for Wholeness and Salvation.* Grand Rapids: Baker Academic, 2003.

Sider, J. Alexander. *To See History Doxologically: History and Holiness in John Howard Yoder's Ecclesiology.* Grand Rapids: Eerdmans, 2011.

Simon, Caroline J. "What Wondrous Love Is This? Meditations on Barth, Christian Love, and the Future of Christian Ethics." In *For the Sake of the World: Karl Barth and the Future of Ecclesial Theology*, edited by George Hunsinger. Grand Rapids: Eerdmans, 2004.

Smedes, Lewis B. *Forgive and Forget: Healing the Hurts We Don't Deserve.* New York: Harper & Row, 1984.

Smith, Gordon T. *A Holy Meal: The Lord's Supper in the Life of the Church.* Grand Rapids: Baker Academic, 2005.

Smith, Nick. *I Was Wrong: The Meanings of Apologies.* Cambridge: Cambridge University Press, 2008.

Smyth, Geraldine. "Brokenness, Forgiveness, Healing, and Peace in Ireland." In *Forgiveness and Reconciliation: Religion, Public Policy, and Conflict Transformation,* edited by Raymond G. Helmick and Rodney L. Petersen. Philadelphia: Templeton Foundation Press, 2001.

Soares-Prabhu, George. "'As We Forgive': Interhuman Forgiveness in the Teaching of Jesus." *Concilium* 184 (1986): 57-66.

Sonderegger, Katherine. "For Us and for Our Salvation: A Response to Timothy Gorringe." In *Commanding Grace: Studies in Karl Barth's Ethics,* edited by Daniel L. Migliore. Grand Rapids: Eerdmans, 2010.

Swinburne, Richard. *Responsibility and Atonement.* Oxford: Clarendon, 1989.

Swinton, John. *Raging with Compassion: Pastoral Responses to the Problem of Evil.* Grand Rapids: Eerdmans, 2007.

Sykes, S. W., ed. *Karl Barth: Centenary Essays.* Cambridge: Cambridge University Press, 1989.

Taylor, Charles. *Hegel and Modern Society.* Cambridge: Cambridge University Press, 1979.

———. *Sources of the Self: The Making of the Modern Identity.* Cambridge, MA: Harvard University Press, 1989.

Taylor, Vincent. *Forgiveness and Reconciliation: A Study in New Testament Theology.* London: Macmillan, 1941.

Telfer, W. *The Forgiveness of Sins: An Essay in the History of Christian Doctrine and Practice.* London: SCM Press, 1959.

Tilley, Terrence W. *The Disciples' Jesus: Christology as Reconciling Practice.* Maryknoll, NY: Orbis Books, 2008.

Torrance, Alan J. "Christian Experience and Divine Revelation in the Theologies of Friedrich Schleiermacher and Karl Barth." In *Christian Experience in Theology and Life,* edited by I. Howard Marshall. Edinburgh: Rutherford House Books, 1988.

———. *Persons in Communion: Trinitarian Description and Human Participation, with Special Reference to Volume One of Karl Barth's Church Dogmatics.* New York: Continuum International, 1996.

Torrance, Alan J., and Michael Banner, eds. *The Doctrine of God and Theological Ethics.* London: T&T Clark, 2006.

Torrance, James B. *Worship, Community and the Triune God of Grace.* Downers Grove, IL: InterVarsity Press, 1996.

Torrance, James B., Trevor A. Hart and Daniel P. Thimell, eds. *Christ in Our Place: The Humanity of God in Christ for the Reconciliation of the World: Essays Presented to Professor James Torrance.* Allison Park, PA: Paternoster, 1990.

Torrance, T. F. *Karl Barth, Biblical and Evangelical Theologian.* Edinburgh: T&T Clark, 1990.

———. *Reality and Evangelical Theology. The Realism of Christian Revelation.* Philadelphia: Westminster, 1982.

———. *Royal Priesthood: A Theology of Ordained Ministry.* 2nd ed. Edinburgh: T&T Clark, 1993.

———. *Theology in Reconciliation: Essays Towards Evangelical and Catholic Unity in East and West.* London: G. Chapman, 1975.

Tutu, Desmond Mpilo. *Hope and Suffering.* Grand Rapids: Eerdmans, 1983.

———. *No Future Without Forgiveness.* New York: Doubleday, 1999.

Van Gelder, Craig. *The Missional Church in Context: Helping Congregations Develop Contextual Ministry.* Grand Rapids: Eerdmans, 2007.

Volf, Miroslav. *After Our Likeness: The Church as the Image of the Trinity.* Grand Rapids: Eerdmans, 1998.

———. *The End of Memory: Remembering Rightly in a Violent World.* Grand Rapids: Eerdmans, 2006.

———. *Exclusion and Embrace: A Theological Exploration of Identity, Otherness, and Reconciliation.* Nashville: Abingdon, 1996.

———. "Forgiveness, Reconciliation, and Justice: A Christian Contribution to a More Peaceful Social Environment." In *Forgiveness and Reconciliation: Religion, Public Policy, and Conflict Transformation,* edited by Raymond G. Helmick and Rodney L. Petersen. Philadelphia, PA: Templeton Foundation Press, 2001.

———. *Free of Charge: Giving and Forgiving in a Culture Stripped of Grace.* Grand Rapids: Zondervan, 2006.

———. "Theology for a Way of Life." In *Practicing Theology: Beliefs and Practices in Christian Life,* edited by Miroslav Volf and Dorothy Bass. Grand Rapids: Eerdmans, 2001.

———. "The Trinity is Our Social Programme: The Doctrine of the Trinity and the Shape of Social Engagement." In *The Doctrine of God and Theological Ethics,* edited by Alan J. Torrance and Michael Banner. London: T&T Clark, 2006.

von Balthasar, Hans Urs. *The Theology of Karl Barth: Exposition and Interpretation.* San Francisco: Ignatius Press, 1972.

Von Meding, W., and D. Müller. "Bind." In *The New International Dictionary of New Testament Theology*, edited by Colin Brown. Vol. 1, *A–F*, Exeter, UK: Paternoster, 1975.

Wadell, Paul J. *Becoming Friends: Worship, Justice, and the Practice of Christian Friendship*. Grand Rapids: Brazos Press, 2002.

Waldron, Vincent R., and Douglas L. Kelly. *Communicating Forgiveness*. Los Angeles: Sage Publications, 2008.

Wannenwetsch, Bernd. *Political Worship: Ethics for Christian Citizens*. Translated by Margaret Kohl. Oxford: Oxford University Press, 2004.

Watson, Francis. *Agape, Eros, Gender: Towards a Pauline Ethic*. Cambridge: Cambridge University Press, 2000.

Watson, Gordon. "A Study in St. Anselm's Soteriology and Karl Barth's Theological Method." *Scottish Journal of Theology* 42 (1989): 493-512.

Webb, Stephen H. *Refiguring Theology: The Rhetoric of Karl Barth*. Albany: State University of New York Press, 1991.

Webber, Robert E. *The Younger Evangelicals: Facing Challenges of the New World*. Grand Rapids: Baker Books, 2002.

Webster, John. "'Assured and Patient and Cheerful Expectation': Barth on Christian Hope as the Church's Task." *Toronto Journal of Theology* 10 (1994): 35-52.

———. *Barth's Earlier Theology*. London: T&T Clark, 2005.

———. *Barth's Ethics of Reconciliation*. Cambridge: Cambridge University Press, 1995.

———. *Barth's Moral Theology: Human Action in Barth's Thought*. New York: Continuum International, 2004.

———, ed. *The Cambridge Companion to Karl Barth*. Cambridge: Cambridge University Press, 2000.

———. "The Church as Witnessing Community." *Scottish Bulletin of Evangelical Theology* 21, no. 1 (2003): 21-33.

———. "'The Firmest Grasp of the Real': Barth on Original Sin." *Toronto School of Theology* 4, no. 1 (1988): 19-29.

———. "Response" to "What Wondrous Love Is This?" In *For the Sake of the World: Karl Barth and the Future of Ecclesial Theology*, edited by George Hunsinger. Grand Rapids: Eerdmans, 2004.

———. *Word and Church: Essays in Christian Dogmatics*. Edinburgh: T&T Clark, 2001.

Werkman, L. A. "Forgiveness as a Political Virtue: The Case of Srebrenica." *Zeitschrift für dialektische Theologie* 18, no. 3 (2002): 270-75.

Werpehowski, William. "Command and History in the Ethics of Karl Barth." *Journal of Religious Ethics* 9, no. 2 (1981): 298-320.

————. "Divine Commands, Philosophical Dilemmas: The Case of Karl Barth." *Dialog* 201, no. 1 (1981): 25-30.

————. *Karl Barth and Christian Ethics: Living in Truth*. Surrey, UK: Ashgate, 2014.

————. "Narrative and Ethics in Karl Barth." *Theology Today* 43 (1986): 334-53.

West, Charles C. *Communism and the Theologians*. Philadelphia: Westminster Press, 1958.

Wiéner, Claude. "Love." Translated by John J. Kilgallen. In *Dictionary of Biblical Theology*, edited by Xavier Léon-Dufour. 2nd ed. New York: Seabury Press, 1973.

Wiersbe, Warren W. *Be Free: Exchange Legalism for True Spirituality*. NT Commentary, Galatians. Colorado Springs, CO: David C. Cook, 1975.

Wiesel, Elie. "Ethics and Memory." In *Ernst Reuter Vorlesungs im Wissenschafts-kolleg zu Berlin*. Berlin: Walter de Gruyter, 1977.

————. *From the Kingdom of Memory: Reminiscences*. New York: Summit, 1990.

————. *Night*. Translated by Stella Rodway. New York: Bantam Books, 1982.

Wiesenthal, Simon. *The Sunflower: On the Possibilities and Limits of Forgiveness*. New York: Schocken Books, 1998.

Wilken, Robert Louis. *The Spirit of Early Christian Thought: Seeking the Face of God*. New Haven, CT: Yale University Press, 2003.

Willard, Dallas. *The Spirit of the Disciplines: Understanding How God Changes Lives*. San Francisco: Harper Collins, 1988.

Williams, Rowan. *Resurrection*. New York: Pilgrim, 1982.

Williams, Rowan, and Mark Collier. *Peacemaking Theology: A Study Book for Individuals and Groups*. London: Dunamis, 1984.

Williams, Stephen N. "What Christians Believe About Forgiveness." *Studies in Christian Ethics* 24, no. 2 (May 2011): 147-56.

Willis, Robert. *The Ethics of Karl Barth*. Leiden, Netherlands: E. J. Brill, 1971.

Wingren, Gustaf. *Theology in Conflict, Nygren, Barth, Bultmann*. Translated by Eric H. Wahlstrom. Edinburgh: Oliver and Boyd, 1958.

Wink, W. *When the Powers Fall: Reconciliation in the Healing of Nations*. Minneapolis: Fortress, 1998.

Worthington, Everett L., Jr. *Forgiveness and Reconciliation: Theory and Application*. New York: Taylor & Francis Group, 2006.

————. "Unforgiveness, Forgiveness, & Reconciliation and Their Implications for Societal Interventions." In *Forgiveness and Reconciliation: Religion, Public Policy, and Conflict Transformation*, edited by Raymond G. Helmick and Rodney L. Petersen. Philadelphia: Templeton Foundation Press, 2001.

Wright, Christopher J. *The Mission of God: Unlocking the Bible's Grand Narrative.* Downers Grove, IL: InterVarsity Press, 2006.

Wright, N. T. *Jesus and the Victory of God.* Vol. 2 of *Christian Origins and the Question of God.* Minneapolis: Fortress, 1996.

Yocum, John. *Ecclesial Mediation in Karl Barth.* Aldershot, UK: Ashgate Publishing, 2004.

Yoder, John Howard. "Binding and Loosing." In *The Royal Priesthood: Essays Ecclesiological and Ecumenical.* Grand Rapids: Eerdmans, 1994.

———. *Body Politics: Five Practices of the Christian Community Before the Watching World.* Scottdale, PA: Herald Press, 1992.

———. *For the Nations: Essays Evangelical and Public.* Grand Rapids: Eerdmans, 1997.

———. *Karl Barth and the Problem of War, and Other Essays on Barth.* Edited by Mark Thiessen Nation. Eugene, OR: Cascade Books, 2003.

———. *The Politics of Jesus.* 2nd ed. Grand Rapids: Eerdmans, 1994.

Zahl, Simeon. "Reformation Pessimism or Pietist Personalism?" In *New Perspectives on Evangelical Theology: Engaging with God, Scripture and the World,* edited by Tom Greggs. New York: Routledge, 2010.

Žižek, Slavoj. *Living in the End Times.* London: Verso, 2011.

———. *The Neighbor: Three Inquiries in Political Theology.* Chicago: University of Chicago Press, 2005.

Zizioulas, John D. *Being as Communion.* Crestwood, NY: St. Vladimir's Seminary Press, 1985.

Author Index

Subject Index

New Explorations in Theology

Theology is flourishing in dynamic and unexpected ways in the twenty-first century. Scholars are increasingly recognizing the global character of the church, freely crossing old academic boundaries and challenging previously entrenched interpretations. Despite living in a culture of uncertainty, both young and senior scholars today are engaged in hopeful and creative work in the areas of systematic, historical, practical and philosophical theology. New Explorations in Theology provides a platform for cutting-edge research in these fields.

In an age of media proliferation and academic oversaturation, there is a need to single out the best new monographs. IVP Academic is committed to publishing constructive works that advance key theological conversations. We look for projects that investigate new areas of research, stimulate fruitful dialogue, and attend to the diverse array of contexts and audiences in our increasingly pluralistic world. IVP Academic is excited to make this work available to scholars, students and general readers who are seeking fresh new insights for the future of Christian theology.

DISTINCTIVES OF NEW EXPLORATIONS IN THEOLOGY:

- Best new monographs from young and senior scholars
- Volumes explore systematic, historical, practical and philosophical theology

VOLUMES INCLUDE:

- *Karl Barth's Infralapsarian Theology: Origins and Development, 1920–1953*, Shao Kai Tseng
- *The Reality of God and Historical Method*, Samuel V. Adams
- *A Shared Mercy: Karl Barth on Forgiveness and the Church*, Jon Coutts